Children's Catholic Encyclopedia of Geography

Senior Editor
Esther Moon, Ph.D.

Contributors
Amy Gamez, M.A. • Janelle Green • AnneMarie Johnson, B.A. •
Sara Johnson • Susan McCoy, M.A. • Nathaniel Maresh, M.A. •
Kandy Mathis, B.A. • Esther Moon, Ph.D. • Elizabeth L. Pratt, B.A. •
Kathleen Solis, B.A. • Leta Sundet, Ph.D.

Fact Checkers
Mary Heipel, B.A. • John Iachetta • Maria T. Johnson, B.A. •
Elizabeth Kelly, B.A. • Maria Miller, B.A. • Helen Ott, B.A. •
Matthew Reiner, Ph.D. • Marcin Wolski, B.A.

Maps
Mapping Specialists, Ltd.

Graphic Design
Maria T. Johnson

Children's Catholic
Encyclopedia of

GEOGRAPHY

Image credits can be found on pages 313-316.

Special thanks to Kiddle.co for articles that were used as the starting point for some of the entries in this encyclopedia. All content from Kiddle encyclopedia articles can be freely used under CC BY-SA 3.0.

Catholic Heritage Curricula
1-800-490-7713 • chcweb.com

ISBN: 978-1-946207-73-9

Printed by Transcontinental Interglobe
Beauceville, Quebec, Canada
June 2025

Contents

Introduction

The *Children's Catholic Encyclopedia of Geography* is a fabulous reference tool, meticulously crafted for young explorers. Designed for grades 2–8, the encyclopedia features 15 detailed maps and 400 age-appropriate entries on saints, shrines, landmarks, animals, historical people and places, contemporary activities, countries, continents, and definitions of key geography terms.

Discover:

- Majestic animals and their God-given habitats
- Catholic saints and shrines across every continent
- Natural wonders that reveal the splendor of creation
- Historic landmarks and world-changing figures
- Cultural traditions that reflect global diversity in God's family

Use with CHC's Hands-on Geography Courses

The *Children's Catholic Encyclopedia of Geography* stands alone as a rich resource, but it is especially valuable when paired with *Explore the Continents* and *Tour a Country*. These hands-on courses for second and third graders guide students through an engaging, step-by-step exploration of geography.

All the required information for completing *Explore the Continents* and *Tour a Country* is included in the *Children's Catholic Encyclopedia of Geography*. This means that students can complete the research independently, without needing assistance from a parent or teacher. There is no need to monitor the students' internet use or worry about biased information in secular reference materials!

Explore the Continents

Students journey through all seven continents, learning about their geography, landmarks, saints, and wildlife. As they gather information, they create a colorful poster display to showcase what they've learned.

Tour a Country

As a follow-up to *Explore the Continents*, students "tour" one country per month by researching its saints, Catholic shrines, animals, natural wonders, and historical landmarks. As they study different aspects of the country, they compile a report in the format of a travel brochure. They then use the travel brochure to give an oral presentation—while dressed up in the "native garb" of the country they have been studying!

Features

Four Hundred Entries on:

Animals from around the world
Saints
Catholic shrines and churches
Natural wonders
World-renowned landmarks
Historical figures
Historical events
Activities, traditions, and celebrations in
different cultures

The Seven Continents:
Africa
Antarctica
Asia
Australia
Europe
North America
South America

A Selection of Countries from Around the Globe:
Canada
China
France
India
Italy
Peru
Spain
United Kingdom

Lessons on How to Use an Encyclopedia and Glossary

The encyclopedia begins by teaching
critical research skills:
- Alphabetization to the third and
  fourth letter
- Using encyclopedia guide words
- Using a glossary

15 Detailed Maps of Continents and Countries

A colorful map of each continent,
displaying the terrain and vegetation in a
child-friendly style

A topographical map of each featured
country, displaying mountains, rivers,
cities, and key locations referenced in
other entries

Illustrated Glossary of Key Geography Terms

How to Use an Encyclopedia

Alphabetical Order

Dictionaries and encyclopedias use ABC order. ABC order is also called alphabetical order. Learning how to put words in alphabetical order will help us to find words and topics easily.

Letters can be put in alphabetical order. These letters are mixed up: Q M P. When they are put in alphabetical order, they are written like this: M P Q.

Words can be put in alphabetical order, too. See?

> cave
> desert
> earthquake
> jungle

When you put words in alphabetical order, start by looking at the first letter of the word.

Alphabetizing Words that Begin with the Same Letter

To alphabetize words that all begin with the same letter, look at the second letter.

Not in alphabetical order:

> gulf   glen   gorge

In alphabetical order:

> glen   gorge   gulf

How do you alphabetize words that have the same first and second letters? You look at the third letter! See?

Not in alphabetical order:

> hemisphere   harbor   habitat

In alphabetical order:

> habitat   harbor   hemisphere

Sometimes, words have the same letters for three or more letters. You alphabetize these words by looking at the first letter that is different. "Canal" and "canyon" have the same first three letters. "Canyon" goes after "canal" because "y" comes after "a" in the alphabet. "Marsh" and "marsupial" begin with the same four letters. "Marsupial" goes after "marsh" because "u" comes after "h" in the alphabet.

Alphabetizing Titles with More than One Word

In this encyclopedia, you will often need to look up topics with long names, like "Basilica of Saint Anthony." How would you alphabetize these names?

> Basilica of Our Lady of the Pillar
> Basilica of Lourdes
> Basilica of Saint Francis of Assisi
> Basilica of Saint Anthony

The first two words are the same in each name, so you don't look at them. The first letters that are different are "O" in "Our Lady," "L" in "Lourdes," and "S" in "Saint Francis" and "Saint Anthony".

"L" comes before "O," which comes before "S," so you know that "Basilica of Lourdes" comes first, "Basilica of Our Lady of the Pillar" comes next, and "Basilica of Saint Anthony" and "Basilica of Saint Francis" come next. Since "Anthony" begins with an "A" and "Francis" begins with an "F," "Basilica of Saint Anthony" comes before "Basilica of Saint Francis." See?

> Basilica of Lourdes
> Basilica of Our Lady of the Pillar
> Basilica of Saint Anthony
> Basilica of Saint Francis of Assisi

Encyclopedia Guide Words

Alphabetizing is useful when you use encyclopedia guide words. **Guide words** show which topics can be found on the pages you are looking at. The guide word in the top left-hand corner tells which topic comes first on the left page. The guide word in the top right-hand corner tells which topic comes last on the right-hand page.

"Hippopotamus" is the first topic found on the pages below. "Humpback Whale" is the last topic found on the pages. The second letter in "Hippopotamus" is "i." The second letter in "Humpback Whale" is "u." All the rest of the words on these pages must have second letters between "i" and "u."

Using a Glossary

A **glossary** is like a little dictionary in the back of another book. The words in a glossary are in alphabetical order. There is a glossary at the end of this encyclopedia. It gives definitions for important geography terms.

Cross-References

As you read your encyclopedia, you will notice that some words are in different colors. When you come across a word in **blue**, it means it is a glossary word. You can look this word up in the glossary to find its definition.

If the word is **green**, it means that this topic has its own entry in the main part of the encyclopedia, which starts on page 59.

Orange words are the names of continents and countries that have their own entries in the front of the encyclopedia. The Continents section starts on page 7 and the Country section starts on page 31.

---

be thrown onto the enemy below.

It is amazing that the castle is so strong and so beautiful at the same time. The castle is sometimes called *Hakuro-jō*, meaning "White Egret Castle," because the white walls and curved roofs remind people of a white bird flying. Himeji Castle is Japan's largest and most visited castle.

Hippopotamus

The common hippopotamus (or hippo) is a large, heavy animal that lives in Africa, mostly south of the Sahara Desert. It can grow to be 15 feet long and weighs 7,000 pounds on average. It's one of the biggest mammals on earth—and one of the meanest!

Hippos have very strong mouths with two huge tusks inside them. Tusks are teeth that are sharper and longer than the other teeth. Hippos use their tusks to fight off crocodiles and lions. Hippos can be very dangerous to humans too. They think humans are just another predator that wants to attack their babies. They will do anything to protect their young, so be careful if you meet a hippopotamus.

Hippos live both in the water and on the land. As you know, it is very hot in Africa, so in the daytime, they keep cool by staying in the muddy waters of shallow rivers and lakes. When night comes and it is cooler, they go on

land to eat plants. Hippos are herbivores and can eat around 88–110 pounds of grass in one night!

Fun Facts:

- Hippos can run faster than most people.
- Hippos have webbed feet but are not good swimmers and can't float.
- A hippo's nostrils, eyes, and ears are on top of its head so its body can be under the water while it watches for predators.
- Hippos can close their nostrils underwater and hold their breath for five minutes at a time.
- Hippopotamus means "river horse" in Greek.

Howler Monkey

The howler monkey can be found in South America and some parts of North America. It is the loudest monkey in the world. Its howl can be heard from as far as three miles away, and it sounds like a loud growl or a roar.

Howler monkeys live together in groups high in the trees of rainforests. They have a big bone in the front of their necks that enables them to howl so loudly. They howl to defend their territory, and sometimes groups of howler monkeys howl back and forth as a kind of discussion to

• • •

---

decide where each group's territory ends.

The howler monkey is one of the largest monkeys in the Americas. It can grow up to three feet long. Its tail can be as long as its body, or even longer! Its tail is quite strong and can wrap around things, so howler monkeys often use it to hold onto branches and pick fruit from trees.

There are many different types of howler monkeys. Most are black or a deep reddish brown, but some are golden brown or black with reddish hands. They mostly eat leaves from trees, as well as flowers, buds, and fruits. Because leaves don't give them much energy, howler monkeys usually move slowly and spend a lot of time resting and sleeping. Howler monkeys are hunted by jaguars and other large cats, eagles, and large snakes. They can live for 15–20 years.

Huascaran

Huascaran is not only the tallest mountain in Peru but also the fourth-tallest mountain in all of the Americas. It is part of the Andes mountain range.

The Quechua people (the native people of Peru) have their own name for it. They call it *Mataraju*, which means "twin snow peaks." This is because Huascaran actually has two peaks, not one! (A peak is the pointed top

of a mountain.) The taller peak is toward the south, so it is called Huascaran Sur. Its summit is 22,204 feet in elevation, the highest point in Peru. The shorter peak is called Huascaran Norte. It is pretty tall too, at 21,833 feet.

Huascaran is mostly covered in snow and ice. Mountain climbing can be a fun challenge on this mountain, but it can also be very dangerous. It takes five to seven days to climb to the top of Huascaran Sur, and sometimes there are earthquakes and avalanches. (An avalanche is when large amounts of snow, ice, and rocks fall down a mountain.) In 1970, an earthquake shook Huascaran and made a giant avalanche. The falling rocks and ice gathered mud as they slid all the way to the bottom of the mountain. An entire town and several villages were buried, and thousands of people died. An avalanche this large is very rare, but mountain climbers still have to watch out for smaller avalanches on Huascaran.

Visitors to Huascaran also hike, ski, and watch the amazing mountain wildlife, like the Andean condor and spectacled bear.

Humpback Whale

The humpback whale is a very large whale found in every ocean, but it is very commonly seen along the coasts of North America.

• • •

Continents

Africa

Africa is the second-largest **continent** in the world. There are 54 countries in Africa, and over a billion people live there! Africa has very dry areas—big, sandy **deserts**—and very wet areas—**rainforests**. It is also home to the **Nile River**, which is the longest **river** in the world, running through eleven countries.

The people of Africa speak many different languages. Nearly one-third of all the languages in the world are spoken in Africa. Most people in Africa are Christian or Muslim. If you visit North Africa, the region of Africa closest to the **Mediterranean Sea**, you'll find more people who are Muslim. In southern and eastern Africa, more people are Christian. But many Christians in Africa are persecuted for their faith.

Much of Africa is very poor. Some places don't have good houses, food, or water available to the people who live there. Some people have to dig deep wells to get water. African governments do their best to provide an education for children, but not everyone can go to school. Many people in Africa can't read or write. Africa does have some rich countries

A coffee farmer shows her coffee cherries on her farm in Kenya.

like Nigeria, Egypt, Algeria, and Botswana. Nigeria has one of the largest cities in the world—Lagos.

Farming is one of the most important jobs in Africa. Depending on which part of Africa you visit, you can find crops like rice, millet, corn, tea, coffee, and yams. The most important of all foods grown in Africa is the cocoa bean. This bean is very important because it's used to make chocolate! Africa produces the most cocoa beans in the world. Mining is also an important job in Africa. Minerals, metals, and gems are mined there.

Children playing in clean water in Nigeria

Three African farmers show cocoa pods and seeds.

EUROPE

ASIA

Mediterranean Sea

ATLANTIC OCEAN

MOROCCO

Atlas Mts.

TUNISIA

Alexandria

Giza

ALGERIA

Ahaggar Mts.

LIBYA

EGYPT

Western
Sahara

Sahara Desert

Nile River

Red Sea

CABO
VERDE

MAURITANIA

MALI

NIGER

Tibesti
Mts.

CHAD

SUDAN

ERITREA

SENEGAL

GAMBIA

GUINEA-BISSAU

GUINEA

Niger River

BURKINA
FASO

BENIN

NIGERIA

DJIBOUTI

Ethiopian
Highlands

SIERRA
LEONE

CÔTE
D'IVOIRE

GHANA

Lagos

CENTRAL AFRICAN
REPUBLIC

SOUTH
SUDAN

ETHIOPIA

LIBERIA

TOGO

CAMEROON

SOMALIA

EQUATORIAL GUINEA

SÃO TOMÉ AND PRÍNCIPE

Congo River

Rwenzari Mts.

UGANDA

KENYA

Equator

GABON

CONGO

DEMOCRATIC
REPUBLIC OF
THE CONGO

Lake
Victoria

RWANDA

BURUNDI

Mt. Kilimanjaro

SEYCHELLES

ANGOLA

Lake
Tanganyika

TANZANIA

INDIAN
OCEAN

COMOROS

ATLANTIC OCEAN

ANGOLA

Lake Malawi

Zambezi River

ZAMBIA

MALAWI

Mozambique Channel

MADAGASCAR

MAURITIUS

Victoria
Falls

ZIMBABWE

MOZAMBIQUE

NAMIBIA

BOTSWANA

Kalahari
Desert

ESWATINI

LESOTHO

Drakensberg Mts.

SOUTH
AFRICA

Arts and crafts are a big part of African culture. Africans make beautiful pottery, wood-carvings, sculptures, paintings, woven baskets, and dyed fabrics. Jewelry is often made by hand, sometimes with small cowry shells. Lots of colorful clothing and headdresses are made for cultural ceremonies and dances!

An African woman weaves a blue and yellow raffia mat.

Women sell handicrafts with national Tanzanian themes at a market in Tanzania.

Pilgrims around the cross-shaped *Biete Giyorgis* (Church of Saint George) in Lalibela, Ethiopia

A *Bedouin* (nomadic Arab of the desert) with a camel at the Great Pyramids of Giza and the Great Sphinx in Egypt

Antarctica

Antarctica is the southernmost **continent**, surrounding the **South Pole**. It is often called the "Frozen Continent" because it's covered almost entirely in ice and snow. This continent is the fifth largest, and it has the smallest population—zero!

Antarctica's **ice sheet** is the largest in the world, holding nearly 60% of Earth's fresh water. This ice holds fresh water, not salt water, because it is made of snow that has been pressed down over time by the weight of new snow falling on top. The ice sometimes extends over the **ocean**, too, in ice shelves that look like cliffs. Under the ice that covers 98% of the continent, there are lakes, rocky ground, and even dormant **volcanoes**. The Transantarctic Mountains divide Antarctica into two parts: East Antarctica and West Antarctica.

The continent is surrounded by the Southern Ocean. The **sea** ice that forms there each winter holds mostly fresh water, similar to Antarctica's ice sheet, because as salt water freezes, most of the salt is pushed out of the ice. Under the ice, this leaves very salty, heavy water called Antarctic Bottom Water that sinks to the ocean floor. It carries oxygen and heat to the deepest places in the world and is an

Adélie Penguins jump off Paulet Island in Antarctica.

important part of balancing earth's climate.

Antarctica is the coldest place on earth. Winter temperatures can drop below -100°F in some areas, and even in summer, it's often below freezing. It is also the driest continent, meaning there's little rain or snowfall despite all the ice. In fact, Antarctica is considered a **desert**! The wind can be very strong, and the sunlight during summer lasts for 24 hours a day, while winter brings long periods of darkness. Because Antarctica is in the Southern **Hemisphere**, its summer starts on December 21 and ends on March 20.

No one lives in Antarctica permanently. Instead, scientists and researchers from countries all over the world visit Antarctica to study its unique environment. During the warmer summer months, there may be around 5,000

A penguin on an ice shelf

The South Pole with the flags of the 12 nations who signed the Antarctic Treaty for peace and scientific exploration

SOUTHERN
OCEAN

*Weddell
Sea*

A n t a r c t i c   P e n i n s u l a

Q u e e n   M a u d   L a n d

*Ronne
Ice Shelf*

ANTARCTICA

T r a n s a n t a r c t i c   M o u n t a i n s

*Bellingshausen
Sea*

• South Pole

*EAST
ANTARCTICA*

*Ellsworth
Land*

Vinson Massif

*WEST
ANTARCTICA*

*Amundsen
Sea*

Marie Byrd Land

Wilkes Land

*Ross
Ice Shelf*

*Ross
Sea*

SOUTHERN
OCEAN

people working in research stations, but that number drops to fewer than 1,000 in winter when conditions get even harsher.

If you visited Antarctica, you would see penguins, seals, whales, and many birds. You might explore giant **glaciers**, hike in the snow, or ride in boats to get a closer look at **icebergs**. You could attend Mass in the world's only permanent ice chapel, the **Chapel of Our Lady of the Snows**. A highlight for many visitors is seeing the Aurora Australis, or "southern lights," a display of colorful lights in the sky that is similar to the **northern lights**.

Brown Station, an Argentinian base and scientific research station in Paradise Bay, Antarctica

Argentinian icebreaker ship breaking the ice platform

A breaching humpback whale near the Antarctic Peninsula

The southern lights over Larsemann Hills, Prydz Bay, Antarctica

Asia

Asia is the largest **continent** in the world. It's also home to the largest number of people on the planet: more than 4.8 billion! The largest country in Asia is Russia, which is so big that part of it is in **Europe** too. The smallest country is the Maldives, which is a collection of **islands**.

Since Asia is so large, there are many different cultures and people groups in the continent. Southeast Asia is the name of the region south of **China** and east of **India**, including Korea, Japan, Thailand, Vietnam, and Indonesia. Each of these countries are fascinating: for example, Indonesia is made up of over 17,000 islands and has the fourth-largest population of any country in the world! South Asia is the name of the southwest region, where you will find India and surrounding countries such as Nepal and Pakistan. In the central and northern regions are China, Mongolia, and Russia, which stretches all the way across the western border between Asia and Europe at the Ural River.

Asia is known for having the most oil in the world, especially in Saudi Arabia. The Middle East produces lots of oil and sells it to the

The Royal Banquet Hall of Gyeongbokgung Palace and a cherry tree in Seoul, South Korea

A camel near the *Al Khazneh* or the Treasury, a tomb in the ancient city of Petra in Jordan

A traditional floating market selling produce on the canals of Thailand

Dubai, a modern city in the United Arab Emirates on the Arabian Peninsula

ARCTIC OCEAN

Bering Sea

EUROPE

Ural Mts.

Siberia

RUSSIA

Lena River

Sea of Okhotsk

Irtysh River

Black Sea

Caucasus Mts.

TURKEY

GEORGIA

The Steppes

Lake Baikal

PACIFIC OCEAN

CYPRUS
LEBANON
ISRAEL

ARMENIA

AZERBAIJAN

Caspian Sea

KAZAKHSTAN

JAPAN
Tokyo

SYRIA

Sea of Japan

JORDAN

Zagros Mts.

TURKMENISTAN

UZBEKISTAN

MONGOLIA

Gobi Desert

NORTH KOREA

Himeji

IRAQ

KYRGYZSTAN

Red Sea

IRAN

TAJIKISTAN

Beijing

SOUTH KOREA

Nagasaki

KUWAIT

Arabian Peninsula

BAHRAIN

AFGHANISTAN

Tibetan Plateau

CHINA

Yellow River

Yellow Sea

SAUDI ARABIA

QATAR

U.A.E.

Indus River

PAKISTAN

Shanghai

East China Sea

OMAN

Himalaya Mts.

Delhi

Mt. Everest

NEPAL

BHUTAN

Yangtee River

TAIWAN

Guam

YEMEN

Ganges River

BANGLADESH

MYANMAR

Hong Kong

Philippine Sea

AFRICA

Arabian Sea

INDIA

Kolkata (Calcutta)

LAOS

Manila

Mumbai

VIETNAM

PHILIPPINES

Bay of Bengal

THAILAND

Bangkok

CAMBODIA

South China Sea

Velankanni

SRI LANKA

Equator

MALDIVES

BRUNEI

MALAYSIA

Borneo

SINGAPORE

Sumatra

INDIAN OCEAN

INDONESIA

Jakarta

TIMOR-LESTE

world. Asian countries also mine many useful metals out of the ground, such as aluminum, tin, and iron. China is particularly famous for being a world leader in manufacturing. People who work in manufacturing help make just about anything you can imagine: toys, clothes, electronics, machinery—you name it!

There are still many poor people in Asia. In India, for example, many people do not have enough food to eat, and one out of every four people do not know how to read or write because they can't go to school. Some families in Asia are so poor that the children need to work instead of going to school. Asia also has some very wealthy cities and countries. The richest of these countries is Singapore, a small island country in Southeast Asia that has very advanced technology.

Several religions are practiced in Asia. The most practiced religions are Hinduism, Buddhism, Taoism, Confucianism, and Islam—the most popular religion in Asia. You can find practicing Jews and Christians, but there are very few of them and they are often persecuted for their faith.

One very interesting activity that you will find in many different countries in Asia is the practice of **martial arts**—a type of fighting technique that uses the human body and sometimes weapons. While martial arts started in China, other countries have their own styles and techniques. For example, Japan developed *aikido* and *karate*, Korea started *tae kwon do*, and in the Philippines, you can learn a martial art called *escrima* that uses wooden sticks.

A woman floating in the salty water of the Dead Sea in Israel

A nomad traveling in inner Mongolia

A street vendor in Hanoi, Vietnam

Australia

Australia is different from other **continents** because it is both a country and a continent! It is close to three million square miles, making it the sixth-largest country in the world. There are around 27 million people living in Australia, and most of them live on the eastern coast. Even though it is so big, Australia is one of the least populated continents in the world.

Australia has an interesting history: the **United Kingdom** made it a penal colony in the eighteenth century, meaning that it was a place where criminals were sent as punishment. Later, other people moved to Australia from **Europe**, **North** and **South America**, and **Asia** to be farmers or to mine for gold. But there were already native people in Australia called Aborigines. There was a lot of conflict between the Aborigines and the newcomers. Today, you can find Aboriginal communities that still practice some of their old ways of

A kangaroo at Lucky Bay near Esperance in Western Australia

living, but most of Australia is very modern and European. Australia became independent of the United Kingdom in 1986.

A lot of Australians don't practice any religion, but Christianity is the most practiced religion there. Twenty percent of Australians are Catholics. After World War II, more and more people of different non-Christian backgrounds began moving to Australia. Now you can find Judaism, Hinduism, Islam, and other religions practiced there.

There is plenty of wealth in Australia, and most people have comfortable homes and plenty of food to eat. Australian children are

An Aborigine father and son in a dance festival in Cape York, Australia

A cowgirl rides in a campdrafting event at a country rodeo. Campdrafting is a unique Australian sport involving a horse and rider working cattle.

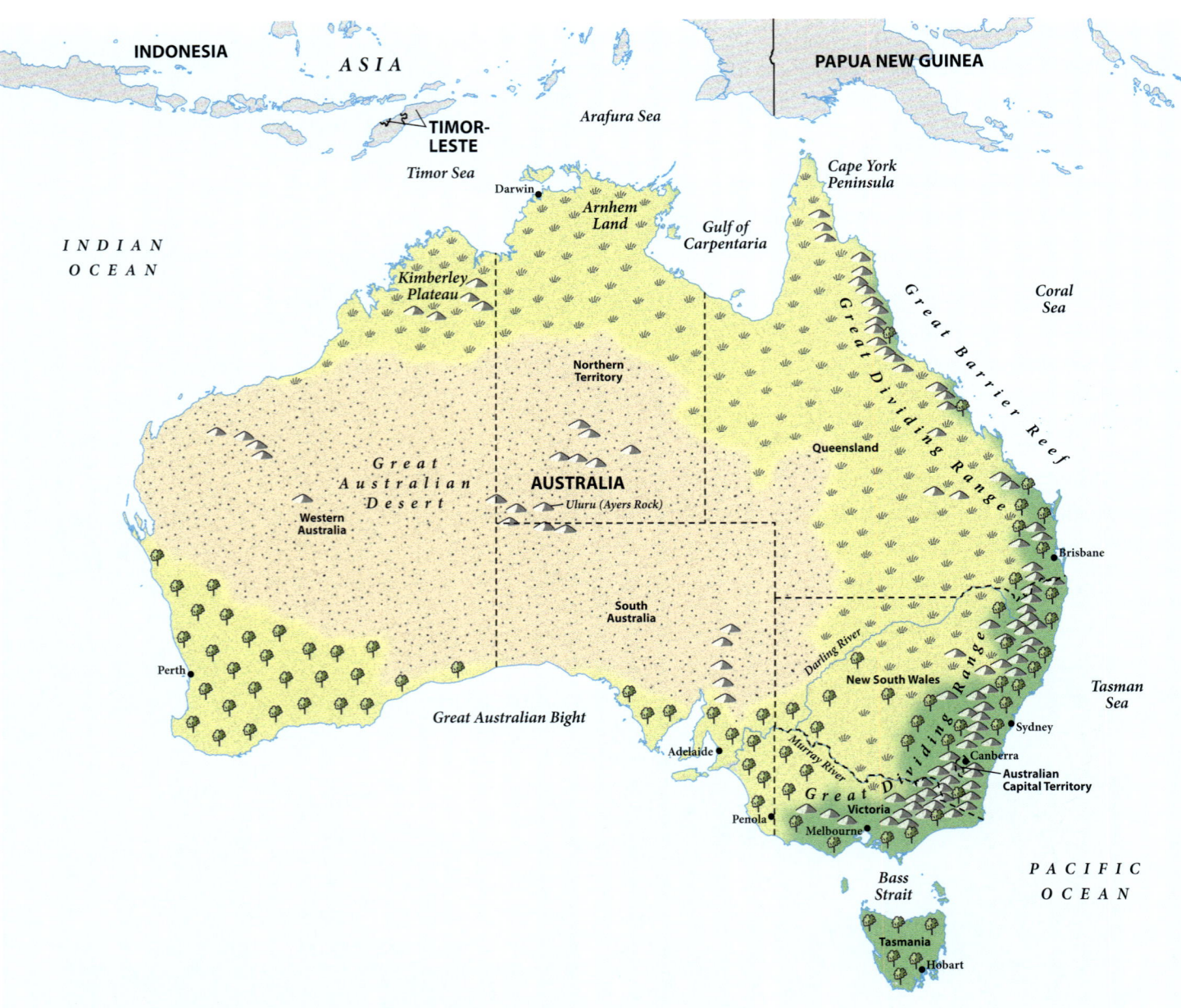

expected to go to school for an education, and older teenagers can go to college or attend vocational school to learn special skills.

Overall, Australia is a very flat, dry place. It is so dry that it can be difficult to grow things in Australian soil. Australia is known for mining minerals and ores that are traded around the world. Australia has some of the most advanced mining techniques in the world, like drones and remote-controlled vehicles! The most important mined materials are iron ore, which can be used to build tools and machines, and coal, which is burned to produce energy. Other important industries include manufacturing, banking, and even international education.

Because Australia is in the Southern **Hemisphere**, seasons are reversed from what you would experience in the United States. For example, when Australians celebrate Christmas in December, they are also beginning their summer vacation! Can you imagine singing Christmas carols when it's hot enough to go swimming at the beach?

Ngilgi Cave in Western Australia

Dingo puppies

A crowd gathers to see the summertime Christmas tree at Martin Place in Sydney, Australia.

Australian water dragon

Europe

Europe is one of the smallest **continents** in the world. There are over 40 countries in Europe, including the western part of Russia, which is in two continents. The world's smallest country is located in Europe inside of **Italy**—**Vatican City**! Most of the 740 million people living in Europe are Christian, but there are also Jews and an increasing number of Muslims there. Many of the countries in Europe have their own language, and because these countries are so close to each other, it is easy to find people who speak more than one language.

Since there are so many countries in Europe, you will find many different traditions from one country to the next. These differences can be found in how people wear their clothes, what their homes and buildings look like, the languages they speak, and how they make their food. Europe is often divided into two areas, Eastern and Western Europe. While all countries are different, the ones in Eastern Europe all share many similar traditions and culture, while the countries in Western Europe share other traditions and culture.

The Winged Victory of Samothrace, also called Nike of Samothrace, a marble sculpture in the Louvre Museum in Paris

The Passion Play, repeated every ten years with over 2000 performers, in Oberammergau, Germany

A mother and her children shop for Christmas tree ornaments at a traditional German Christmas street market.

A bagpipe regiment in Edinburgh, Scotland

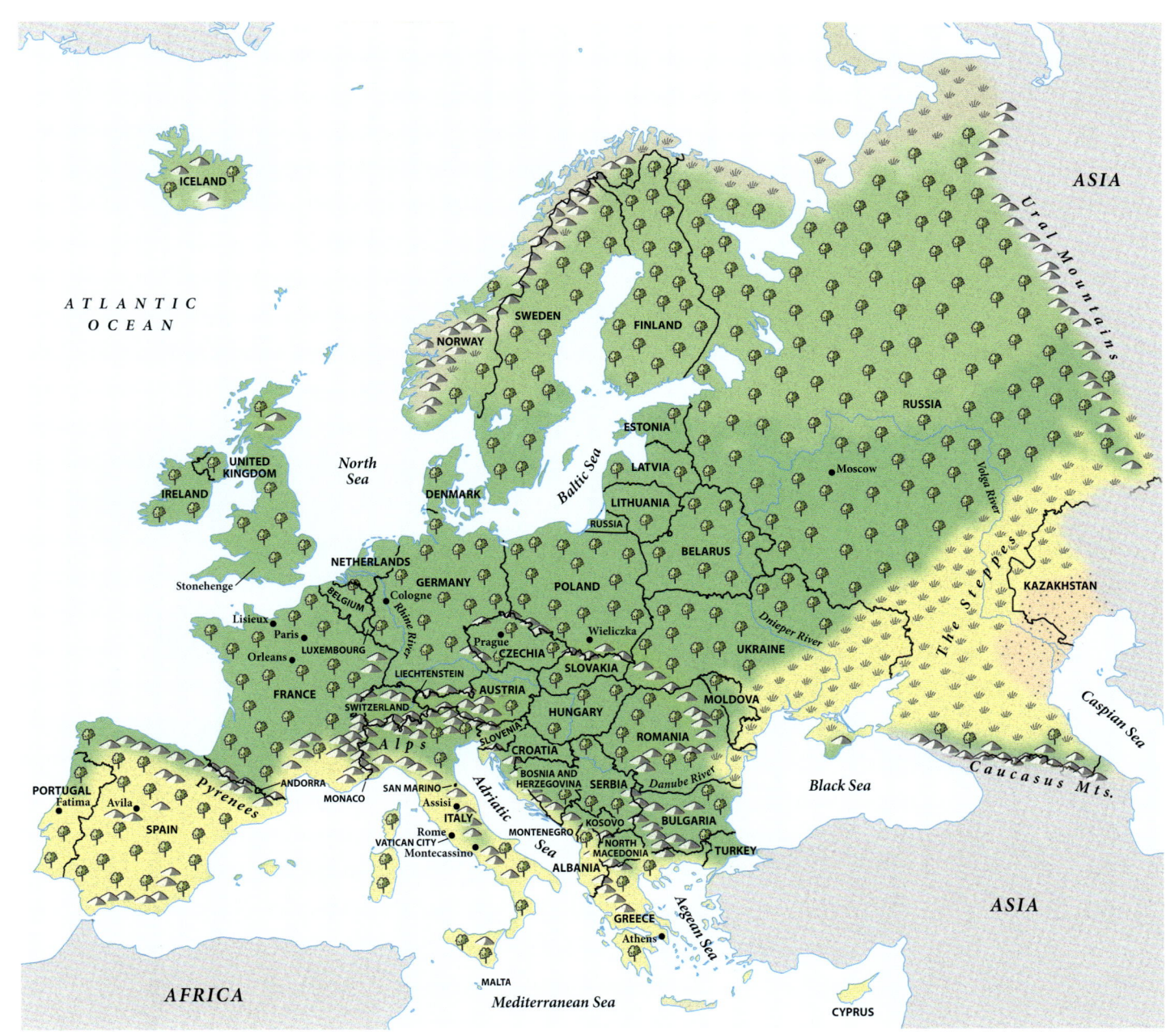

Europe is one of the wealthiest continents in the world. In fact, a good portion of the world's wealth is in Europe. People who live in Europe usually have safe homes, nice clothes, and plenty of good food to eat.

There is a lot of good soil in Europe, so close to 40% of Europe is used to grow all kinds of crops. Some of the most important foods grown in Europe are wheat, barley, vegetables, fruits, and grapes, which are used to make wine, too. **France** produces the most food of any European country.

Europe is visited by millions of people from all over the world who want to see the many beautiful landscapes and historical sites. Much of Western civilization came from Europe, so there is always plenty to see. You can find ancient architecture and sculptures in Greece and Rome, beautiful paintings from France and Italy, and historic churches all over Europe.

Svartifoss Waterfall in Iceland

The vineyards of Saint Emilion, a village in Bordeaux, France

A man with a truffle-hunting pig searches for truffles at the Uzes Truffle Festival in France.

Frederiksborg Castle in Denmark

Inside Westminster Abbey in London, England, United Kingdom

North America

North America is the third-largest **continent** in the world and is home to 23 countries. There are more than 590 million people living in North America. You'll find people of every race and background here, especially in the United States. This means that in the United States, you have the chance to experience many cultures mixing in one place. The largest country in North America is **Canada**, and the largest city is Mexico City, which is home to more than 20 million people! North America is also home to the world's largest **island** that isn't its own continent—Greenland.

In Canada, the United States, and Mexico, the most practiced religion is Christianity. Mexico has the greatest number of Catholics in North America, and the United States is home to more Christians than anywhere else in the world. You can still find plenty of other religions across the continent, though.

A cable car and Alcatraz Island, San Francisco, California

Women making tortillas in Yucatán, Mexico

Old Faithful Geyser erupting in Yellowstone National Park, Wyoming, United States of America

ASIA

ARCTIC OCEAN

EUROPE

*Chukchi
Sea*

*Bering
Sea*

*Beaufort
Sea*

Greenland
(DENMARK)

*Baffin
Bay*

Yukon River

Alaska (U.S.)

*Mt McKinley
(Denali)*

*Gulf of
Alaska*

Mackenzie River

*Labrador
Sea*

Arctic
Circle

*Hudson
Bay*

CANADA

R o c k y

G r e a t

Great Lakes

St. Lawrence River

●Quebec City

●Montreal

Missouri River

Yellowstone
National Park

●Auriesville

Niagara Falls

●New York City

●Philadelphia

●Washington, D.C.

M o u n t a i n s

Mt. Rushmore

P l a i n s

Appalachian Mts.

ATLANTIC
OCEAN

*San Francisco
Bay*

Colorado River

**UNITED STATES
OF AMERICA**

*Grand
Canyon*

●St. Louis

Mississippi River

Rio Grande

●New Orleans

*Gulf of America
(Gulf of Mexico)*

BAHAMAS

ST. KITTS
& NEVIS

ANTIGUA
& BARBUDA

Puerto Rico
(U.S.)

CUBA

PACIFIC
OCEAN

MEXICO

●Mexico City

DOMINICAN
REPUBLIC

HAITI

DOMINICA
ST. LUCIA
BARBADOS
ST. VINCENT & THE GRENADINES
GRENADA

JAMAICA

Caribbean Sea

TRINIDAD
AND TOBAGO

BELIZE

HONDURAS

GUATEMALA

EL SALVADOR

NICARAGUA

*Panama
Canal*

COSTA RICA

PANAMA

C e n t r a l   A m e r i c a

SOUTH
AMERICA

North America is one of the richest continents in the world, and Canada and the United States are the wealthiest of the countries there. People in these countries are usually able to go to school and live in a home with electricity and running water. There are many great jobs in these countries, from farming to working in some of the biggest industries (groups of businesses that make similar goods or provide similar services) in the world, such as vehicle manufacturing and technology. In many of these North American countries, a lot of minerals are mined, including copper, iron ore, and even gold and silver. These minerals are used to create all kinds of things that we use every day, from car parts to watches. The United States is special because it is one of the world's biggest producers of oil, which is important for making cars and machines run.

North American countries love watching and playing sports. For example, Canada enjoys hockey, the United States enjoys baseball and basketball, and Mexico enjoys soccer, which is actually called **football** in that country—it's definitely different from football in the United States. These sports bring people of all kinds of backgrounds together for a fun time!

A worker preparing to catch a fish at the Pike Place Fish Market in Seattle, Washington, United States of America

People playing street hockey in Ottawa, Ontario, Canada

The Alamo, a historic fort in San Antonio, Texas, United States of America

Bald cypress trees with hanging Spanish moss in Lake Martin, Louisiana, United States of America

South America

South America is the **continent** below **North America**. The Panama Canal separates these two continents from each other. South America is very long, and it is the continent closest to **Antarctica**. There are twelve countries in South America, and three dependencies, which are areas of land run by another larger country or government. The largest country is Brazil, which is only slightly smaller than the United States. The largest city in South America is São Paulo in Brazil, and it is one of the largest cities in the world.

Over 430 million people live in South America, and about half of those people live in Brazil! There are many poor people throughout the continent. Food and clean water can be

An indigenous South American girl in traditional clothing

Mount Fitz Roy, Patagonia, Argentina

Traditional *quadrilha* dances in Campina Grande, Brazil

A cable car to Sugarloaf Mountain in Rio de Janeiro, Brazil

Caribbean Sea

Panama Canal

VENEZUELA

Angel Falls

GUYANA

SURINAME

French Guiana

COLOMBIA

Sanctuary of Las Lajas

Equator

ECUADOR

Amazon River

Amazon Rainforest

PERU

BRAZIL

Lima

Machu Picchu

Brazilian Highlands

BOLIVIA

Parinacota Volcano

PACIFIC OCEAN

PARAGUAY

Rio de Janeiro

Sao Paulo

Iguazu Falls

Itaimbezinho Canyon

Parana River

URUGUAY

CHILE

Buenos Aires

ARGENTINA

ATLANTIC OCEAN

Marble Caves

Cave of the Hands

Andes Mountains

Cape Horn

Christ the Redeemer statue overlooking Rio de Janeiro, Brazil

hard to find sometimes. There is also a lot of crime, which can make life difficult. In places like Brazil, most people get to go to school, so most know how to read and write.

Most people in South America are Christian. Some of the countries even have the Roman Catholic Faith as their official religion, but people in those countries are still allowed to practice other religions. It should come as no surprise that the giant **Christ the Redeemer Statue** stands at the top of a **mountain** in Brazil, looking over the city of Rio de Janeiro. It is a beautiful symbol of Christianity in South America and across the world.

The tropical **rainforests** in South America produce some of the world's most valuable trees, like mahogany, ebony, and even rubber. South America also has some of the best soil

A hiker looks at a glacier at Mount Fitz Roy in Patagonia, Argentina.

poorer and live in the country. Your home uld be a hut or a house on stilts if you lived the **river**.

The official language of China is Mandan Chinese. There are many versions of the Chinese language, including Cantonese and Mongolian. Chinese writing isn't written with the same alphabet that you're reading right now. Instead, Chinese writing is made with signs and symbols called characters rather than individual sounds. It is written from top to bottom instead of left to right like English. Chinese writing is the world's oldest system of writing!

China is a communist state. Even though its full name is the People's Republic of China, it isn't a **republic**. Ordinary Chinese people don't have any say in how their country is run, and they are not allowed to criticize the government. The government takes away some freedoms from people who don't behave as the government wants them to. For example, a Chinese person might be punished for saying the wrong things on social media, buying too many video games, or eating on public buses and trains! This is called the Social Credit

A young woman picking tea near Sishuanbanna

System. People who do things the government doesn't like will often have a lower social credit score. This can cause many problems for them. For instance, people with a lower score might not be able to travel or get good jobs, and they might have to wait longer for service at the hospital.

China doesn't have any official religion, but the group that runs the government is atheist (meaning they don't believe in God). There are Christian churches in China, but they are controlled by the government. They can only say and do things that the atheist government says are okay, and churches must include Chinese

Tiananmen Gate, the entrance to the Forbidden City in Beijing, with a portrait of Mao Zedong, founder of the communist People's Republic of China

Communist Party ideas in their homilies. If you lived in China, you might go to a secret church that the government doesn't know about to practice your faith freely. Missionaries in China are not allowed to preach, start religious schools, print or sell religious books, or try to convert Chinese people without special permission from the government.

Chinese culture has been shaped by the teachings or religions of Confucianism, Taoism, and Buddhism. Confucianism is especially important in Chinese culture. It teaches that people are good and that we can always be better people with the help of virtue. The most popular religion that follows Confucian teaching is called Chinese folk religion.

China is known for some delicious foods that are different depending on what part of the country you're in. If you lived in the northern part of China, you'd likely have breads and noodles, vegetables, and pork, which is the most popular meat in China. If you lived in the southern part of China, you'd enjoy rice, vegetables, and seafood. The Chinese also like food made from beans like tofu and soy milk. You would eat your food with chopsticks instead of a fork or a spoon. It takes practice to learn how to eat with chopsticks, but once you know how to use them, you can eat just about anything with them!

When You Visit China:

If you are one of the millions of tourists who visit China every year, you'll find that tea is very important to Chinese culture. Serving tea can be a way to say thank you or even say that you're sorry if you've hurt someone's feelings. When you are served tea in a Chinese house, accepting it and taking a sip shows appreciation to the host. Make sure to tap two fingers on the table every time tea is poured into your cup. It's a proper way of saying "thank you" without words.

The Chinese calendar looks different from the regular calendar you might know. Twelve animals—including the tiger, the rabbit, and the monkey—take turns representing the year on the calendar. This calendar is based on the cycles of the moon. It is important in Chinese culture for helping people decide when to do important things like having a wedding or moving to a new home.

The colors of your clothes can have special meanings in China, too! Green represents good health, and red represents good luck. You will see lots of red at big celebrations like **Chinese New Year**. If you're in China during Chinese New Year, you'll celebrate with a giant festival that lasts for fifteen days. On the last night of the celebration, you'll get to stay up until midnight to watch the **fireworks** while enjoying some sweet dumplings that are shaped like little white moons.

A Chinese girl in traditional dress plays with sparklers at a Chinese New Year celebration

France

France is the largest country in Western **Europe**. It gets more visitors than any other country in the world! France borders eight other countries. It is known for its rich history and culture, especially its art, architecture, and food.

Weather and Climate:

France's many different land formations, including **mountains** and beaches, affect the climate across the country. The country has a mostly oceanic climate, especially near its coasts. This means that winters are cool and mild, and summers are warm and windy. The farther south you go toward the **Mediterranean Sea**,

A cheese maker cleaning cheeses in his workshop

The village of Hunawihr in the middle of vineyards in Alsace, a region of France close to Germany

the hotter and dryer it becomes. In France's mountain ranges, the weather is very cold and snowy—great for **skiing**!

Natural Resources and Important Industries:

France has always been famous for its farming and for the delicious foods French people make from their fresh farm produce. It is one of the top 10 exporters of farmed foods in the world. French foods are enjoyed in many places around the world. You just might have something in your kitchen that was brought into the United States from France! France is known for its wonderful wine, and it exports the most wine of any country. Many fancy items like watches, jewelry, and perfume are also made in France. France is also known for building airplanes, spaceships, and even rockets.

Life in France:

If you lived in the French countryside, you'd probably live on a farm. If you lived in a city, you'd probably live in one of the three biggest cities in France—Paris, Lyon, or Marseilles. The largest is Paris, the capital of France. Most

French people have good food and homes to live in and nice clothing.

French is the official language of France, but because France is close to many other European countries, you might hear people speak other languages, like Spanish or Italian.

France is a **republic**. It has a parliament, which is an elected group of people that makes laws and decides what the government spends money on. But unlike most parliamentary republics, the prime minister and the president share power in France. The president is elected by the people, and then he appoints a prime

A mechanical elephant walking around the the Île de Nantes, an island in the middle of the city of Nantes

minister to help him govern the country. France used to be a **monarchy**, but since the **French Revolution**, France has most often been a republic. However, **Napoleon Bonaparte** ruled France like a **dictatorship** for a time.

Traditionally, France is Catholic, but there is no official religion. Catholicism has become less popular in France in the twenty-first century: in 2023, only 25% of French people said they were Catholic. You can also find a few other religious groups, such as Muslims.

French people wear many of the same kinds of clothes you might see worn in the United States. But France is also known for its fashion and fancy clothing. Beautiful and expensive clothes are designed and made to perfectly fit the person wearing them. This fashion style is known around the world as *haute couture*, French for "high fashion." French fashion design is an art, and clothing designers display their work at big fashion shows every year.

Dresses designed by Coco Chanel, a famous French *haute couture* designer

A pastry chef making tarts in Paris

The French are well-known for making some of the most delicious food in Europe. The French enjoy freshly baked bread, especially long, thin loaves called baguettes and pastries (including croissants). French food includes tasty, simple dishes like roasted chicken with vegetables and also complicated dishes that take a long time to make but taste amazing. The French invented many foods, including the soufflé (a fluffy, baked egg dish), creamy soup known as bisque, and many delicious desserts and pastries like crêpes, éclairs, and sweet macarons, which are small and colorful sandwich cookies that come in many flavors.

When You Visit France:

When you visit France, you will be one of the 100 million people who visit every year! Whether you enjoy skiing in the mountains, playing on the beach, bicycling in the quiet countryside, or exploring a big city, you can do it all in France.

There are many famous buildings and monuments built throughout France that are worth a visit. If you like castles and palaces, you can visit a French château (castle) or a palace like Versailles, where many French kings and

The glass pyramids at the entrance to the Louvre Museum in Paris

queens lived. You can also find many famous pieces of art inside the **Louvre Museum** in Paris, the most famous art museum in France. And don't forget about the most recognizable landmark in all of France—the **Eiffel Tower**!

In France, instead of a big breakfast, you would enjoy a small breakfast of toast and jam or a croissant with a cup of coffee or hot chocolate. Lunch will usually be a much bigger meal in the middle of the day, and it lasts about two hours. Dinner is often a special occasion where family and friends come together to spend time with each other. If you are invited to someone's home in France for dinner, it is polite to bring a gift, like flowers, chocolates, or a bottle of wine. People in France believe that relaxation is very important and do their best not to work on the weekends or into the evenings. This way, they can relax, play, and spend time with family and friends.

When friends say hello in France, instead of shaking hands or hugging, they kiss each other lightly on the cheek. Well, they really just touch cheeks and make a kissing sound with their lips. In some places, it's traditional to kiss each cheek twice—four kisses total! This greeting is why you may hear French family members or friends say hello and goodbye with the word *bisous,* which means "kisses."

A Parisian café

India

India is a country located in South **Asia**. It is the seventh-largest country in the world. It even has its own **ocean** named after it—the Indian Ocean. India has a very rich culture with many old traditions, fun celebrations, and lots of delicious food!

Weather and Climate:

India has a mostly tropical climate, which means that the weather is hot for much of the year, but it can cool off a bit in the winter. Summer in India comes early, from March to June. Then, there is the **monsoon** season. In monsoon season, it rains a lot from June or July through September. The summer heat and winds blowing in from the nearby Indian Ocean cause this rainy season. If you are in India during monsoon season, you'll probably get pretty wet—but without the monsoons, the land would get very dry and the crops wouldn't grow.

Natural Resources and Important Industries:

India produces many wonderful things that other countries buy, including tea, rice, salt,

Sisters of the Missionaries of Charity walking with a child in Chunakhali, West Bengal

and spices. Today, it also makes electronics, cars, and even medicine. India is also famous for making more movies than anywhere else in the world. Its movie industry makes around 2,000 movies every year—twice as many as the United States!

Life in India:

There are about 1.5 billion people living in India, which is more people than in any other country in the world! Many people in India are poor, and some don't have enough food to eat or good homes to live in. **St. Teresa of Calcutta** (Mother Teresa) and her Missionaries of Charity were famous for helping the poorest of the poor in Calcutta, India. These missionaries still help the poor today.

With so many people living in India, it's not surprising that there are many languages spoken there. In fact, there are hundreds of languages in India, including English. Of all of the languages, Hindi is the most common language. But India has 22 official languages!

A mother guides her son through a flooded street during monsoon season in Kolkata

AFGHANISTAN

CHINA

PAKISTAN

Amritsar

H I M A L A Y A S

New Delhi

Mt. Kangchenjunga

NEPAL

BHUTAN

Taj Mahal

Thar Desert

Yamuna River

Ganges River

Brahmaputra River

Loktak Lake

BANGLADESH

Narmada River

Kolkata
(Calcutta)

MYANMAR

INDIA

Lonar Lake

Mumbai
(Bombay)

Godavari River

Western Ghats

Goa

Eastern Ghats

Borra
Caves

Krishna River

Bay of Bengal

Arabian Sea

Jog Falls

Kerala

Chennai

Andaman Islands

Andaman Sea

Lakshadweep

Malabar Coast

Vailankanni

Laccadive Sea

Nicobar Islands

SRI LANKA

MALDIVES

INDIAN OCEAN

| 0 | 200 | 400 Miles |
| 0 | 200 | 400 Kilometers |

India is a **republic**, but its people aren't all equally served by the government. India has a caste system, which is a way of ranking people based on what family they are born into. If you are born into a high-caste family in India, you will probably have plenty of food, go to a good school, and be able to get a good job. But if you are born into a low caste, you will probably be very poor and may not be able to go to school or get a good job. The government is trying to stop Indians from treating lower-caste people badly, but it is still a problem. Lower-caste Indians don't have as much influence in the government because they don't have enough money or power.

A little Indian girl sleeping on the street in Kolkata

be poorer and live in the country. Your home would be a hut or a house on stilts if you lived by the **river**.

The official language of China is Mandarin Chinese. There are many versions of the Chinese language, including Cantonese and Mongolian. Chinese writing isn't written with the same alphabet that you're reading right now. Instead, Chinese writing is made with signs and symbols called characters rather than individual sounds. It is written from top to bottom instead of left to right like English. Chinese writing is the world's oldest system of writing!

China is a communist state. Even though its full name is the People's Republic of China, it isn't a **republic**. Ordinary Chinese people don't have any say in how their country is run, and they are not allowed to criticize the government. The government takes away some freedoms from people who don't behave as the government wants them to. For example, a Chinese person might be punished for saying the wrong things on social media, buying too many video games, or eating on public buses and trains! This is called the Social Credit

A young woman picking tea near Sishuanbanna

System. People who do things the government doesn't like will often have a lower social credit score. This can cause many problems for them. For instance, people with a lower score might not be able to travel or get good jobs, and they might have to wait longer for service at the hospital.

China doesn't have any official religion, but the group that runs the government is atheist (meaning they don't believe in God). There are Christian churches in China, but they are controlled by the government. They can only say and do things that the atheist government says are okay, and churches must include Chinese

Tiananmen Gate, the entrance to the Forbidden City in Beijing, with a portrait of Mao Zedong, founder of the communist People's Republic of China

Communist Party ideas in their homilies. If you lived in China, you might go to a secret church that the government doesn't know about to practice your faith freely. Missionaries in China are not allowed to preach, start religious schools, print or sell religious books, or try to convert Chinese people without special permission from the government.

Chinese culture has been shaped by the teachings or religions of Confucianism, Taoism, and Buddhism. Confucianism is especially important in Chinese culture. It teaches that people are good and that we can always be better people with the help of virtue. The most popular religion that follows Confucian teaching is called Chinese folk religion.

China is known for some delicious foods that are different depending on what part of the country you're in. If you lived in the northern part of China, you'd likely have breads and noodles, vegetables, and pork, which is the most popular meat in China. If you lived in the southern part of China, you'd enjoy rice, vegetables, and seafood. The Chinese also like food made from beans like tofu and soy milk. You would eat your food with chopsticks instead of a fork or a spoon. It takes practice to learn how to eat with chopsticks, but once you know how to use them, you can eat just about anything with them!

When You Visit China:

If you are one of the millions of tourists who visit China every year, you'll find that tea is very important to Chinese culture. Serving tea can be a way to say thank you or even say that you're sorry if you've hurt someone's feelings. When you are served tea in a Chinese house, accepting it and taking a sip shows appreciation to the host. Make sure to tap two fingers on the table every time tea is poured into your cup. It's a proper way of saying "thank you" without words.

The Chinese calendar looks different from the regular calendar you might know. Twelve animals—including the tiger, the rabbit, and the monkey—take turns representing the year on the calendar. This calendar is based on the cycles of the moon. It is important in Chinese culture for helping people decide when to do important things like having a wedding or moving to a new home.

The colors of your clothes can have special meanings in China, too! Green represents good health, and red represents good luck. You will see lots of red at big celebrations like **Chinese New Year**. If you're in China during Chinese New Year, you'll celebrate with a giant festival that lasts for fifteen days. On the last night of the celebration, you'll get to stay up until midnight to watch the **fireworks** while enjoying some sweet dumplings that are shaped like little white moons.

A Chinese girl in traditional dress plays with sparklers at a Chinese New Year celebration

France

France is the largest country in Western **Europe**. It gets more visitors than any other country in the world! France borders eight other countries. It is known for its rich history and culture, especially its art, architecture, and food.

Weather and Climate:

France's many different land formations, including **mountains** and beaches, affect the climate across the country. The country has a mostly oceanic climate, especially near its coasts. This means that winters are cool and mild, and summers are warm and windy. The farther south you go toward the **Mediterranean Sea**,

A cheese maker cleaning cheeses in his workshop

The village of Hunawihr in the middle of vineyards in Alsace, a region of France close to Germany

the hotter and dryer it becomes. In France's mountain ranges, the weather is very cold and snowy—great for **skiing**!

Natural Resources and Important Industries:

France has always been famous for its farming and for the delicious foods French people make from their fresh farm produce. It is one of the top 10 exporters of farmed foods in the world. French foods are enjoyed in many places around the world. You just might have something in your kitchen that was brought into the United States from France! France is known for its wonderful wine, and it exports the most wine of any country. Many fancy items like watches, jewelry, and perfume are also made in France. France is also known for building airplanes, spaceships, and even rockets.

Life in France:

If you lived in the French countryside, you'd probably live on a farm. If you lived in a city, you'd probably live in one of the three biggest cities in France—Paris, Lyon, or Marseilles. The largest is Paris, the capital of France. Most

French people have good food and homes to live in and nice clothing.

French is the official language of France, but because France is close to many other European countries, you might hear people speak other languages, like Spanish or Italian.

France is a **republic**. It has a parliament, which is an elected group of people that makes laws and decides what the government spends money on. But unlike most parliamentary republics, the prime minister and the president share power in France. The president is elected by the people, and then he appoints a prime

A mechanical elephant walking around the the Île de Nantes, an island in the middle of the city of Nantes

minister to help him govern the country. France used to be a **monarchy**, but since the **French Revolution**, France has most often been a republic. However, **Napoleon Bonaparte** ruled France like a **dictatorship** for a time.

Traditionally, France is Catholic, but there is no official religion. Catholicism has become less popular in France in the twenty-first century: in 2023, only 25% of French people said they were Catholic. You can also find a few other religious groups, such as Muslims.

French people wear many of the same kinds of clothes you might see worn in the United States. But France is also known for its fashion and fancy clothing. Beautiful and expensive clothes are designed and made to perfectly fit the person wearing them. This fashion style is known around the world as *haute couture*, French for "high fashion." French fashion design is an art, and clothing designers display their work at big fashion shows every year.

A pastry chef making tarts in Paris

Dresses designed by Coco Chanel, a famous French *haute couture* designer

The French are well-known for making some of the most delicious food in Europe. The French enjoy freshly baked bread, especially long, thin loaves called baguettes and pastries (including croissants). French food includes tasty, simple dishes like roasted chicken with vegetables and also complicated dishes that take a long time to make but taste amazing. The French invented many foods, including the soufflé (a fluffy, baked egg dish), creamy soup known as bisque, and many delicious desserts and pastries like crêpes, éclairs, and sweet macarons, which are small and colorful sandwich cookies that come in many flavors.

When You Visit France:

When you visit France, you will be one of the 100 million people who visit every year! Whether you enjoy skiing in the mountains, playing on the beach, bicycling in the quiet countryside, or exploring a big city, you can do it all in France.

There are many famous buildings and monuments built throughout France that are worth a visit. If you like castles and palaces, you can visit a French château (castle) or a palace like Versailles, where many French kings and

The glass pyramids at the entrance to the Louvre Museum in Paris

queens lived. You can also find many famous pieces of art inside the **Louvre Museum** in Paris, the most famous art museum in France. And don't forget about the most recognizable landmark in all of France—the **Eiffel Tower**!

In France, instead of a big breakfast, you would enjoy a small breakfast of toast and jam or a croissant with a cup of coffee or hot chocolate. Lunch will usually be a much bigger meal in the middle of the day, and it lasts about two hours. Dinner is often a special occasion where family and friends come together to spend time with each other. If you are invited to someone's home in France for dinner, it is polite to bring a gift, like flowers, chocolates, or a bottle of wine. People in France believe that relaxation is very important and do their best not to work on the weekends or into the evenings. This way, they can relax, play, and spend time with family and friends.

When friends say hello in France, instead of shaking hands or hugging, they kiss each other lightly on the cheek. Well, they really just touch cheeks and make a kissing sound with their lips. In some places, it's traditional to kiss each cheek twice—four kisses total! This greeting is why you may hear French family members or friends say hello and goodbye with the word *bisous,* which means "kisses."

A Parisian café

India

India is a country located in South **Asia**. It is the seventh-largest country in the world. It even has its own **ocean** named after it—the Indian Ocean. India has a very rich culture with many old traditions, fun celebrations, and lots of delicious food!

Weather and Climate:

India has a mostly tropical climate, which means that the weather is hot for much of the year, but it can cool off a bit in the winter. Summer in India comes early, from March to June. Then, there is the **monsoon** season. In monsoon season, it rains a lot from June or July through September. The summer heat and winds blowing in from the nearby Indian Ocean cause this rainy season. If you are in India during monsoon season, you'll probably get pretty wet—but without the monsoons, the land would get very dry and the crops wouldn't grow.

Natural Resources and Important Industries:

India produces many wonderful things that other countries buy, including tea, rice, salt,

A mother guides her son through a flooded street during monsoon season in Kolkata

Sisters of the Missionaries of Charity walking with a child in Chunakhali, West Bengal

and spices. Today, it also makes electronics, cars, and even medicine. India is also famous for making more movies than anywhere else in the world. Its movie industry makes around 2,000 movies every year—twice as many as the United States!

Life in India:

There are about 1.5 billion people living in India, which is more people than in any other country in the world! Many people in India are poor, and some don't have enough food to eat or good homes to live in. **St. Teresa of Calcutta** (Mother Teresa) and her Missionaries of Charity were famous for helping the poorest of the poor in Calcutta, India. These missionaries still help the poor today.

With so many people living in India, it's not surprising that there are many languages spoken there. In fact, there are hundreds of languages in India, including English. Of all of the languages, Hindi is the most common language. But India has 22 official languages!

Map of India

AFGHANISTAN

CHINA

HIMALAYAS

Amritsar

PAKISTAN

Mt. Kangchenjunga

New Delhi ★

NEPAL

BHUTAN

Taj Mahal

Brahmaputra River

Thar Desert

Yamuna River

Ganges River

Loktak Lake

BANGLADESH

Narmada River

Kolkata (Calcutta)

MYANMAR

INDIA

Lonar Lake

Mumbai (Bombay)

Godavari River

Eastern Ghats

Borra Caves

Western Ghats

Arabian Sea

Goa

Krishna River

Bay of Bengal

Jog Falls

Andaman Islands

Andaman Sea

Chennai

Malabar Coast

Kerala

Lakshadweep

Vailankanni

Nicobar Islands

Laccadive Sea

SRI LANKA

0   200   400 Miles
0   200   400 Kilometers

MALDIVES

INDIAN OCEAN

India is a **republic**, but its people aren't all equally served by the government. India has a caste system, which is a way of ranking people based on what family they are born into. If you are born into a high-caste family in India, you will probably have plenty of food, go to a good school, and be able to get a good job. But if you are born into a low caste, you will probably be very poor and may not be able to go to school or get a good job. The government is trying to stop Indians from treating lower-caste people badly, but it is still a problem. Lower-caste Indians don't have as much influence in the government because they don't have enough money or power.

A little Indian girl sleeping on the street in Kolkata

There are many religions practiced in India, but the main religion is Hinduism. Hinduism was actually started in India. Buddhism, Sikhism, and Islam are also popular—in fact, India has the third-largest Muslim population in the world. You can be a Christian in India, but it can be hard. Some Christians there are persecuted for their faith.

While Indians often wear modern clothing, their traditional clothes look very different. Both men's and women's traditional clothing is made of long drapes of fabric that can measure between 15–27 feet long! It's a little like dressing in a very long bedsheet that has many colors and designs. Men wear bottoms called dhotis, and women wear dresses called **saris**.

A lot of food in India is vegetarian, which means it doesn't have meat. Foods like rice, vegetables, and lentils are very common in Indian cooking. You can still find some meats like chicken or fish, but you'll never find beef on the menu since Indians do not eat cow meat. This is because the cow is an important and respected animal in Hinduism. Indian food has lots of tasty spices that give it a special flavor. The most common spices are curry, turmeric, coriander, and ginger. See if you can find these spices the next time that you go to the grocery store!

When You Visit India:

To say hello to people in India, it is common to put the palms of your hands together and then make a slight bow to the person in front of you. This is how Indians respectfully say hello to each other. Before entering a home or one of the historic temples throughout the country, you'll want to remember to take your shoes off and leave them at the door to be polite. It is also polite to use your right hand when

School children having lunch at school in Kolkata

giving and receiving things. Don't be surprised if someone shakes their head in a way that looks like "no" when they really mean "yes" or "I understand." When you visit a home in India, you will be treated very well as a guest.

See if you can visit India during one of their many festivals. There are hundreds of celebrations throughout the year with parades, music and dancing, and many bright colors. Perhaps the most colorful one is the celebration known as Holi, or the Festival of Colors. Holi celebrates the beginning of spring, and it is a whole day of laughter and play. Wherever you are in India during this festival, whether you are a stranger or a friend, you get to be a part of the celebration by throwing colorful powders until everyone is covered from head to toe in a rainbow of bright, happy colors.

Girls in traditional costumes dancing at Holi, a festival celebrating the arrival of spring

Italy

Italy is located in southwestern **Europe** on a **peninsula** surrounded by the **Mediterranean Sea**. Italy is beautiful and full of history, since it was the center of the ancient Western world for centuries.

Weather and Climate:

The weather in Italy, especially near the coast, is hot and dry. The summers are long and hot, and the winters are mild and wet. The rainy season is during the autumn and winter months. It can get cooler in the northern **mountain** regions.

Natural Resources and Important Industries:

There are many different jobs in Italy. Some Italians are farmers and grow olives, grains, almonds, figs, and grapes for wine. Some farmers have cows and make dairy products like milk and cheese. Italy has many factories that make cars, machinery, medicines, plastics, and food, such as Nutella (a chocolate hazelnut

Piazza San Marco in Venice, with a winged lion, the symbol of St. Mark and of Venice, on a pillar in front of the Church of San Giorgio Maggiore

An Italian woman making homemade *gnocchi* pasta

spread) and pasta. Another popular industry there is the Italian fashion industry. It is one of the largest in the world. Many leather purses, shoes, and fancy clothes are designed and made in Italy.

Life in Italy:

Most children in Italy have plenty to eat and can go to school, but many people in the south of the country are poorer than those in the north. This is partly because there is more manufacturing in the north, such as fashion houses and factories that make fancy cars. In the south, more people are farmers or have tourism jobs, and they don't make as much money.

Italian people like to spend time together, and children gather with friends to play. Each afternoon or evening, many families and friends meet at the main square of their town, called a *piazza*. A very popular sport in Italy is soccer. It is called **football** there. Many people play it, but they also get very excited to cheer on their favorite team!

Italian food is one of the most popular kinds of food in the world. Most of their meals are simple, home-cooked dishes made with fresh produce. In the south, you will find lots and lots of pasta. In the north, you can still find lots of pasta, but polenta is more popular. Polenta is creamy boiled cornmeal. Italy is also famous for its pizza, which is often made in a wood-fired stove. You definitely have to try delicious Italian ice cream, called *gelato*.

A lot of Italians are Christians, and most are Catholic. **Vatican City** in Rome is home to the pope, the head of the Catholic Church.

Italy is a **republic**. It has an elected parliament and a president who doesn't have governing power but is an important public figure.

A boy eating ice cream (*gelato*) near the Trevi Fountain in Rome

One of the Italian government's hardest jobs is balancing the different wants and needs of northern Italy and southern Italy. Since each part lives and makes money in different ways, sometimes the same laws don't work well for both.

If you lived in Italy, you would speak Italian. The Italian language has twenty-one letters. The letters j, k, w, x, and y are not in their alphabet. In the United States, we use many Italian words! Many Italian words for food have become part of the English language, including pizza, spaghetti, and ravioli. Italian musical terms and instruments such as *forte* (loud), *piano* (soft), *allegro* (quick), cello, and tuba have become part of our language too. You've been speaking Italian and probably didn't even realize it!

A mother and child looking out at the old town of Trento and the Dolomite mountains from Buonconsiglio Castle in northern Italy

When You Visit Italy:

Many Italians have a very relaxed lifestyle. They have flexible schedules, and it is acceptable for things to start later than planned. Italians do not rush through meals. Lunch or dinner could last for several hours, with lots of talking and laughter. Italian people also like to show their excitement by moving their hands while talking.

Family is very important to Italians. Grandparents, parents, aunts, uncles, and children often live close to each other or even in the same house. Family ties are strong, and there are many family gatherings, such as getting together each Sunday for lunch.

Italy has a long, interesting history that can be seen in the many ancient buildings there. You can step back in time when you visit places like the **Colosseum**, **St. Peter's Basilica**, and the **Leaning Tower of Pisa**. You may even walk in the same places **Julius Caesar**, **Caesar Augustus**, **St. Benedict and St. Scholastica**, and **St. Francis and St. Clare** did! When you leave, you can say goodbye in Italian to this beautiful country and its people. Italians say *arrivederci* or *ciao* for "see you later!"

Gondolas at the Rialto Bridge in Venice

Peru

Peru is located in western **South America** and touches the Pacific Ocean. Here, you will find the **Andes mountains** and the Amazon River. This is an amazingly diverse country with mountains, beaches, **deserts**, and **rainforests**.

Weather and Climate:

The weather and climate in Peru can change by location and season. The areas along the coast have warmer temperatures. It doesn't rain a lot there, but it is very humid. The mountain regions are rainy, but cooler and drier. Lastly, the Peruvian **Amazon rainforest** has lots of rain and is very hot. Like **Australia**, Peru is in the Southern **Hemisphere**, so the seasons in Peru are opposite to what they are in the United States. This means when it is winter in the United States, it is summer in Peru!

Natural Resources and Important Industries:

Jobs in Peru can be hard to find, especially if you are not in a city like Lima or Arequipa. Many Peruvians are farmers and grow quinoa, avocados, blueberries, potatoes, asparagus, coffee, cocoa, rice, or bananas. Some raise chickens, and others are fishermen. There are many natural

Peruvian girls with alpacas at Sacsayhuaman, an ancient stone site near Cusco

resources found in Peru, such as gold, silver, copper, zinc, lead, iron, oil, and natural gas.

Life in Peru:

Many people in Peru are very poor and live in very tiny houses with no running water. Peru is a **republic**, but government corruption and political and social conflict have made it hard for the government to serve its people well. One in three Peruvians is poor, and many families don't have enough money to send their children to school.

Spanish is the main language spoken in Peru. Peruvian Spanish is a little different from the Spanish spoken in **Spain**: the most noticeable difference is that in Spain, "z" and "c" before "i" and "e" are often pronounced with a soft "th" sound, as in "think," but in Peru, you'll hear an "s" instead.

Most people in Peru are Christians, and many are Catholic. Religious traditions are very important, and there are many religious festivals. These festivals are colorful and exciting. One festival, for the Feast of Corpus Christi, honors the Holy Eucharist. It is the largest

Rainbow Mountain in Vinicunca in the Cusco Region

COLOMBIA

ECUADOR

Iquitos • Amazon River

Piura •

Sechura Desert

Chiclayo •

Chicama •
• Trujillo

Pucallpa •

Chimbote • ▲ Mt. Huascarán

Marañón River

Ucayali River

BRAZIL

PERU

LA MONTAÑA

Callao •⊕ Lima • Huancayo
Machu Picchu

Apurímac River

• Cusco

Huacachina •

PACIFIC OCEAN

BOLIVIA

Toro Muerto petroglyphs

Lake Titicaca

Arequipa •

ANDES MOUNTAINS

0   100   200 Miles
0   100   200 Kilometers

CHILE

religious festival in Peru. There are also festivals to honor the Virgin Mary and a **Saint Rose of Lima** Day. You will find lots of music, dancing, parading of statues through the streets, and delicious food.

Traditional Peruvian clothing has very colorful, bright patterns woven into it, and **Peruvian weaving** is famous for its colors and designs. Women wear dresses or skirts, blankets to carry children, wool jackets, and hats called *monteras*. Men wear brightly colored ponchos. Many children wear a handmade hat with tassels called a *chullo*.

A native *Quechua* man in a poncho and a *chullo* cap playing a *quena*, a traditional wooden flute, in the Cusco Region

Peru was the home to the ancient civilization known as the Inca Empire. The **Incas** built beautiful buildings and found creative ways to live in the region's **rainforests** and mountains. For example, they built terraces (flat areas of land) into the sides of mountains to grow food on. Money wasn't used in the Inca Empire because people traded goods and services for what they needed. Today, money called the *sol* is used in Peru.

Peru's culture is a blend of ancient civilizations, most importantly the Incas, and Spanish and African culture brought by the **Spanish Conquistadors**, slaves, and settlers. Peru has unique styles of dance and music that came from this exotic blend of cultures.

When You Visit Peru:

If you walk through the towns in Peru, you will see many people selling handmade goods on the street or in markets. Hats, scarves, purses, sweaters, and coats are made from the wool from alpaca, **llama**, or vicuña—local wooly animals—and are very soft. Alpacas, llamas, and vicuñas can be found grazing in the countryside high in the mountains. Don't get too close to them, though. They may spit at you if you make them angry!

One of the first things you'll want to see in Peru is **Machu Picchu**, a city built on the side of the Andes mountains by the ancient Incas. You might also want to try **surfing** on Peru's famous waves.

The pace of life in Peru is more relaxed, and people often show up late to scheduled events. When they do show up, Peruvian men greet each other with a handshake, while Peruvian women greet women and men with a kiss on the cheek in less formal settings.

A Peruvian woman weaving

Gathering with family is very important to people in Peru. In the United States, we usually eat our biggest meal in the evening. Peruvians slowly eat their biggest meal at lunchtime. If you are invited to lunch at someone's house in Peru, you can expect to be there for hours and leave happy and well-fed.

Potatoes, corn, quinoa, and beans are a part of most meals in Peru. There are lots of potatoes grown in Peru, and you can find them in bags outside of many restaurants. Peru's national dish is *ceviche*, which is like a salsa that has fresh fish or shellfish in it. Instead of using cooked fish, *ceviche* mixes raw fish with lemon or lime juice, which keeps the fish tender while partly "cooking" it in the acidic juice. You can find many tasty versions of *ceviche* in Peru. One special drink that children in Peru enjoy is Inca Kola. Inca Kola is a soda that is bright yellow and has a sweet bubblegum taste.

Machu Picchu, a city built by the Incan Empire

Map labels:

Cathedral Beach
Bay of Biscay
FRANCE
— CAMINO DE SANTIAGO
Santiago de Compostela
Cave of Altamira
Loyola
Pamplona
PYRENEES
Mt. Aneto
ANDORRA
Ebro River
Zaragoza
Barcelona
Duero River
Segovia
Ávila
Madrid
SPAIN
Toledo
PORTUGAL
Tajo River
Valencia
BALEARIC ISLANDS
Mérida
Guadiana River
Cartagena
Mediterranean Sea
Seville
Guadalquivir River
Granada
El Torcal
Málaga
Gibraltar (U.K.)
Strait of Gibraltar
ALGERIA
ATLANTIC OCEAN
MOROCCO

0   50   100 Miles
0   50   100 Kilometers

Spain

Spain is located in southwestern **Europe**. Its official name is the Kingdom of Spain. You can see the **Mediterranean Sea** to the south and east, and the Atlantic Ocean to the west.

Weather and Climate:

The weather in Spain can vary. The northern areas along the Atlantic Ocean can be cool and rainy. The winters are mild and humid with lots of rain. June, July, and August can be cool with lots of clouds. Along the coast of the Mediterranean Sea, winters are mild and less rainy, and there is lots of sunshine. Summers are hot and very sunny. The middle of Spain is dry and very hot in the summer and very cold in the winter. The **mountain** areas get colder and have more snow.

Camino de Santiago pilgrims passing a flock of sheep near the village of Astorga in Leon

There are many religions practiced in India, the main religion is Hinduism. Hinduism actually started in India. Buddhism, Sikh and Islam are also popular—in fact, India the third-largest Muslim population in the world. You can be a Christian in India, but it can be hard. Some Christians there are persecuted for their faith.

While Indians often wear modern clothing, their traditional clothes look very different. Both men's and women's traditional clothing is made of long drapes of fabric that can measure between 15–27 feet long! It's a little like dressing in a very long bedsheet that has many colors and designs. Men wear bottoms called dhotis, and women wear dresses called **saris**.

A lot of food in India is vegetarian, which means it doesn't have meat. Foods like rice, vegetables, and lentils are very common in Indian cooking. You can still find some meats like chicken or fish, but you'll never find beef on the menu since Indians do not eat cow meat. This is because the cow is an important and respected animal in Hinduism. Indian food has lots of tasty spices that give it a special flavor. The most common spices are curry, turmeric, coriander, and ginger. See if you can find these spices the next time that you go to the grocery store!

When You Visit India:

To say hello to people in India, it is common to put the palms of your hands together and then make a slight bow to the person in front of you. This is how Indians respectfully say hello to each other. Before entering a home or one of the historic temples throughout the country, you'll want to remember to take your shoes off and leave them at the door to be polite. It is also polite to use your right hand when

School children having lunch at school in Kolkata

giving and receiving things. Don't be surprised if someone shakes their head in a way that looks like "no" when they really mean "yes" or "I understand." When you visit a home in India, you will be treated very well as a guest.

See if you can visit India during one of their many festivals. There are hundreds of celebrations throughout the year with parades, music and dancing, and many bright colors. Perhaps the most colorful one is the celebration known as Holi, or the Festival of Colors. Holi celebrates the beginning of spring, and it is a whole day of laughter and play. Wherever you are in India during this festival, whether you are a stranger or a friend, you get to be a part of the celebration by throwing colorful powders until everyone is covered from head to toe in a rainbow of bright, happy colors.

Girls in traditional costumes dancing at Holi, a festival celebrating the arrival of spring

Italy

Italy is located in southwestern **Europe** on a **peninsula** surrounded by the **Mediterranean Sea**. Italy is beautiful and full of history, since it was the center of the ancient Western world for centuries.

Weather and Climate:

The weather in Italy, especially near the coast, is hot and dry. The summers are long and hot, and the winters are mild and wet. The rainy season is during the autumn and winter months. It can get cooler in the northern **mountain** regions.

Natural Resources and Important Industries:

There are many different jobs in Italy. Some Italians are farmers and grow olives, grains, almonds, figs, and grapes for wine. Some farmers have cows and make dairy products like milk and cheese. Italy has many factories that make cars, machinery, medicines, plastics, and food, such as Nutella (a chocolate hazelnut

Piazza San Marco in Venice, with a winged lion, the symbol of St. Mark and of Venice, on a pillar in front of the Church of San Giorgio Maggiore

An Italian woman making homemade *gnocchi* pasta

spread) and pasta. Another popular industry there is the Italian fashion industry. It is one of the largest in the world. Many leather purses, shoes, and fancy clothes are designed and made in Italy.

Life in Italy:

Most children in Italy have plenty to eat and can go to school, but many people in the south of the country are poorer than those in the north. This is partly because there is more manufacturing in the north, such as fashion houses and factories that make fancy cars. In the south, more people are farmers or have tourism jobs, and they don't make as much money.

Italian people like to spend time together, and children gather with friends to play. Each afternoon or evening, many families and friends meet at the main square of their town, called a *piazza*. A very popular sport in Italy is soccer. It is called **football** there. Many people play it, but they also get very excited to cheer on their favorite team!

Italian food is one of the most popular kinds of food in the world. Most of their meals are simple, home-cooked dishes made with fresh produce. In the south, you will find lots and lots of pasta. In the north, you can still find lots of pasta, but polenta is more popular. Polenta is creamy boiled cornmeal. Italy is also famous for its pizza, which is often made in a wood-fired stove. You definitely have to try delicious Italian ice cream, called *gelato*.

A lot of Italians are Christians, and most are Catholic. **Vatican City** in Rome is home to the pope, the head of the Catholic Church.

Italy is a **republic**. It has an elected parliament and a president who doesn't have governing power but is an important public figure.

A boy eating ice cream (*gelato*) near the Trevi Fountain in Rome

One of the Italian government's hardest jobs is balancing the different wants and needs of northern Italy and southern Italy. Since each part lives and makes money in different ways, sometimes the same laws don't work well for both.

If you lived in Italy, you would speak Italian. The Italian language has twenty-one letters. The letters j, k, w, x, and y are not in their alphabet. In the United States, we use many Italian words! Many Italian words for food have become part of the English language, including pizza, spaghetti, and ravioli. Italian musical terms and instruments such as *forte* (loud), *piano* (soft), *allegro* (quick), cello, and tuba have become part of our language too. You've been speaking Italian and probably didn't even realize it!

A mother and child looking out at the old town of Trento and the Dolomite mountains from Buonconsiglio Castle in northern Italy

When You Visit Italy:

Many Italians have a very relaxed lifestyle. They have flexible schedules, and it is acceptable for things to start later than planned. Italians do not rush through meals. Lunch or dinner could last for several hours, with lots of talking and laughter. Italian people also like to show their excitement by moving their hands while talking.

Family is very important to Italians. Grandparents, parents, aunts, uncles, and children often live close to each other or even in the same house. Family ties are strong, and there are many family gatherings, such as getting together each Sunday for lunch.

Italy has a long, interesting history that can be seen in the many ancient buildings there. You can step back in time when you visit places like the **Colosseum**, **St. Peter's Basilica**, and the **Leaning Tower of Pisa**. You may even walk in the same places **Julius Caesar**, **Caesar Augustus**, **St. Benedict and St. Scholastica**, and **St. Francis and St. Clare** did! When you leave, you can say goodbye in Italian to this beautiful country and its people. Italians say *arrivederci* or *ciao* for "see you later!"

Gondolas at the Rialto Bridge in Venice

Peru

Peru is located in western **South America** and touches the Pacific Ocean. Here, you will find the **Andes mountains** and the Amazon River. This is an amazingly diverse country with mountains, beaches, **deserts**, and **rainforests**.

Weather and Climate:

The weather and climate in Peru can change by location and season. The areas along the coast have warmer temperatures. It doesn't rain a lot there, but it is very humid. The mountain regions are rainy, but cooler and drier. Lastly, the Peruvian **Amazon rainforest** has lots of rain and is very hot. Like **Australia**, Peru is in the Southern **Hemisphere**, so the seasons in Peru are opposite to what they are in the United States. This means when it is winter in the United States, it is summer in Peru!

Natural Resources and Important Industries:

Jobs in Peru can be hard to find, especially if you are not in a city like Lima or Arequipa. Many Peruvians are farmers and grow quinoa, avocados, blueberries, potatoes, asparagus, coffee, cocoa, rice, or bananas. Some raise chickens, and others are fishermen. There are many natural

Peruvian girls with alpacas at Sacsayhuaman, an ancient stone site near Cusco

resources found in Peru, such as gold, silver, copper, zinc, lead, iron, oil, and natural gas.

Life in Peru:

Many people in Peru are very poor and live in very tiny houses with no running water. Peru is a **republic**, but government corruption and political and social conflict have made it hard for the government to serve its people well. One in three Peruvians is poor, and many families don't have enough money to send their children to school.

Spanish is the main language spoken in Peru. Peruvian Spanish is a little different from the Spanish spoken in **Spain**: the most noticeable difference is that in Spain, "z" and "c" before "i" and "e" are often pronounced with a soft "th" sound, as in "think," but in Peru, you'll hear an "s" instead.

Most people in Peru are Christians, and many are Catholic. Religious traditions are very important, and there are many religious festivals. These festivals are colorful and exciting. One festival, for the Feast of Corpus Christi, honors the Holy Eucharist. It is the largest

Rainbow Mountain in Vinicunca in the Cusco Region

COLOMBIA

ECUADOR

Iquitos • *Amazon River*

Piura •

Sechura Desert

Chiclayo •

Marañón River

Chicama • Trujillo •

Pucallpa •

Ucayali River

Chimbote • ▲ *Mt. Huascarán*

PERU

L A   M O N T A Ñ A

BRAZIL

Callao • ✦ Lima • Huancayo •

Apurímac River

Machu Picchu

• Cusco

Huacachina •

PACIFIC OCEAN

A N D E S   M O U N T A I N S

Toro Muerto petroglyphs

Lake Titicaca

BOLIVIA

Arequipa •

CHILE

0   100   200 Miles
0   100   200 Kilometers

religious festival in Peru. There are also festivals to honor the Virgin Mary and a **Saint Rose of Lima** Day. You will find lots of music, dancing, parading of statues through the streets, and delicious food.

Traditional Peruvian clothing has very colorful, bright patterns woven into it, and **Peruvian weaving** is famous for its colors and designs. Women wear dresses or skirts, blankets to carry children, wool jackets, and hats called *monteras*. Men wear brightly colored ponchos. Many children wear a handmade hat with tassels called a *chullo*.

A native *Quechua* man in a poncho and a *chullo* cap playing a *quena*, a traditional wooden flute, in the Cusco Region

Peru was the home to the ancient civilization known as the Inca Empire. The **Incas** built beautiful buildings and found creative ways to live in the region's **rainforests** and mountains. For example, they built terraces (flat areas of land) into the sides of mountains to grow food on. Money wasn't used in the Inca Empire because people traded goods and services for what they needed. Today, money called the *sol* is used in Peru.

Peru's culture is a blend of ancient civilizations, most importantly the Incas, and Spanish and African culture brought by the **Spanish Conquistadors**, slaves, and settlers. Peru has unique styles of dance and music that came from this exotic blend of cultures.

When You Visit Peru:

If you walk through the towns in Peru, you will see many people selling handmade goods on the street or in markets. Hats, scarves, purses, sweaters, and coats are made from the wool from alpaca, **llama**, or vicuña—local wooly animals—and are very soft. Alpacas, llamas, and vicuñas can be found grazing in the countryside high in the mountains. Don't get too close to them, though. They may spit at you if you make them angry!

One of the first things you'll want to see in Peru is **Machu Picchu**, a city built on the side of the Andes mountains by the ancient Incas. You might also want to try **surfing** on Peru's famous waves.

The pace of life in Peru is more relaxed, and people often show up late to scheduled events. When they do show up, Peruvian men greet each other with a handshake, while Peruvian women greet women and men with a kiss on the cheek in less formal settings.

A Peruvian woman weaving

Gathering with family is very important to people in Peru. In the United States, we usually eat our biggest meal in the evening. Peruvians slowly eat their biggest meal at lunchtime. If you are invited to lunch at someone's house in Peru, you can expect to be there for hours and leave happy and well-fed.

Potatoes, corn, quinoa, and beans are a part of most meals in Peru. There are lots of potatoes grown in Peru, and you can find them in bags outside of many restaurants. Peru's national dish is *ceviche*, which is like a salsa that has fresh fish or shellfish in it. Instead of using cooked fish, *ceviche* mixes raw fish with lemon or lime juice, which keeps the fish tender while partly "cooking" it in the acidic juice. You can find many tasty versions of *ceviche* in Peru. One special drink that children in Peru enjoy is Inca Kola. Inca Kola is a soda that is bright yellow and has a sweet bubblegum taste.

Machu Picchu, a city built by the Incan Empire

Map of Spain:

— CAMINO DE SANTIAGO

Bay of Biscay
Cathedral Beach
Santiago de Compostela
Cave of Altamira
Loyola
Pamplona
PYRENEES
FRANCE
Mt. Aneto
ANDORRA
Ebro River
Zaragoza
Barcelona
Duero River
Segovia
Ávila
Madrid
SPAIN
Toledo
Valencia
BALEARIC ISLANDS
PORTUGAL
Tajo River
Mérida
Guadiana River
Guadalquivir River
Seville
Cartagena
Granada
El Torcal
Málaga
Gibraltar (U.K.)
Strait of Gibraltar
ATLANTIC OCEAN
Mediterranean Sea
ALGERIA
0   50   100 Miles
0   50   100 Kilometers
MOROCCO

Spain

Spain is located in southwestern **Europe**. Its official name is the Kingdom of Spain. You can see the **Mediterranean Sea** to the south and east, and the Atlantic Ocean to the west.

Weather and Climate:

The weather in Spain can vary. The northern areas along the Atlantic Ocean can be cool and rainy. The winters are mild and humid with lots of rain. June, July, and August can be cool with lots of clouds. Along the coast of the Mediterranean Sea, winters are mild and less rainy, and there is lots of sunshine. Summers are hot and very sunny. The middle of Spain is dry and very hot in the summer and very cold in the winter. The **mountain** areas get colder and have more snow.

Camino de Santiago pilgrims passing a flock of sheep near the village of Astorga in Leon

they like to eat tall grasses and don't eat any meat. They are grazers, just like cows.

Oxpeckers, small gray birds with brightly colored beaks, warn the buffalo about predators. They sit on the buffaloes' backs, eating insects off of them, and hiss if there is danger nearby. Buffaloes defend themselves by keeping close together in huge herds. If a buffalo wanders away from the rest of the herd, it may become a tasty meal for a pride (a group) of lions!

African buffaloes are part of the African Big Five, which are known as the five hardest animals to hunt. The buffalo is on this list because of how dangerous it can be when it is hunted.

Fun Facts:
- Buffaloes are excellent swimmers.
- They can run fast—up to 35 miles per hour!
- They are much stronger than an ox.
- They have smooth tongues.
- They can drink over nine gallons at a time in just a few minutes, and up to 30 gallons a day!

African Elephant

African elephants are found almost everywhere in **Africa** except in the **Sahara Desert**. They live in scrublands (areas covered with small bushes and short grass), dry areas, tropical **rainforests**, and woodlands.

African elephants are giant creatures. In fact, they are some of the largest mammals on earth. Male elephants are 10–13 feet tall and weigh from 5,000 to 14,000 pounds. A car only weighs about 3,000 pounds!

African elephants have large flapping ears, long swinging trunks (noses), and big tusks. Their large ears not only help them hear better, but they also help keep them cool under the hot African sun. Elephants do a lot more with their trunks than just smell: they also eat, drink, make sounds, pick things up, and protect themselves.

Did you know that elephants' tusks are actually teeth? They use them for fighting each other and defending themselves against predators. They also use their tusks to dig up roots and strip bark off trees to eat. Elephants are herbivores, meaning they eat plants, roots, bark, and fruit—and they eat a lot!

Fun Facts:
- African elephants are very smart.
- They can run as fast as 25 miles per hour.
- When they swim underwater, they use their trunks as snorkels.
- They only sleep about two hours a day.
- They take mud and dust baths to cool off.
- Their ears are shaped a lot like the **continent** of Africa.
- A single tusk weighs an average of 100 pounds and is about 7 feet long.

Alfred the Great

Alfred the Great was a king in England in the ninth century. (England is part of the **United Kingdom**.) When Alfred became king, England was made up of smaller kingdoms. Alfred ruled one of those kingdoms, called Wessex. Later, he became king of all the **Anglo-Saxons** (the English people).

Alfred liked learning and poetry. He did not expect to be king when he was growing up because he had four older brothers. Each one became king but then died. In the year 871, when Alfred was only 22 years old, he became king! It wasn't an easy time to start ruling. England faced great danger. The Vikings (Danes), a group of warriors from **Europe**, were attacking England and trying to take it over. They were taking everyone's food and money, making some people their slaves, and destroying churches and monasteries. Alfred had to help his people.

At first, Alfred was defeated in battle, but he kept trying even when victory seemed impossible. Eventually, he won a huge victory over the Vikings in the Battle of Edington. Guthrum, the Viking king, and 30 of his most powerful warriors were baptized after losing this battle. Many other Vikings became Christians afterward.

After defeating the Vikings, Alfred made good laws and encouraged people to learn. England became a wonderful, rich country. But when Alfred was old, the Vikings attacked again! At that time, Alfred united all the kingdoms of England, and together they defeated the Vikings again at London. Today, England is a unified Christian country because of Alfred the Great.

Alhambra

The Alhambra is a large fortress and palace in Granada, **Spain**. It is on a hill near the Sierra Nevadas, the tallest **mountain range** in the country. In the year 1238, when this area of Spain was ruled by the Muslims, Muhammad I of Granada started building the Alhambra. Over the years, Muslim rulers added to it until it had six palaces, a strong fortress called Alcazaba, courtyards with fountains and pools, mosques (places where Muslims pray), towers, and more.

The Alhambra is decorated very beautifully with geometric patterns and other designs. The walls are covered with colorful tiles and stucco (plaster) carved in fancy patterns. Some of the ceilings are carved in a special way that makes them look like a honeycomb when you look up at them. Because they used reddish clay for building, the Muslims called their palace-fortress al-Hamra, which means "the red fortress." Over time, al-Hamra became Alhambra.

In 1492, the Catholic rulers **Ferdinand and Isabella** defeated the Muslims in Spain. When King Ferdinand and Queen Isabella were at the Alhambra, they met with **Christopher Columbus**! It was here that Columbus asked for ships for his trip across the Atlantic Ocean. Over many years, the Spanish rebuilt parts of the Alhambra and added Catholic churches where there used to be mosques.

Alpine Ibex

Alpine ibexes (or *steinbocks*) are a type of wild mountain goat. They can be found high up in the **Alps** in **Europe**. Their natural **habitat** is steep, rocky land and open meadows.

Ibexes are excellent climbers! Their sharp hooves help them to move about the **mountains** easily. Females and kids (young ibexes) weigh less, so they are able to climb higher and steeper mountains than adult males.

Wolves, bears, foxes, and lynxes like to hunt Alpine ibexes. But ibexes are hard to catch because their predators can't jump and climb as well as they can. Ibex kids are always in danger from large birds like the golden eagle.

Alpine ibexes grow ridged horns all through their lives. Males' horns grow much longer than those of the females—a little over three feet long! Male ibexes use them against each other in battles of strength to find out who will be the leader of the group.

Alpine ibexes are herbivores, so they feed on grass, mosses, flowers, leaves, and twigs. Although they live where it is very cold and snowy, they do not hibernate. Instead, they find shelter when it is cold and come out when the sun is shining.

Although adult males and females live apart from each other for most of the year, they are social animals. Adult male Alpine ibexes talk to each other by short whistles. Females and their young communicate by bleating.

Have you read a fairy tale about goats like these animals, "The Three Billy Goats Gruff"?

Alpine Marmot

The Alpine marmot is a large ground squirrel found in **Italy** and throughout **Europe**, particularly in **mountain ranges** like the **Alps**. Alpine marmots live in meadows and other flat, grassy, or rocky areas in the mountains.

Alpine marmots can dig with both their front and hind feet. They are very good at digging and can even burrow into hard, rocky soil that would be difficult to dig even with a shovel or pickax. Alpine marmot families live together. Young marmots don't start new families until they are about three years old, so as many as 20 marmots can live together in one big burrow!

Alpine marmots spend most of the year in their burrow. They can hibernate for up to nine months every year. To survive their long hibernation, marmots have to eat a lot during the summer and grow a thick layer of fat. Alpine marmots eat mostly grass and other plants, but they will also eat bugs, worms, and seeds.

Alpine marmots often stand on their hind legs to watch for predators, much like prairie dogs and other ground squirrels. They make several warning sounds when threatened, including whistling and chattering their teeth.

Alps

The Alps are the highest **mountain range** in **Europe**, and they are mostly in **Italy**. But the Alps are so large that they are part of eight countries—Monaco, **France**, Switzerland, Italy, Liechtenstein, Germany, Austria, and Slovenia. The tallest mountain in the Alps is Mont Blanc, which is French for "white mountain." It stands at an enormous 15,771 feet! There are 82 **mountains** in the Alps with peaks that measure taller than 13,000 feet. Can you imagine

how far you could see if you stood at the top of one of these mountains? If you were that high up, you would see beautiful white snow on the peaks of each mountain because of how cold it is at that height. It's not surprising, then, that the original meaning of the word *alps* is "white."

Many of the mountains in the Alps offer fun things for visitors to do during the summer and winter months. If you like playing in the snow, visit the Alps between December and April for some exciting **skiing**, snowboarding, snowshoeing, and many other winter sports. In the summer, you can hike, mountain bike, and even paraglide over the forests of oak, spruce, and fir trees. If it's warm enough, you can even go swimming in the alpine **lakes** at the bottoms of the mountains. Every year, around 100 million people visit the Alps from all over the world!

Amazon Basin

The Amazon basin is the area of land where streams and **lakes** drain into the Amazon River. This area covers most of the top half of **South America**. Think of a bowl: if you pour water into the bowl, it will collect in the bottom. A river basin is like a huge bowl in the earth, and all the water ends up in the **river** at the bottom.

The Amazon River is one of the longest

rivers in the world. It starts high up in the **Andes** and winds around for 4,000 miles before emptying into the **ocean**! It moves the largest amount of water of any river system, and the Amazon basin is the world's largest river basin. A Spanish soldier named the river after he fought local tribes led by female warriors who reminded him of the Amazons of Greek mythology.

The trees and plants in the basin grow wild and close together. It is usually hot and humid there. Many interesting animals live in the Amazon basin. There are bats, frogs, parrots, snakes, and between 4,000 and 7,000 types of butterflies! Some humans live there, too, but not many. They live in homes shaped like beehives with slanted roofs. They survive by farming and fishing, and they use the river to travel and move goods from place to place. Can you imagine floating down the Amazon River on a raft or canoe, surrounded by a thick forest and strange creatures?

Scientists believe it is the biggest collection of plants and animals on earth. For every one human on the planet today, there are nearly 50 trees in this rainforest!

The Amazon rainforest is a tropical rainforest. This means that, if you were there, you would never feel cold, the sun would shine straight down on you at midday, and you'd probably be out in the rain—a lot! In some parts of Peru, it rains about every other day. The rainfall adds up to hundreds of inches a year! Still, even in the Amazon rainforest, some months have more rainfall than others. Scientists study these small changes in rainfall. They look at how the changes affect the rainforest and, in turn, how this might affect the rest of our planet.

If you visit the Amazon rainforest, having a flashlight could be more helpful than an umbrella. This is because its giant trees grow branches with big leaves at their tops, which act a little like a roof. These thick treetops block a lot of the sunshine so that most of the forest floor is pretty dark, even during the day. When it rains, the treetops also catch a lot of the water. It can take several minutes for any rainwater to drip down to the ground!

Amazon Rainforest

The Amazon **rainforest** covers more than half of **Peru** and also grows across the lands of eight other countries in **South America**. It is the largest of all existing rainforests! The Amazon rainforest is also filled with life of all kinds.

American Bison

Is that a giant, fuzzy cow? No, it's an American

bison, though some people confuse them with buffaloes. Bison are found in **North America** and **Europe**. They have large humped shoulders, very big heads, horns, and beards. They are the biggest animals found in North America.

In the 1700s, there were many millions of bison, especially in the Great Plains area of the United States. They were one of the main food sources for Native American Indians. Sadly, so many bison were hunted and killed that, for a time, bison were at risk of disappearing forever. Today, there is an especially large herd of bison at Yellowstone National Park in Wyoming.

Bison travel together in herds and have excellent senses of smell and hearing, but they have very poor eyesight. Never get too close to bison. If just one or two get startled, an entire herd can stampede (run wild)! They can gallop for long distances and run much faster than a human.

Bison are herbivores, meaning they only eat plants. When snow covers the ground in the winter, bison will use their giant heads like snowplows to push snow out of the way and look for grass to eat. At other times of the year, they like to roll around in shallow holes and cover themselves with dust or mud.

Fun Fact:

- Bison don't moo, but they do snort, bellow, and grunt! Can you imagine what that might sound like?

Anaconda

The anaconda is a large snake found in **South America**. There are four different kinds of anacondas, but the most common one is the green anaconda. It is dark green with black splotches all along its body. It is the second-longest snake in the world, reaching lengths of up to nearly 30 feet. And it is the heaviest snake in the world, weighing up to 500 pounds! Because it is so heavy, it likes to spend a lot of its time in the water. Have you ever noticed that you feel a little bit lighter whenever you are swimming in the water? Anacondas know this, so swimming in swamps and **rivers** makes it easier for them to get around and hunt for food.

Anacondas are carnivores, which means they eat meat. Some of their favorite foods are **capybaras** (giant rodents), fish, deer, river reptiles, and even **jaguars**! Even though anacondas eat meat, they don't attack their prey with venomous teeth, as many dangerous snakes do. Instead, an anaconda will wrap its body around the animal it has caught and squeeze it tightly. The anaconda will then eat its food whole. An anaconda's jaw can stretch very wide to fit large animals into its mouth. Its body stretches around its food, too. Once the anaconda has eaten a very large meal, it can go for weeks and even months without food! Can you imagine eating a meal so big that you wouldn't be hungry again for months?

Andean Condor

Andean condors are giant black and white birds, also called vultures. The name "Andean" tells us that they are found mostly in the **Andes** of **South America**. They are the largest flying land bird in the Western **Hemisphere**. Their wings measure over 10 feet wide. This means their wings can stretch out farther than the length of a ping-pong table!

Condors are scavengers, so they feed on carrion (dead animals). Condors like to be in open grasslands and high **mountain** areas. That way, they can spot carrion from the air. They prefer large animals like deer or cattle. The condor's beak is hooked so that it can be used to tear meat off of bones. They help the land by getting rid of carrion, which can be a source of disease.

Condors will fly more than 120 miles a day. When they take off, they flap their wings a lot, but once they're up in the air, they don't flap their wings very much at all. So how do they stay in the air? It's science! They glide on air currents, which are like **rivers** of wind.

Fun Facts:
- Males have a large red comb on their heads and a red wattle on their necks.
- It is the longest-living bird, living as long as 50 years.

- The birds keep their heads and necks extremely clean. The condors' baldness makes this easier because they don't have any feathers to trap germs!
- They can go a few days without eating.
- Andean condors are the national bird of Bolivia, Chile, Colombia, and Ecuador.

Andes Mountains

The Andes **mountains** stretch across seven countries on the western edge of **South America**. It is the longest mountain range on earth at almost 6,000 miles long. It is also the tallest mountain range outside **Asia**. If you plan on hiking it, be prepared for a tough hike with beautiful views!

Weather in the Andes varies depending on the region. In the north, it is warm and rainy, although the mountains get cold at night. In the south, it is cool and rainy; the mountains get lots of wind and rain from the Pacific Ocean. As you travel south in the Andes, it can get very cold since it is farther from the **Equator**. In the central region of **Peru**, the weather is mostly dry. There are trees, shrubs, and lots of animals. You can find many mammals, such as **llamas** and alpacas. The **Andean condor** lives here and soars through the **canyons**. You can also find reptiles and amphibians.

A long time ago, the **Incas** and other civilizations lived in the Andes Mountains. They built cities in the big **valleys** and made roads through the mountain passes. The Amazon River, which starts in the Andes, was their main water source. These people cut terraces, or flat steps, into the mountainsides to grow food on, and some of them are still in use. Since the Andes have lots of **volcanoes**, the soil is very fertile, meaning it is full of nutrients and plants grow well there. Many foods are grown in the Andes in Peru, including cocoa in the foothills, coffee high up in the mountains, and special potatoes that are blue, yellow, pink, and bright purple. (In fact, potatoes and tobacco were first grown in the Andes!) If you ever visit Peru, you should take a hike in the Andes and try a purple potato at dinner!

reaches the bottom. If you could stand right under the waterfall, you'd be drenched by a wet fog!

Angel Falls is named after an American gold hunter named Jimmie Angel. In 1937, Jimmie was flying his airplane to land on Auyán-tepui when he crash-landed near the top of the waterfall. Don't worry—he and his companions were not hurt! They had to hike down the mesa and through **jungle** for days. When Jimmie and his companions made it back safely, they told people of their adventure and of the amazing waterfall.

If you visit Angel Falls today, you'll need to take a plane ride over **jungles**, **rivers**, and **mountains** to see it. There are no hiking trails in the surrounding national park, so you can't hike to it. But at certain times of year, you can take a riverboat to the bottom of the falls!

Angel Falls

Angel Falls is a famous waterfall located in the country of Venezuela in **South America**. Angel Falls flows from the Auyán-tepui **mesa** and plunges down a sheer cliff. The water falls more than 2,600 feet, making it the tallest uninterrupted waterfall on earth! This height is taller than almost every skyscraper that has ever been built. Angel Falls is so tall that as the water pours down, it turns into mist before it

Anglo-Saxons

The Anglo-Saxons were a group of people who settled in Britain (now part of the **United Kingdom**) in the early Middle Ages. They spoke Old English, the earliest form of the English language, and lived in England and southern Scotland.

Originally, the Anglo-Saxons were just called Saxons. Saxons came from central

Europe. When the soldiers of the **Roman Empire** left Britain, many Saxons started moving there. After the Saxons settled in Britain, they developed a different culture and language (Old English) from what their ancestors had. Eventually, these British Saxons came to be known as Anglo-Saxons.

It wasn't always peaceful as the Saxons settled in Britain. The Celts, who lived in Britain before the Saxons came, were unhappy that the Saxons were taking over. They saw the Saxons as enemies and called them *Sassenach*, the Celtic word for "Saxon." Stories say the Celts in Britain united under **King Arthur** to defeat the Saxons.

Eventually, the Anglo-Saxons became a part of the British people, and everyone started speaking Old English. The Anglo-Saxons then became the main people group in Britain. From AD 650–800, there were seven different Anglo-Saxon kingdoms in Britain: Kent, Mercia, Northumbria, East Anglia, Essex, Sussex, and Wessex. United by **Alfred the Great**, the Anglo-Saxons ruled England until William the Conqueror invaded in 1066 and brought the Norman people to Britain.

Are you curious about what the Anglo-Saxons were like? You can discover more by learning about the Sutton Hoo treasures. Sutton Hoo is the site of an Anglo-Saxon king's burial, where archeologists (people who practice **archaeology**) dug up beautiful gold treasures, a wooden ship, weapons, and other interesting things.

Arabian Horse

The Arabian horse comes from the **deserts** of Arabia in southwest **Asia** and was bred by the Bedouin people. With its arched neck and high tail, it is famous for its beauty, speed, and endurance. Of all the horse breeds in the world, the Arabian is one of the oldest.

A horse is measured by hands. Each hand is four inches. The height of an Arabian horse is about 15 hands, so it is 60 inches tall at the shoulder. That's five feet, which is probably taller than you! But compared to other horse breeds, this is a smaller horse. It may be small, but its bones are very dense and its back is broad and short. This makes it a very strong animal. Even the smallest Arabian horse can carry a heavy rider.

Arabians can have different colored coats: gray, bay (reddish-brown coat and black mane), chestnut (reddish-brown coat and mane), roan (white hairs mixed in with a colored coat), and sometimes black. No matter their coat color, all Arabian horses have black skin except in spots where they have white markings. Their black skin provides protection from the hot desert sun.

Arabian horses eat at least 10–15 pounds of grass or pasture plants each day. That's a lot of food and a lot of chewing! It's a good thing that their teeth never stop growing, or else they would get worn down in no time.

The Arabian horse is smart and full of life. It can be a racehorse, a workhorse, or a show horse. It is intelligent, spirited, and also gentle and cooperative when trained well.

Arc de Triomphe

The Arc de Triomphe is a large arch in Paris, **France**. Its name means "Arch of Victory." The arch is decorated with sculptures that show famous French military victories and inspiring pictures of heroism, victory, and peace. The Arc de Triomphe is in the center of a very large, long street that runs through Paris. The arch is big enough for cars to drive through, but they are not allowed to.

The arch was ordered to be built by **Napoleon Bonaparte** in 1806 as a monument to celebrate and remind people of his victory in an important battle, the Battle of Austerlitz. But it was not completed until 1836, after Napoleon had died. It is a tradition for the French army to march under or around the arch to celebrate winning a battle or war.

In 1920, just after World War I, France placed the tomb of an unknown soldier under the Arc de Triomphe. This was to honor the soldier and ensure that he was always remembered, even though he could not be identified. Every evening at sunset, a flame is lit on his tomb. It is called the "eternal flame," or the Flame of the Nation, and it shows that the French people do not forget any soldiers who died for their country. Since the unknown soldier was buried under the arch, military parades do not march through the arch out of respect. Instead, they now march around it.

Ardennes Horse

Ardennes horses are from a land of thick forests and rough hills named the Ardennes. The Ardennes is in Belgium, Luxembourg, western Germany, and northeastern **France**. The winters in the Ardennes are severe. These horses are very hardy to live in such weather. Thankfully, their thick coats and the feathering (long hair) over their hooves help them stay warm.

When we talk about horses, there are three kinds. Light horses are used for easier work and speed, and then there are small horses, which we call ponies. Heavy horses, also known as draft horses, are used for hard work. This is what an Ardennes horse is.

Although their legs are short, Ardennes horses are still about five feet high. They also have short backs. With all their muscles, they can weigh 2,200 pounds. That's about twice the weight of a light horse! They use this weight, as well as their thick-boned legs and strong joints, to pull heavy loads. Do they sound a bit like tractors to you?

Ardennes horses love people and are very patient and very smart. They are easy to take care of and surprisingly don't need a lot of food. They enjoy water, hay, and grass.

Ardennes horses are one of the oldest draft horses in history. In the past, they were used as war horses to carry men in full armor and haul heavy artillery weapons like cannons. They can pull thousands of pounds! Today, Ardennes horses are mainly bred for forestry, farming, and driving competitions. Because of their calm, gentle nature, they also make great therapy horses. They are like big teddy bears!

Fun Fact:

- Did you know that a horse's eyes can each be looking at a different object at the same time?

Asian Elephant

The Asian elephant lives in **India** and other parts of **Asia**. It is one of the biggest and strongest land animals. It has very thick, tough skin that protects it from the weather and bug bites! Male Asian elephants have tusks: long, white teeth that stick out of their mouths.

They use their tusks for digging in the ground, scratching trees to mark their **territory**, and even fighting enemies.

Their long noses, called trunks, are very useful. They use their trunks to do many different things: breathe, communicate, play and wrestle, hold water to drink and bathe with, and gather food. Asian elephants usually eat grass, leaves, and roots. Bananas and sugarcane are some of their favorite treats.

Asian elephants like to stay together in groups, just like you enjoy playing with friends. Usually, a grandmother elephant is in charge of the group. Elephants are very smart and can learn to carry heavy things, like big logs to build forts and houses. Some elephants have even marched into battle or carried royal kings and queens on their backs in parades.

Asian elephants are different from **African elephants**. If you meet an elephant, how can you tell whether it is an Asian elephant? Look closely at its ears. Are they small and straight across the bottom, like someone just gave the elephant a haircut? That's an Asian elephant.

Attila the Hun

Attila the Hun was a warrior and king during the fifth century AD. He was the ruler of the

Hunnic Empire, which covered much of central and Eastern **Europe**. From an early age, Attila and his brother, Bleda, became excellent warriors. They learned how to ride horses, throw javelins, and shoot with a bow and arrow. Attila even learned Latin and Gothic languages. Attila and Bleda became leaders of the Huns in AD 434 after their uncle died.

Attila's empire was made up of several tribes, including the Ostrogoths, the Alans, and the Bulgars. Attila was one of the biggest enemies of the **Roman Empire**, crossing the Danube River twice to attack the Balkans, an area in southeastern Europe. He eventually invaded **Italy** and **France** as well. When Attila planned to invade Paris, the people of the city were terrified. However, a woman we know today as St. Genevieve helped to calm people down and encouraged everyone to pray rather than run away in panic. Amazingly, Attila and his Huns did not attack Paris. Thanks to St. Genevieve's intercession, the people of Paris were saved from invasion!

Attila the Hun continued his quest to conquer France until his defeat at the Battle of the Catalaunian Plains in AD 451. Even though Attila's army was mostly made of horsemen, which would usually be helpful in a battle, the Huns lost too many men. In the end, Attila lost the battle. This battle marked the end of Attila's empire. While he did invade Italy afterwards, he did not take Rome. In AD 452, Pope Leo the Great spoke with Attila and convinced him not to attack the city. It is said that while the pope spoke persuasively, Attila was also convinced by a vision of St. Peter and St. Paul with drawn swords behind the pope during this meeting.

Ayers Rock

Ayers Rock (also known as *Uluru*) is a natural landmark in Northern Territory, **Australia**. It is a huge **mountain** of sandstone that reaches 1,142 feet into the sky—that's as tall as seven and a half Statues of Liberty stacked on top of each other! Believe it or not, it is even deeper underground. If you were to walk around the entire mountain, you would have hiked 5.8 miles!

Ayers Rock is a special kind of rock formation called an inselberg, which means that it is a mountain standing by itself. Ayers Rock is very special because the ground around it is not made of sandstone like the mountain is. It is like an **island**! The ground around it is much softer and wears away slowly by erosion, but the rock itself remains in its place.

Ayers Rock is sacred to the Aboriginal people, the native people who lived in Australia even before the British came there. Because of this, visitors are not allowed to climb it. All around the rock are springs, water holes, rock **caves**, and ancient paintings. It even changes color at different times of the day because of the lighting. The most beautiful times to visit are in the morning at dawn and in the evening at sunset, when it glows red.

This natural landmark is protected as a national park. Thousands of visitors see it every year.

Aylesford Priory

If you find yourself in Kent, England, be sure to visit the Aylesford Priory and the friars who live there! A priory is a name for a small monastery or nunnery. The friars are part of the Carmelite religious order, which goes back hundreds of years. The beautiful buildings and grounds tell the story of the people who built it.

You'll be able to see what life was like in the thirteenth century as you explore the medieval courtyard, thatched-roof barns, beautiful grounds, and medieval buildings. The buildings have uneven floors and tiny doors, some of which have shells above them (an old symbol of pilgrims). The Peace Garden offers a wonderful place to enjoy nature and pray and reflect on God's goodness. The priory also features a wide variety of modern-day religious artwork including paintings, sculptures, ceramics, and colorful stained glass.

One addition to the priory, called Rosary Way, is a series of shrines that show 15 mysteries of the Rosary. Each mystery is made out of ceramic and sits on a stone pedestal. Pilgrims can walk, pray the Rosary, and then arrive at the main shrine, where they can attend Mass. There is also a statue in Rosary Way showing the Blessed Virgin Mary appearing to St. Simon Stock and giving him the brown scapular, part of the habit worn by Carmelite monks.

Each of the friars at the priory has a special job to do. Some keep the grounds tidy, some teach about the history of the order, and some offer counseling to those in need. Others work outside the order in prisons, schools, hospitals, and more.

Badger

A badger is a mammal that is about the size of a large, heavy cat. They are found in almost every part of **Europe**, from Ireland to Russia. They are so widespread that they are also in parts of western **Asia**. They live in small forests and woodlands, as well as in clearings and pastures.

Badgers live underground in a home called a sett. It is very large and can have a thousand feet of tunnels. Their strong claws and pointed noses allow them to dig through the dirt, which is called burrowing. Badgers are very dedicated to keeping themselves clean. They keep their setts just as clean and never let too much mess pile up. What a good example they set for us!

Badgers live together in groups of six to twenty. In the cold winters, they sleep in their setts but don't hibernate. They cuddle up underground and survive on food they've stored up.

As omnivores, badgers eat both plants and animals, but they eat a lot of earthworms. They can even eat wasps! The wasps can't sting them because they have very thick skin and fur.

Badgers get quite angry when they are attacked and use their powerful jaws to protect themselves. People need to be careful around them because their jaws are strong enough to crush bones. When they are left alone, though, they are calm and peaceful animals.

Bald Eagle

The bald eagle is a large bird that is found all across **North America**. It is the national bird of the United States of America. It stands up to three feet high and has a seven-foot wingspan as well as strong legs and sharp talons on its feet.

The bald eagle is a bird of prey. Eagles have extremely good vision for spotting their food. As soon as they see a tasty meal, they swoop down toward it with great speed. They swiftly grab their prey without landing and fly off with it. They carry it to a place where they can eat without worrying if their food will be stolen by a predator. Bald eagles usually eat fish but also enjoy small mammals, snakes, and other birds.

Bald eagles live in forests near the shores of **lakes** and **rivers**. If you go camping in such a place, be sure to bring your binoculars! Bald eagles hunt for food during the daytime, so you have a good chance of spotting one.

Fun Facts:
- A bald eagle's nest can be eight feet across and weigh one ton (that's as heavy as two pianos!).
- The females are about 30% larger than the males.
- The eagle is related to the hawk.
- A bald eagle can live 20 to 30 years.

Basilica of Bom Jesus

The Basilica of Bom Jesus is in Goa, a small state on the coast of **India**. This basilica is a beautiful church in the Baroque style, which is a style of art that is very detailed and fancy. It was built in 1594, and it is also India's first basilica. *Bom Jesus* means "good Jesus" or "infant Jesus" in Portuguese.

When **St. Francis Xavier** began his missionary work, he first sailed to Goa because it was the capital and main Indian **port** of Portugal, a European country that ruled over certain parts of India at that time. He started his mission there.

When St. Francis was made a saint, his tomb was put in the basilica so pilgrims could pray for his intercession. His tomb is made of bronze, silver, and marble to honor his incorrupt body. ("Incorrupt" means that, because of God's grace, St. Francis' body will never decay.)

St. Francis Xavier is considered the patron saint of Goa. Thousands of people visit the Basilica of Bom Jesus every year on December 3, his feast day! The people of Goa honor him by calling him *Goemcho Saib*, or the "Lord of Goa."

Basilica of Our Lady of Good Health

The Basilica of Our Lady of Good Health is found in Velankanni, **India**. It is also called the Basilica of Our Lady of Velankanni. It is dedicated to the Virgin Mary due to several appearances she made near the site.

In the sixteenth century, Mary appeared to a shepherd boy who was delivering milk. As he walked, he met a beautiful woman holding a child who asked for milk. He gave her some and continued walking in the hot, tropical weather. At the end of all his deliveries, he was surprised to find the milk jug was still full of fresh, cool milk!

The second appearance occurred a few years later when a beautiful woman with a child in her arms appeared to a crippled boy who was selling buttermilk. After the child asked for and received a drink, the woman told the crippled boy to visit a man in the next town and ask him to build a chapel in her honor. When the boy jumped up to take her message, he discovered he could walk! The man obeyed the message and built the chapel, where people started honoring Mary as Our Lady of Good Health.

In the seventeenth century, there was another miracle. Portuguese sailors were saved from a terrible storm by asking Mary, Star of the Sea, to help them. They landed safely at Velankanni on Mary's birthday, September 8. The sailors were so grateful that they rebuilt the small chapel into a wonderful church.

Today, over three million pilgrims visit the shrine every year on September 8. They come from all over India and other parts of the world. In 1962, Pope St. John XXIII made the church a basilica. Because of the huge number of pilgrims that visit and the miracles that have happened there, the basilica is known as the "Lourdes of the East."

Basilica of Our Lady of Guadalupe

The Basilica of Our Lady of Guadalupe is a Catholic church in Mexico City, Mexico in **North America**. It is a special church that we call a Marian shrine. The shrine was built to give glory to God and to honor our Blessed Mother under the title Our Lady of Guadalupe.

In 1531, our Blessed Mother appeared to **St. Juan Diego**. She asked him to have a church built on Tepeyac Hill. A few days later, she appeared to him again, and a miraculous image appeared on his cloak. It was a beautiful picture of Our Lady of Guadalupe. Because of this miracle, the church was built and this same image was hung inside for all to see and venerate.

About 400 years later, there were some people who wanted the image destroyed. A bomb was hidden in a vase of flowers near the image. When it exploded, it caused a lot of damage—but not to the image. The glass protecting it didn't even shatter!

Today, there is a much larger church built in its place. It is shaped like a circle so that when one is inside, the miraculous image of Mary can be seen from any angle. It is now called a basilica, and at least a dozen Masses are offered there every day of the week. Millions of people come to pray and give thanks to God and His Mother, Mary, for all their blessings.

Basilica of Our Lady of Ransom

The Basilica of Our Lady of Ransom is a Marian pilgrimage site in southern **India**. It is on an **island** in the Arabian Sea. The island is called *Vallarpadam*, so the shrine is also known as Our Lady of Vallarpadam.

The original church was built by missionaries from Portugal in 1524. When the missionaries finished building the church, they hung a picture of Our Lady above the main altar to dedicate the church to Our Lady of Ransom. In 1676, a terrible flood came and destroyed the beautiful church. After the flood, the picture of Our Lady was miraculously saved from the **river**—and it wasn't even wet!

The church became a popular pilgrimage site after another miracle. In the eighteenth century, a young Hindu woman from Vallarpadam was traveling by boat with her baby son. A storm came, turning their boat over, and they sank to the bottom of the **sea**. She promised to serve Mary for the rest of her life if she and her child were saved. Then, a local priest was told in a dream to have fishermen throw their nets in the water to find the missing woman and child. Three days after they sank into the water, they were found alive! They were baptized and spent the rest of their lives at the shrine in the service of Our Lady.

To this day, Our Lady of Ransom intercedes for seafarers, those who are on the sea a lot. On September 24, most Catholics celebrate Our Lady of Mercy, but Vallarpadam still celebrates Our Lady of Ransom.

Basilica of Our Lady of the Pillar

The Basilica of Our Lady of the Pillar is a shrine in **Spain** dedicated to the earliest Marian apparition. In AD 40, the Blessed Virgin Mary appeared to the Apostle James the Greater as he preached in what is now Spain.

After Jesus' death, Resurrection, and ascension, the apostles traveled to share the Gospel. James encountered difficulties in Spain and was becoming discouraged in his missionary work. Tradition tells us that Mary appeared to him to comfort him and encourage him to keep sharing the Good News about her Son. This is extraordinary because she was

still alive on earth at this time, meaning she was in two places at the same time! Some saints have also been given this supernatural gift.

The basilica is located in Zaragoza in northeastern Spain. Inside the basilica, a wooden statue depicts Mary standing on a pillar, baby Jesus in her left arm, and a dove in His left hand. The pillar is made of jasper, a kind of gemstone. It is protected by two cases, one of bronze and one of silver. A mantle or cloth covers the cases most of the time. The mantle is removed three times a month so people can see the pillar. The feast day of Our Lady of the Pillar is October 12.

Basilica of Saint Anthony of Padua

The Basilica of St. Anthony is located in Padua, **Italy**. It honors **St. Anthony of Padua**. The high altar was created by Donatello, a very famous Italian sculptor, and it features a bronze statue of Mary holding the Child Jesus, as well as other statues. Donatello also created four reliefs (wall carvings) showing events from St. Anthony's life.

If you visited the basilica, one of the first things you'd see is a painting of Our Lady of the Pillar (like the one at the **Basilica of Our Lady of the Pillar**), and after that, you'd see the Chapel of St. Anthony. The Chapel of St. Anthony is referred to as the spiritual heart of the shrine. A slab of green marble covers St. Anthony's burial place, and you can touch the cool marble as you pray silently. Many people also leave prayer cards on the tomb, as well as thank-you notes for answered prayers.

There are several buildings on the basilica property, including five cloisters. A cloister is a home for monks or nuns who vow to leave the rest of the world and remain there praying. There are also several museums on the basilica's grounds that you can visit and learn about the art, St. Anthony's life, and stories of his intercession.

Basilica of Saint Francis of Assisi

The Basilica of St. Francis of Assisi is a large, beautiful church dedicated to **St. Francis** in his hometown, Assisi, in **Italy**. The basilica is the home of the Franciscans.

It is said that St. Francis wanted to be buried on the hill where this church is built. It was called the Hill of Hell because criminals were put to death there. Francis wanted to be buried there to be like Jesus, who was killed on a hill where criminals died.

As soon as St. Francis was canonized in the year 1228, the town of Assisi began to build the church in his honor. The pope ordered it to be built and laid the foundation stone (an important stone at the corner of a building) himself. The basilica was designed by the most famous architect at the time and supervised by one of St. Francis' oldest followers.

There are a few parts to this basilica: the Upper Church, the Lower Church, and a crypt where St. Francis is now buried. (A crypt is an underground chamber.) When the Lower Church was finished in 1230, it was meant to be the crypt. Because people were afraid that someone might try to steal St. Francis' bones, they were buried in a secret location. But the location was so secret, the priests forgot where he was! In 1818, St. Francis' bones were rediscovered under the floor of the Lower Church. Then, the crypt was built so that people could visit his burial place.

Both the Upper and Lower Churches have important fresco paintings on the walls. (Frescoes are paintings made on wet plaster.) Many different artists came to paint the church in honor of St. Francis. If you visit, try to find the painting of Mary, the cow, and the donkey smiling at baby Jesus.

Basilica of Saint Thérèse of Lisieux

The Basilica of St. Thérèse of Lisieux is a shrine that was built to honor the Little Flower, **St. Thérèse of Lisieux**. It stands high on a hill in Lisieux, **France**. Lisieux is where the Carmelite saint lived and died.

The church building is so grand! Four thousand people can fit inside at one time. There is a large side altar that has a beautiful box holding a relic of St. Thérèse. If you look through the glass, you can see the bones of her right forearm. Countless people come to see it, light candles, and ask St. Thérèse to pray for them.

There are also 18 smaller side altars. They are from different countries around the world, like Ireland, Ukraine, **Canada**, Mexico, Germany, and Brazil. Each one is the country's way of saying, "Thank you for your prayers, St. Thérèse. Please shower your roses on our land."

Below the church floor is an underground chamber called a crypt. It holds the relics of St. Thérèse's parents, who also became saints. Do you know their names? (That's right—they are Sts. Louis and Zélie!)

Many people who travel to visit the shrine of Our Lady of Lourdes also visit the Basilica of St. Thérèse. Two million visitors a year means there are a lot of people who love St. Thérèse!

Basilica of the Annunciation

The Basilica of the Annunciation is a large Catholic church in Nazareth, Israel, which is also called the Holy Land. Tradition tells us that this basilica stands on very holy ground. It is believed to be where the Annunciation took place.

Do you remember that the first Joyful Mystery of the Rosary is called the Annunciation? The Annunciation is when the Angel Gabriel appeared to the Virgin Mary. He asked if she would be the mother of the Son of God, Jesus. She said yes! That was the blessed beginning of God becoming man to save us from our sins and opening the gates of Heaven to us.

The Basilica of the Annunciation is not just a big church. It's a special church that was built to help us remember the Annunciation, Our Lady's "yes" to becoming Jesus' Mother—and our Mother too!

On the walls of the two-story basilica, there are dozens of colorful images of Our Lady. They are gifts from different countries around the world. It is beautiful to see so many different cultures honoring Mary, each in their own way.

Over two thousand years, the basilica has been destroyed and rebuilt many times. The one standing today took about 10 years to build.

Basilica of the Holy House of Loreto

Have you ever tried to picture the house the Holy Family lived in? Well, you can see it if you visit the Basilica of the Holy House of Loreto in Italy. This Marian shrine has within it the Holy House of Loreto.

The structure is plain and only has three stone walls, one door, and one window. It is said to be where Mary grew up, where she received the Annunciation from the Angel Gabriel and conceived Jesus by the Holy Spirit, and where the family lived during Jesus' childhood. After Jesus' ascension, the house was made into a church where the apostles celebrated the first Eucharist after the Resurrection.

Tradition teaches that in the year 1291, during the Crusades, the Holy Family's house was in danger of being destroyed by Muslim soldiers. To protect it, angels carried it from Nazareth to Croatia and then to Italy, where it is today.

Our Lady of Loreto is the patroness of air passengers and pilots. Pilot Charles Lindbergh took a small Loreto statue with him on his famous flight across the Atlantic Ocean in 1927, and the crew of Apollo 8 brought a Loreto medallion with them on their flight to the Moon in 1968.

Basilica of the National Shrine of the Immaculate Conception

The Basilica of the National Shrine of the Immaculate Conception in Washington, DC, honors Mary as the patroness of the United States. This shrine is one of the largest shrines in the whole world, and it is the largest Christian church in all of North America. Many special events are held there each year, as well as daily Mass.

The Basilica of the National Shrine of the Immaculate Conception is so big that six thousand people can be inside at the same time! People started building the shrine in 1920. It was built with a beautiful mix of styles, so it has high domes, golden mosaics, Greek-style columns, as well as simpler arches and windows.

The shrine has one of the largest glass mosaics in the entire world—it is made of 24 tons of Venetian glass. Construction was completed in 2017, and the dome was dedicated on December 8, the feast of the Immaculate Conception.

Many popes have visited the shrine, including Pope St. John Paul II and Pope Benedict XVI. In 2013, a special Mass from the basilica was shown on TV as two first-class relics of Americans **St. Kateri Tekakwitha** and St. Marianne Cope were enshrined there. Pope Francis has also visited the shrine, and in 2015, he celebrated a Mass there to canonize St. Junípero Serra.

Beaver

A beaver is a large rodent that lives in **North America** and **Europe**. It has webbed hind-feet and a wide, flat, scaly tail. A beaver lives both on land and in water. When the beaver is on land, he gathers food and uses his powerful front teeth to cut away at tree trunks until the trees fall over. He builds his home, called a lodge, in ponds.

If there is no pond, the beaver must make one! He does this by building a dam. A dam is a strong wall that blocks the flow of water in a **river** or stream. How does a beaver build a wall? Using his teeth again, the beaver drags the trees he has cut down across the water until the logs partly block the flow of the water. The water pools behind the dam and makes a pond.

This lodge built of sticks, mud, and stones gives the beaver protection from wolves, coyotes, and bears. In the winter, beavers do not hibernate. Instead, they live deep inside their lodge, where they have food like bark, plants, and fruits that they stored up during the fall.

Because the beaver eats plants like wood, grass, pondweed, and water lilies, it is called an herbivore. It does not eat fish.

The beaver has been known to live up to 24 years of age in the wild. Unlike humans, a beaver does not stop growing when it reaches a certain age but continues growing all its life. Its teeth also continue to grow because otherwise they would get worn down by chewing on so much wood!

Bengal Tiger

The Bengal tiger is the largest wild cat in the world, and it can be found in the grasslands and forests of **India** and southern **Asia**. Just like human fingerprints, the stripes on a Bengal tiger are unique to each tiger. They have long claws, and their teeth are three inches long, the longest of any cat.

Bengal tigers like to live alone. The males use many methods to mark their **territory**, including scratching trees with special scratches. They spend most of the day resting in the shade. They are most active from dusk to dawn, when they search for food. Bengal tigers like to eat other animals such as water buffaloes, **wild boars**, deer, porcupines, and hares. They hide in tall grasses and trees while stalking their prey.

Bengal tiger cubs are born with thick, wooly fur. During their first month, the cubs quadruple in size! When they are two months old, they begin to follow their mom on her hunting outings. At five or six months old, they begin to help with the hunting. When they are two or three years old, they leave their family and look for an area to make their own territory. Imagine leaving home and being on your own at two years old. Tigers sure grow up fast!

Fun Facts:

- Bengal tigers are the national animal of India.
- They can run at speeds of up to 40 miles per hour.
- Instead of purring, Bengal tigers make a snorting sound where they blow air out of their nose while keeping their mouth shut.
- They can live 10–15 years in the wild, and 15–20 years in captivity.

Big Ben, Big Ben is really the nickname for the large bell inside it. The tower is called Elizabeth Tower after Queen Elizabeth II.

Building the clock tower took 16 years! It was completed in 1859. It is constructed like a layer cake. The first layer is its foundation, a thick concrete base below ground. The second layer, the tower's base, is made of bricks covered with limestone that make the tower seem smooth. Last is the spire, the part that points to the sky. The clock has a Gothic design, so it has lots of fancy details and looks a little like a castle.

Big Ben is famous for telling time accurately. Inside the clock are cables with heavy weights tied to them. There are also three sets of gears in the clock, called trains. The going train makes the clock's hands move. The chiming train makes the sound you hear when the clock chimes every 15 minutes. The striking train makes Big Ben ring each hour. Big Ben rings so loudly that if you stand nearby, you can feel your body shake from the sound!

Big Ben

If you are visiting London in the **United Kingdom** near the Thames River, you can't miss seeing a huge clock tower called Big Ben. No matter where you stand, you can see one of its four faces. Although people call the tower

Bird-watching

Bird-watching is an activity that is popular in the country of **Peru**. A bird-watcher in Peru has a chance to see more species of birds than in all of **North America** combined! In fact, one-sixth

● ● ●   ● ● ●

of the earth's bird species can be found in that one country. Famous birds in Peru include the large **Andean condor**, three different kinds of **flamingos**, and the Andean cock-of-the-rock, which is the national bird of Peru.

If you planned a trip to go bird-watching in Peru, you would probably go with a professional guide. Guides are trained in where and when to look to find the greatest variety of birds. These guides are familiar with the country's many bird-watching regions and trails. They also know the best time of year to find certain birds. For example, the best time to find the three kinds of flamingos all in one place is during the rainy season, which is usually between December and March. Thousands of flamingos will visit the shallow **lakes** formed by the rain.

When bird-watching, don't forget to bring a pair of binoculars to help you to watch birds from far away without scaring them. If you bring a camera, you can take photos of the amazing birds you see!

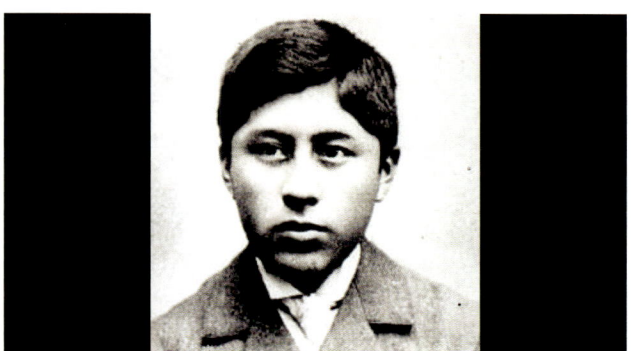

Blessed Ceferino Namuncurá

The life of Bl. Ceferino Namuncurá gives us a good example of virtue and hard work.

Ceferino grew up in a large family in a small town named Chimpay in Argentina, **South America**. His father was chief of the Mapuches, who were some of the first people living in Chile and Argentina. Once Ceferino became a man, his job would be to help his people and try to make their lives easier.

To prepare him for the job, he was sent to school far away at the age of eleven. The other boys were mean to him because he was the only Mapuche at the school. He was very unhappy, so he moved to a Catholic school in Buenos Aires. This is where he learned about St. Dominic Savio and tried to be just like him. Ceferino loved Jesus in the Eucharist and always spoke to Him like a friend. He was an excellent student, sang well in the choir, played sports, did card tricks, and taught the other boys how to shoot a bow and arrow.

After his school days, he wanted to help his people as much as ever. They did not know about the love of God, so he wanted to become a priest for them. But while studying for the priesthood, Ceferino became very sick and died of tuberculosis. The year was 1905, and he was almost 19 years old.

He always loved his nation of Argentina and his Mapuche people. Now, he does indeed help them from Heaven by his prayers. The Church celebrates his feast day on August 26.

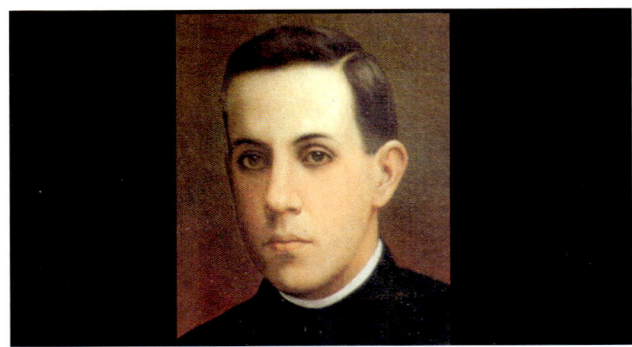

Blessed Miguel Pro

Bl. Miguel Pro Juárez was a young man who was shot for being a Catholic priest in Mexico, **North America**. His brief time as a Jesuit priest was spent during the Cristero War. He was very brave to stay in Mexico during a time when priests and nuns were being killed.

In Mexico, the churches had been closed and their valuable items stolen. It was forbidden to receive the sacraments. Fr. Pro was a priest who loved God's people as a true father. He knew he must bring them the sacraments. But it was too dangerous to be seen dressed as a priest. Instead, he dressed in the clothes of different workmen and went about the streets in disguise.

It was in November of 1927 when Fr. Pro was arrested for a crime he did not do. When led to the prison yard to be shot, he stretched his arms out in the form of a cross, holding a crucifix and rosary. He cried, *"Vivo Cristo Rey!"* (Long live Christ the King!) and was shot by the firing squad.

Miguel Pro had great courage when he faced death. This was because each day of his life was spent praying, doing works of charity, and becoming more in love with God. God's grace was with him to the end. His feast day is celebrated on November 23.

Blue Marlin

The Atlantic blue marlin is a fish that lives in the Atlantic Ocean near **South America** as well as near parts of **North America** and **Africa**. This amazing fish is big and fast, and it can change color when it hunts other fish and squid. One of the blue marlin's special features is its long and pointy upper jaw, called a bill. This bill is like having a sword or spear for a nose. When the blue marlin hunts, it uses its bill to stun or wound its prey. It then swims back for its meal.

Blue marlins are big fish. Females can grow to be as long as 15 feet and weigh more than 5 or even 10 adult human beings combined. One of the biggest blue marlins ever caught weighed more than 1,400 pounds! This big fish is also one of the fastest fish in the **sea**. It can swim at speeds of more than 20 miles per hour.

Blue marlins follow **ocean** currents that help them travel great distances. They like to swim in warmer surface waters at night and often dive deeper during the day. They can dive hundreds of feet below the surface.

Blue Whale

The blue whale is found in most of the world's **oceans**. It doesn't live in the Arctic Ocean, but it does live in the waters around **Antarctica**. It is the largest animal ever known to exist. This **sea** mammal is longer than three school buses. Everything about the blue whale is massive!

Blue whales are usually found alone or in small groups. They migrate to cooler waters in summer and warmer waters in winter. They give birth to their babies, called calves, in winter.

Blue whales eat about 40 million small, shrimp-like animals called krill every day. Instead of teeth, they use something called baleen to help them eat. Baleen acts like a filter. Blue whales swim toward the krill and gulp in a huge amount of water. The water pushes the krill through the baleen, where they are trapped for the whales to swallow.

Blue whales sing! Their voices are very low and very loud—the loudest voice of any animal. Their only natural enemy is the orca whale, also known as the killer whale. Blue whales usually live for 80–90 years.

Fun Facts:

- The blue whale's tongue weighs as much as an elephant!
- The blue whale's heart is about the same size as a Volkswagen Beetle car.
- The age of a blue whale can be estimated by counting the layers in their wax-like earplugs. A layer of wax is added twice a year.

Borra Caves

The Borra Caves are the deepest **caves** in **India**. Located on the east coast of India in a **valley** filled with trees, these caves go down 260 feet. Almost no sunlight gets inside the Borra Caves! Imagine what it would be like to explore a cave in total darkness. You would have to hold your hand out in front of you when you walk so you wouldn't bump your nose into the cave wall!

The word *borra* means "hole." There is a legend that these caves were discovered by a farmer when his cow fell through a hole in the roof of the caves!

The Borra Caves are full of beautiful rock formations. These sculptures are formed when water trickles down from the roof of the caves and dissolves the limestone the caves are made of. The drips of limestone that hang like icicles from the roof are called stalactites, and the drips that build up on the ground are called stalagmites. The stalagmites and stalactites in the Borra Caves have interesting shapes. They have been given funny names based on their shapes, such as "Mother-Child," "Human Brain," "Mushrooms," and "Crocodile."

Even though these caves are so deep and dark, there are some creatures who live in them: the fruit bat and the golden gecko. Both are nocturnal, meaning they are awake at night and sleep during the day. Archaeologists (people who practice **archaeology**) have also found some stone tools in the caves, which means that at some point long ago, humans may have lived in them, too.

Brushtail Possum

The brushtail possum is a **marsupial** found in **Australia** and some of its surrounding **islands**. Brushtail possums have tails with bushy fur that grows only on the top side. They can use their tails to wrap around tree branches like a monkey.

Brushtail possums spend most of their time in trees and eat several types of leaves, fruits, and seeds. Sometimes, they also eat insects, small animals, and birds' eggs. They are nocturnal, meaning they sleep during the day and come out to eat at night.

Brushtail possums make their dens in **caves**, hollow trees, or even the attics of houses.

The brushtail possum has one baby at a time, which stays in its mother's pouch for four to five months. After that, the baby rides on its mother's back, like Virginia opossums do, or it stays home in the den when the mother is away. They usually live alone and can live to be 13 years old.

Buckingham Palace

Buckingham Palace stands in the city of London in the **United Kingdom**. It was built in 1703 as a home for the Duke of Buckingham, and it was bought by King George III in 1761 to serve as a vacation home for Queen Charlotte. Today, the king of England works and lives in it. Queen Victoria was the first king or queen to stand on the balcony and wave to the people. Today, the royal family stands on the balcony and waves to the people on special occasions like coronations, weddings, birthdays, and births.

Buckingham Palace is magnificent—a proper palace. Many famous art pieces are found in its rooms and hallways. It has 775 rooms! You might need a map to find your way around. There are office rooms, royal bedrooms, guest bedrooms, staff bedrooms, and ballrooms. There is also a post office, movie theater, swimming pool, doctor's office, jeweler's workshop, and beautiful gardens.

You can visit Buckingham Palace! You may even get to see the changing of the guards. Guards dressed in red jackets and tall, furry bearskin hats stand in front of the palace, and every morning at eleven o'clock, one set of guards goes off duty while another comes to take its place.

Fun Facts:

- There are about 500 clocks in the palace. It takes 50 hours for the two people who look after the clocks to change the times on them in the spring and fall.
- The famous composer Mozart and many United States presidents have been guests at Buckingham Palace.
- There are 78 bathrooms in Buckingham Palace.
- There are 760 windows, and they are cleaned every six weeks.
- There are over 40,000 lightbulbs.
- Over 450 people work in the palace as servants, chefs, footmen, cleaners, plumbers, gardeners, chauffeurs, electricians, and more.

People watch from the stands to cheer for the brave team of bullfighters as they face a bull.

Today, bullfighting is mostly done on foot with a cape and a dagger. This style started in Spain in the eighteenth century. The bullfighting team is made up of seven men called *toreros*, and the leader is called the *matador*. The bullfighters wear special costumes that look like eighteenth-century Spanish clothing. If you watch a bullfight from the stands, you can tell who the *matador* is because of his shiny gold costume. His costume is called a *traje de luces*, which means "suit of lights."

The *matador* also has a red cape. He waves it around to get the bull's attention. When the bull sees the cape waving around, it charges at the cape. Then, the *toreros* work together to fight the bull. Fighting a bull can be dangerous because the bull has sharp horns. But the *toreros* are very brave and quick, so they jump out of the bull's way at the last second.

Fun Fact:

If you were a *matador*, you would be able to pray in a chapel at the bullring before going to fight the bull.

Bullfighting

Bullfighting is an old sport that is still practiced in **Spain**. It happens in a big, open arena.

Caesar Augustus

Caesar Augustus was the first Roman emperor in **Italy**. He came from an important family and was the great-nephew of **Julius Caesar**, who adopted him because Julius Caesar didn't have any sons. Before Julius Caesar was killed, he named Caesar Augustus as his heir, but it took Augustus almost 20 years of fighting to become Emperor Caesar Augustus, sole ruler of Rome.

Caesar Augustus was intelligent, well-liked, and a great leader. During his 40-year reign, he brought peace and success to the **Roman Empire**. He rebuilt towns that were damaged by wars and built new bridges, roads, and public buildings. He strengthened the army and navy. He expanded the Roman Empire across three different **continents**. Instead of keeping all the power, Caesar Augustus gave some of it to a group of men called senators. He kept the people of Rome happy by giving many people

free grain and holding free gladiator games in the **Colosseum**.

Caesar Augustus' reign and the 160 years after are known as the *Pax Romana*, which means "the peace of the Roman Empire." He died at the age of 75. For 400 years, his title, Augustus, was the title of every Roman emperor. Romans even considered him to be a god after his death, just as they considered Julius Caesar a god. Not many people have a month (August) named after them, but Caesar Augustus does! Caesar Augustus was one of the greatest emperors and played an important role in shaping ancient Rome.

Camargue Salt Marshes

The Camargue salt **marshes** are saltwater pools in the south of **France** where people have been harvesting salt since ancient times.

The Camargue region is the area in and around the delta, or mouth, of the Rhône River. There are many shallow **lakes** here called lagoons. The water is salty because it used to be part of the Mediterranean Ocean. Fortunately, this is the perfect start for making salt.

Salt is known as "white gold" because it used to be very expensive. It was rare and very important for preserving food and other things. Besides, can you imagine what your food would taste like without any salt? Blegh! A very good way to make salt is to collect salt water in shallow ponds and let the sun and wind dry it up until salt crystals form on top. Then, the salt can be collected.

Charlemagne even built a tower here so that guards could protect the workers as they harvested the precious salt. Later, this tower was attached to a Benedictine monastery, then it was replaced by a new tower built by **St. Louis IX** that you can still see today. Many monasteries in the area harvested salt to support themselves.

If you visit the Camargue salt marshes today, you can climb up the medieval walls of the city of Aigues-Mortes. From there, you might be able to see some **flamingos** or some of the special horses and bulls bred here that wander around in herds. Of course, you'll see some salt pools. Guess what? They're pink! The salt water in this area is naturally pink because of tiny algae in the water that produce a reddish substance called beta-carotene.

Camel

Camels live in many **deserts** of **Africa** and also parts of **Asia**. They look a little bit like **llamas**, but they are easy to recognize because they have tall humps on their backs. African camels, called dromedary camels or Arabian camels, have only one hump. But Asian camels, called Bactrian camels, have two humps. Camels like to live in hot deserts. Their thick coats of hair keep the hot sunlight away from their skin, and it keeps them warm during the cooler nights. God also gave camels special ways to keep the sand out: three eyelids, two rows of extra-long eyelashes, and nostrils that shut tight.

Sometimes, camels can go months without water. Even their blood has special properties to make it possible for them to drink and store extreme amounts of water. A camel can safely drink much more water in 10 minutes than a human being can drink in one day! Some camels can drink up to 53 gallons at a time.

The camel's main defense against starvation is its hump (or humps). Whenever it can eat extra food, the excess is stored as fat inside its hump. The fat inside gives them energy for long trips through the hot desert. When food is hard to find, a camel can use the fat stored in its hump for energy. This makes the hump soften and shrink. When a camel's hump droops, it's a sign they need food and water.

It's like having a built-in backpack for food! If this fat was evenly spread around their bodies, they would get too hot.

Camels feed on shrubs, grass, and things that other herbivores (plant eaters) avoid, like thorns. They have very tough mouths that protect them from spiky and dry plants.

Camels are very social and live in herds. Their only predators are wolves. They make a lot of different sounds, including moaning and groaning sounds, high-pitched bleats, loud bellows, and rumbling roars. Mothers and their newborns even hum to each other!

Camels are very helpful to humans, carrying people and supplies for a long way—even across deserts. Since ancient times, camels have been used for travel and to carry goods along the **Silk Road**. Camels can carry loads of up to 900 pounds and travel up to 25 miles a day, even while carrying so much. Their feet are wide so that they can walk through sand without sinking. Camels can be quite fast— they can run up to 40 miles per hour. Dromedary camels are usually faster, while Bactrian camels often run at around 15 miles per hour.

Camino de Santiago

The Camino de Santiago is a popular pilgrimage in **Spain**. People come from all over the world to make this journey. There are different routes to take, but all paths lead to the **Cathedral of Santiago de Compostela** in northwest Spain. Every year, thousands of pilgrims travel on foot, walking many miles per day. They typically travel light, carrying only a walking stick and a backpack with basic needs such as food, water, extra clothes, shoes, and other small items.

The Camino de Santiago is also known as the Way of St. James. St. James was one of Jesus' twelve apostles, and he was the first of the apostles to be martyred. In the first century AD, he traveled to what is now Spain, preaching the Gospel. Later, a tomb was discovered near Santiago de Compostela with remains that are believed to be St. James'. Many pilgrims traveling the Camino de Santiago look forward to visiting the relics of St. James at the end of the journey.

While many people travel the Camino de Santiago for religious reasons, others go for the cultural experience or as a fitness challenge. The journey can take days or even weeks to complete, depending on the route and how fast you walk. Routes can take you through the open countryside, wooded areas, rolling hills, and **valleys**. There are also churches and villages you can visit along the way. The most popular route is the French Way. It begins at the border of **France** and stretches 491 miles across Spain. That might seem long, but it is not the longest route.

A scalloped shell, the common sign of pilgrimage, can be seen throughout the Camino de Santiago, guiding pilgrims on every route. Many people also receive a shell at the beginning of their journey to identify themselves as pilgrims. "*Buen camino!*" means "Happy trails!" or "Good walk!" in Spanish. People say this to greet each other along the Camino de Santiago.

Canada Goose

The Canada goose comes from **North America** and especially **Canada**. You have surely seen flocks of them if you live near the **Great Lakes**. They are some of the best-known water birds and are some of the largest geese in the world.

These wild water birds don't mind living near people, especially if the people feed them. Many people don't want them around, though, because they make a lot of noise and leave the sidewalks messy with their droppings. They also tend to follow people around, begging for food. Have you ever done that to your mother? You goose!

Canada geese are mostly herbivores, so they usually eat green plants and grains. They bite and tear the long grasses with a quick jerk of their head. Because they are water birds, they like to live near fresh water and will eat algae or seaweed. Sometimes they might also eat insects and small fish.

Geese are very protective of their **territory**. If their nest is being attacked or a person gets too close to their territory, they will make a hissing sound to frighten the enemy away. They can be very loud birds, and they have 13 different calls. Their honks can even be heard when they are migrating 3,000 feet overhead!

Migration is when birds fly south in the fall and north in the spring. They do this to move to warmer temperatures where food can be more easily found. A flock of Canada geese will fly together in a V-shape to save their energy. The lead goose at the tip of the V has the hardest job: he breaks through the air, creating a pocket behind him that is easier to fly in. Each goose in the lines behind him finds the right spot so that all the geese can fly more easily. When the lead goose gets tired, he flies to the back of the V and another goose takes a turn. This way, geese are able to fly 70% farther than they could on their own!

Fun Facts:
- Young geese are called goslings.
- The call of a male is called a "honk."
- The higher-pitched call of a female is called a "hrink."

Canals and Gondolas of Venice

In northern **Italy**, there is an unusual city named Venice. Can you imagine a city with no roads and no cars? Venice is like that. Instead of roads, Venice has waterways called **canals**. There are over 175 canals throughout the city.

These canals cross into each other to create many tiny **islands**—126 of them! People have built many bridges and even filled in some canals with land so they can walk between the islands. They also use boats to float on the canals themselves.

The people of Venice have special long rowboats called gondolas that they use on the canals. A gondola is made by hand and is built out of wood. If you were to take a ride on a gondola, you would be greeted by the gondola captain, called a gondolier. The gondolier stands up near the back of the boat and uses a long wooden oar to row, to turn, and to stop the gondola.

Tourists from all over the world like to visit Venice to take a gondola ride and explore the city's many canals. Be sure to stay inside the boat, though! The water in the canals is pretty deep.

Capybara

The capybara is a giant rodent found almost everywhere in **South America**. Rodents include mice, rats, chinchillas, and guinea pigs, and the capybara is the largest of all rodents. How big are they? They can grow to over four feet long and two feet tall! Adult capybaras usually weigh about 100 pounds. They look a lot like giant guinea pigs, don't they?

Capybaras like to live together in groups. They can be found in tropical **rainforests** near **rivers**, **lakes**, and swamps. They like to swim and can even hold their breath for up to five minutes. Most humans can't hold their breath for that long. Can you? Capybaras are plant eaters. They like eating plants that grow in the water and on land, and sometimes they eat fruits and tree bark. Since tropical rainforests have wet and dry seasons, capybaras will change what they eat depending on what is growing at the time. Capybaras don't chew like most animals do, but instead they grind their food between their teeth by moving their jaws sideways.

Fun Facts:

- Capybaras can take naps in the water! They keep their noses above water while they sleep.
- Capybaras can live for up to 12 years, but usually they only live for 4–6 years.

Caracal

The caracal is a wild cat commonly found in southwest **Asia** and **Africa**. It is a medium-sized cat with long, powerful legs for jumping and very sharp teeth for eating birds, rodents, and other smaller animals. What makes the caracal different from other wild cats are its long, pointed ears. Caracals have extra-long bits of dark fur on the tips of their ears. These extra bits of fur are believed to help caracals hear better. Caracals also flick these extra bits of fur on their ears to communicate with each other. They also make other familiar cat sounds, like meowing, purring, and hissing.

Caracals like to live alone or in pairs. They usually hunt after sunset in forests, **savannas**, and other places where there is very little rainfall and plenty of places to hide and wait for their prey to come by. When caracals run after their prey, they make almost no noise. Can you imagine running as fast as you can and making hardly any sound?

Most caracals grow to be about three feet long and can weigh over 40 pounds. However, male caracals are larger in size than females. Although they are tough hunters, mother caracals are very kind to their babies. A mother caracal will usually have two or three babies at a time. Young caracals can expect some excellent cuddle time with their mother and with their other brothers and sisters.

Caribou

Caribou, also known as reindeer, are beautiful mammals in the deer family. You can find them in **North America**, where they are called caribou, and in **Europe** and Russia, where they are called reindeer. Caribou live in herds in **mountains** and forests. They migrate every year between their winter and summer grounds. Their migrations are the longest land migrations on earth. They migrate 2,000 miles each year! Their long, strong legs allow them to walk so far. They are also excellent swimmers.

Caribou have large hooves that help them balance on slippery surfaces like ice and snow. This makes caribou very good at pulling sleighs. Their hooves are also perfect for digging because they are hollow on the bottom. Caribou use their hooves like shovels to dig through snow to find food in the winter: lichen, moss, and fungi (like mushrooms). Caribou like to eat grasses and other plants in the summer.

For most kinds of deer, only the males have antlers. But both male and female caribou have antlers. Antlers take at least six months to grow to full size. Then, they fall off and new ones grow. The males lose theirs in the winter, and the females lose theirs in the spring. Caribou use their antlers to defend themselves, and the males also use their antlers to fight each other.

Caribou noses are covered in short hollow

hairs. This helps warm the cold air they breathe in. Caribou have two layers of fur. The undercoat is thick wool, while the top layer is long. Together, their fur is three inches thick.

Years ago, people hunted caribou for their meat, fur, skin, antlers, and bones. They made warm outer clothing from the fur and skin, and they crafted useful tools from the antlers and bones.

Like horses, caribou can be tamed and made friendly to humans. The first humans to tame caribou were the people of Siberia and Scandinavia. Even today, there are people in the world who keep them as pets.

Baby caribou are called calves. Calves are able to stand an hour after being born, and they can walk just three to six hours after being born. When they are two days old, they can travel 10 miles a day.

Originally, the beach was called *Praia de Augas Santas*, Galician for "Beach of the Holy Waters."

The cliffs were formed like this from erosion, the slow carving away of the rock by **ocean** waves crashing against it over many years. In ancient times, the waves carved **caves** in the cliffs. Then the roofs of some of these caves collapsed, leaving just arches or towers of rock.

At low tide, you can walk along the beach under arches of rock up to 100 feet high and see huge caves carved into the cliffs. There are also narrow spaces with sandy floors between tall cliffs that look like hallways to the ocean. The beach here has fine sand. Visitors must be careful, though, because some areas can only be reached for an hour or so before the tide comes in very quickly! At high tide, the water covers the sand around the cliffs and only a small area of the beach is left.

Cathedral Beach

Cathedral Beach is a beach with beautiful cliffs in Galicia, a region in **Spain**. The cliffs are made from slate and other similar types of rock. As a Natural Monument of Galicia, it draws many visitors. It is commonly called Cathedral Beach because the cliffs are shaped like the huge rounded arches (doorways) and flying buttresses (bridge-like supports) of a cathedral.

Cave of Altamira

The Cave of Altamira in Cantabria, **Spain** is the first place that prehistoric cave paintings were discovered. The **cave** is about 900 feet long and has drawings and paintings of animals on its rock ceilings and walls. Scientists think some of the paintings could have been made up to 36,000 years ago. Objects like tools were also found in the cave, showing that people may have lived there long ago.

The animals in the cave paintings are simple but very beautiful. They include bison, deer, horses, and goats. There are also pictures of human hands and other symbols. Some of the animals were painted onto huge rocks that bulge from the ceiling. This makes them look very round and lifelike.

You might be wondering what people used for paint in prehistoric times. The paintings in Altamira were first outlined with charcoal and then painted with types of yellow and red clay called ochre and hematite. This clay is easily found in the dirt and can be mixed to make paint.

An eight-year-old girl discovered the paintings deep inside the cave in the nineteenth century. No one knows why the paintings in Altamira were made. Can you imagine crawling deep under the ground to paint pictures? The cave must have been a very special place in prehistoric times.

To keep the paintings safe from mold and other problems, the cave is now closed to visitors. However, people can still visit the museum at Altamira and tour the Neocave, an exact copy of the cave and its paintings.

Argentina in **South America**. The opening of the **cave** is 50 feet tall and 50 feet wide. If you step inside, you will find outlines of people's hands stenciled onto the walls of the **cave**. Have you ever placed your hand on a piece of paper and traced around it to make a drawing of your own hand? Imagine over 2,000 drawings like that on the walls of this cave!

The paintings in this cave are very old. Archaeologists (people who practice **archaeology**) also believe that paintings were added over time. They found this out partly by seeing how old the painting tools discovered nearby were. These painting tools were pipes made out of old bones, used to blow paint. What a creative way to spray paint! After blowing the paint, the person would take his hand away, leaving a perfect outline of his hand. Besides hands, there are also drawings of animals, people, and many interesting patterns like circles and zigzags.

These paintings are the oldest known cave paintings in South America. Imagine if you had lived so many years ago that you could say that your painting had been the first to ever exist there. What would your first drawing have been?

Fun Fact:

There are more left hands than right hands drawn in the cave. This means that most painters held the bone pipe in their right hand to spray the paint.

Cave of the Hands

The Cave of the Hands is located in Santa Cruz,

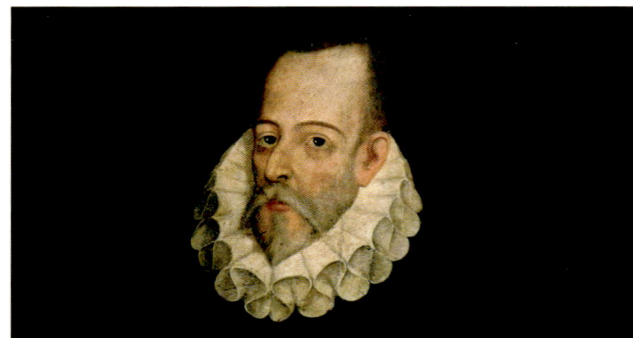

Cervantes

Miguel de Cervantes was an author born in **Spain** in 1547. Though his family was once wealthy, they fell on hard times, so Cervantes grew up poor. In his early twenties, Cervantes was sent to Rome to work for a cardinal, where he learned more about the Faith.

A year later, Cervantes joined the Spanish Navy and fought in many battles. During the Battle of Lepanto, he was wounded and could no longer use his left arm. He became known as the "One-Armed Man of Lepanto."

After fighting so bravely and being injured, Cervantes sailed for home in 1575. On the way, the ship was captured by pirates, and he was sold into slavery. After many escape attempts, his family and a religious order called the Trinitarians were able to buy him back. After five years of slavery, he finally made it home. He soon got a job as a tax collector that allowed him to travel all over Spain and meet many people.

Cervantes learned a lot about people's hopes and dreams. He read a great deal, including adventure stories that inspired his later novels and poems.

Sadly, only a few of his writings still exist. One of these books is Cervantes' greatest work, *Don Quixote.* This book is about an older man named Don Quixote who believes he is a brave knight. Don Quixote spends his last days

fighting for people and for honor. In the end, Don Quixote was honored by the people he had helped and encouraged, just as Cervantes was honored when he died in 1616.

Chapel of Our Lady of the Snows

The Chapel of Our Lady of the Snows is special because it is built entirely out of ice! It is located at Belgrano II Base, one of Argentina's research stations in **Antarctica**. Belgrano II Base is one of the coldest and most remote places on earth. It is near the coast of Antarctica close to **South America**. The Chapel of Our Lady of the Snows is the southernmost church in the world!

The ice chapel is small but very special. The chapel is named "Our Lady of the Snows" because it is surrounded by snow and ice. Inside, the walls, ceiling, and even the floor are made of ice. It's like stepping into a beautiful, icy wonderland!

Visiting the Chapel of Our Lady of the Snows is an amazing experience. You would have to dress in very warm clothes to stay safe from the freezing temperatures outside as you walk to the church. Inside the chapel, it is peaceful and quiet, with soft light shining through the ice. You might hear the sound of the wind outside. The chapel is a place where scientists, explorers, and workers can come to rest and feel close to God. Sometimes, it is used for special events like Christmas services. Would you like to celebrate Christmas in this ice chapel?

Chapel of the Miraculous Medal

Imagine for a moment that you are in prayer, and suddenly the Blessed Mother appears! This is what happened in 1830 at the Chapel of the Miraculous Medal in France. St. Catherine Labouré had recently started studying to become a religious sister. One night, Mary appeared to her.

In her first appearance, Mary gave St. Catherine a special mission. About a year later, Mary appeared again and instructed St. Catherine to create a special medal for the faithful to wear. Mary explained the medal should be an oval shape, with her image on one side and her symbols on the other side. "O Mary, conceived without sin, pray for us who have recourse to thee" is inscribed on the medal. This tells us about one of Mary's most important titles: the Immaculate Conception. Rays of light shine

from Mary's hands, showing that she brings God's graces to us.

Most importantly, Mary said that the purpose of the medal was for people to receive graces from God and to love Him and remember His mercy. Because of St. Catherine's obedience to Mary's instructions, many people have been healed of sickness, and billions of medals have been spread throughout the whole world!

During her life, only a few people knew of St. Catherine's experience. She spent her time quietly, caring for the poor and elderly. Years after she died, her body was found to be incorrupt, meaning it did not decay after her death. Visitors to the chapel can see it today.

Charlemagne

Charlemagne was a king of the Franks, a group of people who lived where France is today. He lived in the eighth and ninth centuries. Eventually, he ruled the Lombards in northern Italy and became the first Holy Roman Emperor.

Charlemagne was really named Charles, or Karl in the Frankish language. *Charlemagne* means "Charles the Great." Charlemagne was a great king because he conquered much of Western Europe and helped their learning and culture grow.

Charlemagne won many battles, and he named his sword *Joyeuse*, which means "joyful." Joyeuse had a gold hilt with jewels in it, and people said that the hilt was made from the spear that pierced Christ's side at the crucifixion. You can still see this sword at the **Louvre Museum** in Paris!

Charlemagne converted the people he conquered to Catholicism and, sadly, killed those who would not convert. He also built many schools so his people could learn. He loved books, and he encouraged monks to copy old books so that they could be saved and read in the future. He also encouraged priests to translate Christian prayers and creeds into languages the people could read. Exciting, beautiful things were achieved in writing, painting, architecture, music, and more during Charlemagne's rule.

The pope saw how successful Charlemagne was. He wanted Western Europe to be united like the **Roman Empire**—but this time, it would be a Christian empire. So the pope crowned Charlemagne as Holy Roman Emperor. This plan didn't entirely work out, but Charlemagne is still remembered for the great things that happened under his rule.

Chartres Cathedral

Chartres Cathedral is a very old Catholic church

in Chartres, **France**. It was built in the twelfth and thirteenth centuries. That means it's been standing for almost a thousand years!

Chartres Cathedral is built on the site of at least five earlier churches. The earliest was built no later than the fourth century. All these earlier churches burned down for different reasons—one was set on fire by Viking pirates. It's a good thing this sixth church is still standing, because it is very beautiful.

Chartres Cathedral is famous for its Gothic architecture, especially its many tall arches and windows and its flying buttresses. A flying buttress is a stone arch that supports some of the weight of the building. This was an important development in architecture because it allowed builders to build much taller buildings with bigger windows. Chartres Cathedral is probably the most beautiful and amazing Gothic building ever built!

Many people have traveled to Chartres over the centuries to see the cathedral. It has an important relic, the *Sancta Camisa*: the tunic that the Virgin Mary wore at the birth of Christ.

On your way in, you will notice many carved statues on the outside of the building showing Bible stories. If you go down to the crypt, you'll see the Well of Strong Saints. This is a very old well, probably built by Celts. It is said that, long ago, the Roman who controlled the town threw **early Christian martyrs** down this well. Make sure that when you return from the dark crypt, you enjoy all the colored light coming through the stained glass windows!

● ● ●

Cheetah

Cheetahs are large wild cats that live in eastern and southern **Africa** south of the **Sahara Desert**. They are slim but strong, with a lot of muscle power in their legs. They have long tails that help them balance when they are running. Cheetahs are the fastest runners on the planet and can run up to 71 miles per hour. That's as fast as a car driving on the highway! Cheetahs run fast to catch their prey, like **gazelles** and wildebeests. When they're chasing prey, cheetahs take over three running steps per second and breathe 60 to 150 times per minute. Can you take 15 breaths in 10 seconds?

Cheetahs are active during the day, which is unusual for cats. In fact, cheetahs are so different from other cats that scientists put them in a different group! They have longer legs and longer backs, which helps them run faster. They even have bigger hearts and nose passages to breathe enough air and pump enough blood when they run really fast.

Many famous people in history have kept cheetahs as pets, including **Charlemagne**. Cheetah pets were trained not to hurt people, but people could take them hunting and watch them run and catch dinner.

Chichen Itza

Chichen Itza was a large city in southeast Mexico, **North America** built by the Maya people. It was an important city between AD 600–900. Today, you can visit the amazing ruins of the city.

One of the first things you can see in Chichen Itza is the Temple of Kukulcán, a large step pyramid. (Step pyramids aren't smooth on the outside but instead are built in layers that look like huge stair steps.) This pyramid was built over another pyramid. You can still get into the old pyramid and reach the throne room.

Chichen Itza has many other interesting structures, including a building with many columns carved into statues of warriors. There are also some courts where people would play a ball game. Players would pass a rubber ball to other players by bouncing it off a wall. But they could not use their hands or feet! Instead, they would use their chest and hips to hit the ball. Many carvings and paintings from Chichen Itza show people playing this game.

Although Chichen Itza is now a popular place to go, it was not always so. By 1100, people began to move away. The beautiful buildings of Chichen Itza began to crumble and become overgrown by bushes and vines.

In the nineteenth century, people in

America saw photos of Chichen Itza and became interested in it. In 1923, the Mexican government allowed American archaeologists (people who practice **archaeology**) to begin uncovering the city and restoring it. Now, over two and a half million people visit Chichen Itza each year.

Chinese Alligator

The Chinese alligator is one of the smallest alligator species in the world. They live in eastern **China**, near the Yangtze River, and are in danger of becoming extinct. This means that there are very few still living in the wild. In fact, more Chinese alligators live in zoos than in the wild.

Most Chinese alligators are normally around five feet long, although they can sometimes be as long as seven feet. They live in freshwater ponds and streams, and they like to eat small animals such as snails, clams, rabbits, fish, birds, and even insects. They can live to be more than 50 years old. Like many other reptiles, Chinese alligators hibernate during the winter in large underground burrows, or tunnels. During the summer, they usually sleep during the day and eat at night.

In the summer, Chinese alligators also mate and lay eggs. Females lay about 10–40 eggs in a nest made of leaves, dead plants,

and soil. Their eggs are smaller than the eggs of any other alligator or crocodile. After the eggs hatch, the mother cares for and protects the baby alligators until they are old enough to care for themselves. That usually takes an entire year!

Chinese alligators make many types of sounds. They can slap their heads on the water, hiss, and whine to talk to other alligators nearby. They also often bellow loudly together. These bellows can be heard from very far away.

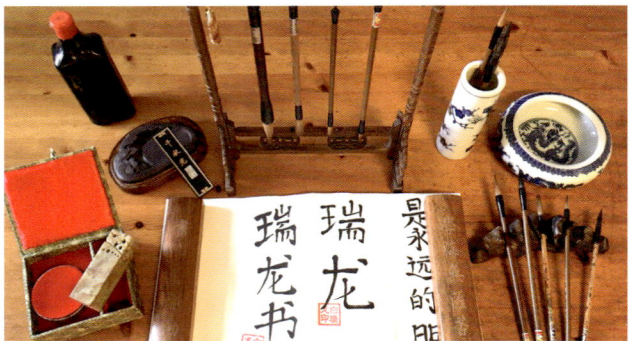

Chinese Calligraphy

Chinese calligraphy is the art of beautiful writing that developed in **China**. In China, the written word is just as important as painting, poetry, and music. The first Chinese writing was found carved on animal bones and turtle shells that are over 3,000 years old. It is the oldest written language in the world.

The four main tools that are used to write Chinese characters are brushes, a stick of ink, an inkstone, and paper. The ink starts as a small, hard stick that is rubbed against the inkstone with some water to make a thick black ink. These tools are called the Four Treasures of the Study (of Chinese calligraphy).

Chinese characters are written in columns, from top to bottom and from right to left. So when you begin writing, the first character is written in the upper right-hand corner of the page. Each of the brush strokes are also painted in a certain direction and in a certain order.

When learning Chinese calligraphy, there is no alphabet to memorize. Instead you learn 214 different basic brush strokes. These are put together to make characters, and those characters are put together to form words. There are over 50,000 words in Chinese calligraphy! But don't worry—you only need to learn 2,000–3,000 in order to read a newspaper. Would you like to be able to read a Chinese newspaper?

of moving from square to square, Chinese chess pieces move along the lines on the board to stop at places where the lines intersect. Also, there are special places on the board called the river and the palace, where not all pieces can move the same way. The river divides the board in half. While soldier pieces who cross the river gain extra strength, elephant pieces can't cross the river.

Chinese chess is a game in which strategy is very important. If you go to China, you might see people playing Chinese chess at little tables in the park.

Chinese Chess

Chinese chess is the most popular board game in **China**. It is quite different from Western chess. For one thing, the playing pieces are small disks that have the name of the piece written on them. There are seven kinds of pieces in Chinese chess: chariot, horse, cannon, soldier, advisor, elephant, and general. The general is sort of like the king in Western chess: whoever captures the other side's general wins. One side is red, and the other side is black.

Some other differences in Chinese chess include the board and how pieces move. Instead

Chinese Junks

A Chinese junk is an ancient sailing ship from **China**. They were first used as early as the second century AD and are still used today. While the word "junk" might make these boats sound like trash, these boats actually have a great design! In fact, junks have one of the simplest and best boat designs ever made. The boats are often made of soft wood that is easy to carve into the shape of the boat. The sails are usually square-shaped, and some even look like large wings. These sails have long, flexible pieces of wood called battens built into them. This helps the sail keep its shape as the wind blows into it, pushing the boat forward.

If you were a sailor aboard a junk, you would find that it is a fun boat to work on, with systems to make sailing easier. For instance, the sail is designed to fold quickly if a sudden storm or strong wind sweeps in. This way, the crew can keep better control over the boat, even in bad weather. Junks were also the first boats to have a rudder, a device used to steer the boat. For a long time, junks were the largest boat on the water.

Many junks are made especially for smaller crews of sailors. A junk can serve as a houseboat or a cargo boat for transporting goods from one place to another. Some are even sailed just for a fun day on the water. The larger junk boats can be used for long **ocean** voyages. What a fun adventure it would be to sail on a junk!

Chinese Martyrs

The Chinese Martyrs were a group of 120 Catholics living in **China**. They were martyred for their faith between 1648–1930. Some were missionaries from different countries, but most were Chinese people.

Let's learn about a few of these brave saints. St. Francisco de Capillas was the first martyr in China. In 1641, he entered China as a Spanish priest to share the Good News. After seven years, he was arrested by soldiers. He

put up with terrible suffering and was finally beheaded.

St. Ann Wang was just 14 years old. When she was about to be beheaded, she bravely said, "The door of Heaven is open to me," and whispered the name of Jesus three times.

St. Chi Zhuzi was a young man preparing to be baptized into the Faith. He was captured one night and ordered by the soldiers to worship idols. He refused to do so. While suffering, he bravely said, "Every piece of my flesh, every drop of my blood will tell you that I am Christian."

St. Augustine Zhao Rong was the first Chinese priest to become a martyr. He was one of the soldiers who led a bishop to his martyrdom. Augustine was so amazed by the bishop's bravery that he, too, became Catholic. He was ordained as a priest five years later and was martyred in 1815.

St. John Gabriel Perboyre was the first martyr of China to be canonized. He suffered and died on a cross. Although he was canonized four years earlier than the other martyrs, he is still counted as one of the 120 Chinese Martyrs. We celebrate their heroic virtue every year on July 9.

Chinese New Year

The Chinese New Year is a huge celebration

in **China** and for Chinese people around the world. It happens on the first new moon of the year. For a long time, China didn't use the same calendar as we do in the West; instead, they used the moon to help them decide when to have important events. The Chinese New Year is also called the Lunar New Year (*luna* means "moon").

Every year, China celebrates the new year with a big party, good food, presents, and more. Chinese New Year is a time to get excited about the next year and prepare for it, as well as remembering family members who have died. Luck, or good fortune, is an important idea to the Chinese, and many new year traditions are meant to bring good fortune. For example, people sweep out their houses to sweep out anything bad from the last year. Then they put away their brooms so they can't sweep out the good fortune that the new year brings!

There is an old story about how the Chinese New Year celebration began. It is said that a monster kept attacking a village, and one man volunteered to stop it. He put up red paper and set off firecrackers. That scared away the monster! Today, red is the color of the Chinese New Year, and the Chinese set off lots of firecrackers. If you were a Chinese child, you would probably get some money in a red envelope or purse. You would eat little dumplings and stay up to watch the **fireworks** and the big parade. Look for the big dragon dancing in the parade!

Christ the Redeemer Statue

The Christ the Redeemer Statue is a large statue of Jesus overlooking the beautiful city of Rio de Janeiro in Brazil, **South America**. It is a well-known symbol of Christianity, a cultural icon, and one of the New Seven Wonders of the World.

In 1859, a missionary priest named Fr. Pierre-Marie Bos had the idea to build a giant statue of Jesus on Corcovado Mountain in honor of Princess Isabel of Brazil. He wanted to show people that Jesus is the way, the truth, and the life and that He welcomes all to come to Him. But Fr. Pierre-Marie died before he could see his dream come true.

About 60 years later, other people began building the statue. It took nine years to complete, opening on October 12, 1931, the feast of Our Lady of the Apparition.

It stands 98 feet tall, which is two-thirds the height of the **Statue of Liberty**. This fantastic landmark is built of concrete, steel, and an outer layer of triangular soapstone tiles. The six million tiles were prepared by local women, and many of them wrote the names of their loved ones on the backs.

The arms are opened wide in the shape of a cross, the hands have nail wounds, and there is a heart upon the chest. After traveling to the top of the **mountain**, you can see the heart more easily. It looks very small from far away, but actually it measures four feet. The statue stands on a base that is also a chapel, where the true Heart of Jesus is found in the Eucharist. From the tabernacle, Christ the Redeemer does indeed overlook the city of Rio de Janeiro.

Christopher Columbus

Christopher Columbus was a famous Italian explorer of **South America**. There are two stories about him that are untrue—that he wanted to prove the earth was round and that he was the first to discover **North America**. There were already many smart Europeans who knew the earth was round. Also, Columbus never landed in North America. He did rediscover it, although it had already been discovered in the eleventh century by the Viking Leif Erikson who sailed there from **Europe**. But Columbus did make it to the **islands** farther south.

Columbus had a very new idea: he wanted to sail west to reach the East Indies (Japan) rather than travel east, which was difficult to do. Columbus was a trader, and he knew how valuable it would be to have an easier way to

get to the Indies. However, the king of Portugal, where Columbus lived at the time, would not support his voyage, so Columbus went to **Spain**. There, Columbus met King **Ferdinand and Isabella**. Queen Isabella thought Columbus' idea was a good one.

Queen Isabella sent Columbus to the New World in three ships named the Niña, the Pinta, and the Santa María. After sailing for a long time, Columbus found land—but it wasn't the East Indies, it was the Bahamas! Columbus thought it was the East Indies, though, because he didn't know that there was more land between Europe and **Asia**. When Columbus returned to Spain as a hero, he brought gold and special things like turkeys, pineapples, and even people he had captured. He called them "Indians" because he thought they were from the Indies, a name for Asia at that time.

On later voyages, Columbus began Spanish colonies in the Bahamas, Cuba, and Jamaica. His third voyage allowed him to find a second **continent**, South America. Just think how much Columbus discovered by following his idea!

Church of La Compañía de Jesús

Have you heard of the **Incas**? You can find

the Church of La Compañía de Jesús at the center of what used to be the Inca Empire. The Church of La Compañía de Jesus is a beautiful old Jesuit church in Cusco, **Peru**. This church is built on the site of an Inca palace where the last ruler of the Inca Empire lived. *La Compañía de Jesús* means "the Society of Jesus," which is the official name of the Jesuit order.

The Jesuits, who came to Peru in 1568 as missionaries, needed a church, and they decided to build a big and beautiful one in Cusco. After a few years, they were able to start building, but the building was badly damaged in an **earthquake** in 1650 and had to be rebuilt. The second church building is even bigger and more beautiful! There are many rounded arches and carved decorations like curlicues and flowers. The local stone carvers who carved all these detailed shapes and arches were very skilled artists!

Today, if you visit the Church of La Compañía de Jesús, you might be able to get a tour from a volunteer student guide. Take a look at the gold altarpiece and see the view from the choir loft. Look for the painting of a group of people, some Spaniards and some Incas, with two Jesuit priests in the middle. It shows the marriage between a Spanish captain who was the nephew of **St. Ignatius of Loyola**, founder of the Society of Jesus, and an Inca princess. How exciting that wedding must have been!

Church of the Holy Sepulchre

Have you ever heard the word sepulchre? A sepulchre is a tomb. For Christians, the Church of the Holy Sepulchre in Israel, southwest **Asia** is one of the holiest places in the world. This is because it was built over the place of Jesus' crucifixion and burial. The church's original Greek name was Church of the Anastasis, which means "Resurrection."

The Via Dolorosa, meaning the Way of Suffering, is a path that marks where Jesus walked as He carried the cross to Calvary. It leads to the church, with the last four Stations of the Cross inside.

The church was built around AD 335. Over the years, it was destroyed and rebuilt several times. As the Bible tells us, the sites of Jesus' crucifixion and burial were near each other. The church was built large enough for both places to be inside it. If you visit, you can see the Rock of Calvary, where the crucifixion is believed to have taken place.

You can also see the Stone of Unction, where Jesus' body was laid and prepared for burial after He died. There are many chapels inside the larger church building. The Angel's Chapel houses the stone where the angel sat as he announced Jesus' Resurrection from the dead. Other chapels are dedicated to various saints and events.

Several churches and monasteries have been designed to look like the Church of the Holy Sepulchre, including Mount St. Sepulchre Franciscan Monastery in Washington, D.C.

Church of the Nativity of Jesus Christ

One of the most popular places for Christians to visit is in the town of Bethlehem in the Holy Land, present-day Israel in western **Asia**. There, you can find the Church of the Nativity of Jesus Christ. This church was built in the fourth century at the place where Jesus was born.

Over time, various groups have wanted to destroy the church. To prevent some of these people from riding through the door on horseback, the doorway was made much smaller. The entry is now just under four feet tall, so most people have to bend over while walking through.

While the main church has stayed mostly the same over the years, some repairs and additions have been made. During the Crusades, two bell towers were added, but they are no

longer there. The size of the church has grown over the centuries. There are three monasteries within the building.

Many mosaics and paintings were made as well, some of which can still be seen today. In recent years, people worked to restore the church so that it would be beautiful and last a long time. They did this by putting in new windows, fixing walls, and cleaning the works of art.

The Church of the Nativity of Jesus Christ is the oldest major church in the Holy Land. The place celebrating Jesus' birthplace is the oldest site of Christian worship.

Cologne Cathedral

Cologne Cathedral is a large Catholic church in Cologne, Germany in **Europe**. Today, it is the church of the Archbishop of Cologne. It was built many years ago to house the golden tomb of the three wise men who brought gifts to Jesus. It was also a place of worship for the Holy Roman Emperor.

It took over 632 years to build Cologne Cathedral. It is the tallest twin-spired church in the world. (Spires look like large stone spikes and are used to show power and strength.)

If you looked down on the cathedral from above, you would see a cross shape. Inside, there are frescoed walls, plastered walls painted with murals. Cologne Cathedral's stained glass windows are amazing! The cathedral has the most windows of any church in the world. They bring color and light into the church, and the pictures tell stories from the Bible, history, and the saints' lives. There is an 800-year-old carved wooden sculpture of Mary and the Christ Child known as the Milan Madonna. Miracles are connected to this statue, and people travel from all over to see it.

During World War II, airplanes hit Cologne Cathedral with 14 bombs. It was badly damaged but remained standing, although the rest of the city was completely flattened. The cathedral was repaired and is still in use today.

If you go and see this magnificent cathedral, be sure to climb the spiral staircase, which has over 500 stone steps! There is a beautiful view of the Rhine River at its top.

Colosseum

The Colosseum is a giant oval-shaped theater built in the time of the **Roman Empire** in the center of Rome, **Italy** in southern **Europe**. Thousands of people—maybe as many as 80,000—would gather in it to see gladiator fights, wild animal hunts, reenactments of famous battles, and plays. The first games were held in AD 80 and ran for 100 days!

There were 80 entrances to the Colosseum so that people could get in and out quickly. The emperor would pay for the event, letting the people attend for free because he wanted them to like him. Small pieces of pottery were used as tickets. Seating was determined by Roman law and the social class people belonged to. There were four main levels of seating. The first level held a special box at either end, one for the emperor and one for the priestesses of the goddess Vesta. Between them sat the senators, and above them were the noblemen. The section for the common people of Rome had two parts: a lower part for rich citizens and a higher part for the poor. The very highest section was for women and slaves, and they had to stand.

The arena had a wooden floor covered by sand. Under this floor were rooms and tunnels that held the animals and gladiators. Today, these passageways are open for the public to walk through—if you buy a ticket!

Some **early Christian martyrs** were probably killed in the Colosseum, which was sometimes used for public executions. We don't know for sure that Christians were martyred here, but many Christians think of the early martyrs when they see the Colosseum. That is why the pope often leads a procession with torches while praying the Stations of the Cross at the Colosseum on Good Friday. Thousands of Christians gather with him to pray and honor the early Christian martyrs.

Crabeater Seal

Crabeater seals are medium- to large-sized seals that live all around the coast of **Antarctica**. They are found on the **islands** of pack ice (ice that is not attached to land) and catch their food in the waters of the Southern Ocean.

From their name, you are probably thinking that these seals eat crabs, but they actually don't! Crabs live much deeper in the **ocean** than these seals will go. Instead, they eat krill, which are called *krebs* in German. This word is where we get the name "crabeater," because they are *krebs*-eaters. Krill are like little shrimp. Crabeater seals are generally about 7 feet long and weigh around 500 pounds. You might wonder how such a big animal can survive on tiny shrimp. It's because there are so many krill! Hundreds of millions of krill live in the Southern Ocean.

Crabeater seals are shaped so that they can swim swiftly away from trouble. Killer whales and leopard seals are their two predators. Leopard seals usually go after the young crabeater seals, which are called pups.

Pups weigh about 50 pounds when they are born. In only a few weeks, they can weigh over 200 pounds! A lot of this weight is fat, which is called blubber. Without their blubber, they would be too cold to live on slabs of ice and swim in the Antarctic waters.

Cricket

Cricket is a ball game that started in England (now the **United Kingdom**) and became popular in **India**, **Australia**, New Zealand, Pakistan, and many other countries that the British settled and ruled in the eighteenth century. This sport is a little like baseball, where there are two teams that take turns batting the ball and fielding (catching) the ball.

However, the rules for cricket are very different from baseball. For instance, cricket teams have 11 players instead of 9, like in baseball. The goal of cricket is to score runs, except in cricket, there are no bases! Instead, two batsmen run back and forth across the cricket pitch (the field) to score runs.

On either end of the cricket pitch is a wicket. A wicket is three sticks stuck into the ground with two short sticks balanced on top of them. The pitcher, called the bowler, bowls the ball at one of the wickets to try to knock it over. The batsman hits the ball with his paddle-shaped bat to keep it away from the wicket. If the ball is caught before it bounces, or if a fielder throws the ball back and hits the wicket, the batsman is "out."

Fun Facts:

- The longest type of cricket game, a test match, is played over five days.

- Cricket was played in England as early as the sixteenth century.
- The name "cricket" may have come from an old word for "staff" or "stick."
- The wicket may have come from actual wicket gates through which **sheep** were herded.

Detian Falls

Detian Falls is a waterfall located on the border between **China** and Vietnam. Detian Falls is sometimes called by its Vietnamese name, *Bản Giốc*. Both names are often combined to make the name *Bản Giốc–Detian*. It's a little like having a person's first and middle name joined together to make one name, like Anne-Marie or John-Paul!

Detian Falls is very beautiful. Many years of running water have washed away tiny bits of limestone rock to create the shape of the waterfall. It often looks like two waterfalls, and sometimes it can look like three waterfalls if there are enough rocks and trees in the way. During the rainy season when there is a lot more water pouring down the falls, it can look like one giant waterfall! Detian Falls is 98 feet at its highest point. It is the fourth-largest waterfall on the border of two countries. With so much water rushing down, the waterfall is loud enough that it can be heard from far away. If you listened for it, you'd hear a sound like distant thunder.

You can visit Detian Falls up close by taking a raft on the water. The question is: how many waterfalls will you see when you visit?

Dingo

The dingo is a wild dog that lives in **Australia**. Dingoes look a lot like regular dogs. But like wolves, dingoes howl—they hardly ever bark like regular dogs. Dingoes are around four feet long and two feet tall. They usually have short, soft, yellowish-red fur, but they can sometimes have tan, black, white, or sand-colored fur. In the wild, dingoes are often seen together in packs of up to 12 dogs.

Dingoes can be found in many different parts of Australia in all kinds of environments, like snowy **mountains**, **deserts**, and wetlands. Dingoes tend to come out at night to hunt and explore. What dingoes eat depends on the part of Australia they live in, but they usually eat smaller animals. For example, in the southwestern deserts, dingoes will eat rabbits. In the northern **rainforests**, dingoes will eat rodents and wallabies, which look like small **kangaroos**. Because dingoes are very strong and can handle the dry heat in Australia, some cattle ranchers bred dingoes with Highland Collies to make the Australian Cattle Dog.

Even though dingoes are a lot like dogs, they are pretty shy around humans. The first dingoes were probably dogs owned by people, but they are wild now. They will usually keep their distance when they see people. If you see a dingo in the wild, you can wave hello from a distance and take a picture of it, but be sure to give it plenty of space!

Dogsledding

Dogsledding was started by the Native American Indians who lived in **Canada**. If you lived in Canada before the French and English came with horses, the only ways to get around in the snow were by snowshoeing or dogsledding. Dogs have helped people out in many ways for a long time. Tying dogs to the front of a sled to pull it across the snow as a team made traveling much faster and easier!

To prepare a dogsled, the human driver, called a musher, chooses several dogs for a team. It is important for the musher to choose dogs that are strong, fast, and can handle the cold. Siberian Huskies and Alaskan Malamutes are the best dogs for this job, especially because they do well in the cold. Every dog on the sledding team has an important job. For instance, a smart dog leads the entire team, while a strong dog is in charge of pulling the sled out of the thick snow when it is stuck.

Dogsleds are used to carry supplies from one place to another in the snow. Dogsledding has also turned into an exciting sport in snowy countries. Mushers race their teams of dogs across many miles. If you were a professional musher and you wanted to raise a team of racing dogs, you would begin training them when they were still puppies. You might tie a small log to a husky puppy and have it practice pulling the log through the snow. This helps young dogs become very strong and fast. With enough training, you could build a team of winning sled dogs!

Duck-billed Platypus

The duck-billed platypus is an odd-looking

mammal that lives in eastern **Australia**. When it was first described in the early nineteenth century, scientists in England thought that it was a made-up creature. Its large rubbery bill is a lot like a duck's bill, and its tail and brown fur coat are a lot like a **beaver's**. It has no toes but instead has webbed feet. Even though it is a mammal, it lays eggs!

If you lived in eastern Australia, you would have some trouble spotting a platypus because it is nocturnal. This means that most of the time, it is only moving about when you are tucked under your covers at night.

It is not only nocturnal, but it also spends most of its time in the water. It is called amphibious because it spends some time on land and some time in water. When it swims, it pushes itself along by moving its front two feet. Its tail and back feet help it to turn left or right.

The platypus eats worms, insect larvae, shrimp, and yabbies, which are a kind of freshwater crayfish. It digs these out of the bottom of the **river** with its bill or catches them while swimming.

When the platypus swims, it keeps its eyes, ears, and nose shut. So how does it hunt? It can sense electricity from other animals. All animals give off some electricity because of their muscles moving and other parts of their bodies working. The platypus has about 40,000 sensors on its bill that pick up this electricity from other animals, even tiny animals like shrimp and insects. This helps the platypus find food in muddy water, where it would be hard to see.

Durdle Door

Durdle Door is a beautiful rock formation on the coast of Dorset, England in the **United Kingdom**. The formation is made of a softer kind of rock called limestone. It looks like a giant stone arch connected to the land. The arch is big enough that a good-sized sailboat could fit through it.

The name Durdle Door is a funny one. The word "durdle" comes from the Old English word *thirl*, which means "to pierce or drill," and the word *thyrel*, which means "hole." It should be no surprise then that these Old English words were used to describe how the rock formation came to be. Over many years, the constant splashing of the **ocean** slowly broke away tiny bits of the limestone until it left a hole in the rock. It's like the ocean drilled a hole in the rock! You would probably win in a drilling competition against the ocean if you used power tools to drill a hole in a giant rock, but the ocean is very good at taking its time to make some of the most beautiful land formations that you can imagine.

Early Christian Martyrs

The early Christian martyrs are Christians who were killed in Rome, **Italy** between AD 30–313. (Find it on your map of Italy!) They lived in the first three hundred years after Jesus was crucified.

The emperor of Rome, who was like a king, ruled the **Roman Empire** and all its people. During those three hundred years, each emperor said that it was against the law to be a Christian. If you believed in Jesus, you had to worship Him in secret. If people found out that you were a Christian, you would be killed.

The Roman emperors were afraid of Christians. They believed that Jesus Christ and the Christians were their enemies. But they were wrong, weren't they? Jesus came to earth to love them and show them the way to Heaven, not to be their enemy.

The emperors tried to force Christians to worship their idols. When the Christians said that they would never do that, they were thrown in jail.

It would have been so easy to worship the Roman idols and be able to go home. But nothing could make them deny the love they had for Jesus. So when they were thrown to the **lions** or crucified like Jesus, they tried hard to be brave.

A few of the early Christian martyrs are Sts. Peter, Tarcisius, Sebastian, Valentine, Polycarp, Ignatius, Catherine, Agnes, and Lucy.

Edinburgh Castle

Edinburgh Castle is a large castle on top of a very tall hill in Scotland in the **United Kingdom**. Parts of the castle are as old as the twelfth century. It was the home of Scotland's kings and queens for many years.

Today, if you visit the city of Edinburgh, you can take a tour of the castle. First, you walk up a long, steep street called the Royal Mile. You are huffing and puffing by the time you get to the castle! This is exactly why the castle was built where it was. Enemies attacking the castle would also have to come up this long, narrow street, and the castle's defenders would have time to shoot them with arrows or prepare to meet them.

Edinburgh Castle is actually built on top of an old **volcano**! The lava inside the volcano's opening turned to stone long ago, and the castle is built on this stone.

Once you get to the castle, you walk through a few gates. These helped Scotsmen keep enemies out. Inside the castle, you can see the Great Hall, a huge room with suits of armor along the walls. You can also see the crown jewels of Scotland: a crown, scepter, and a sword that belonged to the king.

You can also see the Stone of Destiny, which, according to legend, must be there for a Scottish king to be crowned. But the English did not want Scotland to have its own king. King Edward I took the stone and built it into his throne in England. Almost 700 years later, England returned the stone to Edinburgh Castle in 1996. Over 10,000 people stood on the Royal Mile to see this historic moment.

Eiffel Tower

The Eiffel Tower is a world-famous landmark in Paris, **France**. When you think of France or Paris, the Eiffel Tower might be the first thing that comes to mind. It is made of iron and has four separate legs that come together to make one single tower. It was designed by and named after Gustave Eiffel, a French engineer and architect.

When Gustave Eiffel built the tower in 1889 for the World's Fair, many people thought it was a terrible design. Little did those people know that the Eiffel Tower would become one of the most well-loved landmarks in the world. More than 250 million people have visited the tower since it was first built.

The Eiffel Tower is very, very heavy. The iron alone weighs about 7,300 tons! It is also more than 1,000 feet tall. Many people like to climb the Eiffel Tower for its wonderful views. If you ever visit the Eiffel Tower, be ready to wait in line for a while because about 25,000 people go up the tower every day! If you look carefully, you might even spot the names of the 72 French scientists, engineers, and mathematicians who helped to create the tower carved into the metal on the first floor.

Inside the Eiffel Tower, there are shops, restaurants, and even elevators that people can ride to the top. At the very top of the tower, you can find Gustave Eiffel's original office and an observation deck to look out over Paris. At nighttime, 20,000 lights illuminate the Eiffel Tower in a beautiful display.

El Cid and the Reconquista

El Cid was a knight in medieval **Spain** who lived from 1043–1099. His real name was Rodrigo Díaz de Vivar, but he was called *El Cid*, which means "the lord," or *El Campeador*, which means "the valiant."

El Cid lived during the *Reconquista*, which means "reconquest." During this time, Christians in Spain fought to take back land that was conquered by Muslims in the sixth century. With his famous horse, Babieca, and his knights, El Cid conquered the eastern part of Spain.

After serving two Spanish kings as a knight, El Cid was exiled in 1081. There are many different stories about why El Cid was exiled, but we do know that in exile, he offered his service to the Moors (the Muslims in Spain) and fought for them for about six years. Eventually, the Spanish king called him back and offered him lands and wealth. El Cid returned, but he had his own plans. With a combined army of Christians and Moors, he conquered Valencia, a Muslim kingdom on the east coast of Spain. With his wife, Jimena, and his two daughters, El Cid ruled as Valencia's prince until he died.

El Cid is a beloved national hero in Spain and is remembered in many stories and poems.

The *Cantar de mio Cid* is a medieval epic poem that tells the story of his life, but some of the stories are made up. In the poem, El Cid is remembered as the ideal knight: brave, cunning and fierce in battle, kind, just, and pious.

El Escorial

El Escorial is a huge building near Madrid in **Spain**. It is a monastery, royal palace, basilica, library, college, and mausoleum (a fancy tomb) all in one! Its full name is the Monastery of San Lorenzo de El Escorial, because it is dedicated to Saint Lawrence (*San Lorenzo* in Spanish). King Phillip II built it after he won an important battle on the feast of St. Lawrence in 1557.

If you look down on El Escorial from above, it looks like it was built in the shape of a grid. This shape reminds people of St. Lawrence. Do you know the story of St. Lawrence? He was martyred by being burned on a gridiron over a fire! (A gridiron is a grill in the shape of a grid.)

King Phillip, his parents, and almost all the Spanish kings who came later are buried in El Escorial's mausoleum. King Phillip's father, Charles V, had asked to be buried where holy monks could pray for his soul. This was one reason King Phillip built El Escorial. For a long time, monks of the Order of St. Jerome lived at the monastery. Today, Augustinian monks live there.

The basilica is at the center of El Escorial. It has a huge dome on the roof and many beautiful paintings and other works of art. The large library at El Escorial holds more than 400,000 books, including many old and rare handwritten books.

El Greco

El Greco was a famous Greek artist who lived and worked in **Spain**. The name El Greco is actually a nickname for the painter, whose real name was Domenikos. In Spanish, *El Greco* means "the Greek." Domenikos earned that nickname because he was born in Greece in 1541, and he often signed his work with Greek letters.

El Greco became a master painter and sculptor as a very young man. He traveled to Venice, **Italy**, and then to Rome, where he opened a workshop and made many beautiful pieces of art. He learned different styles from other famous artists at the time. Later, he moved to Spain. While he lived there, he made some of his most famous and beautiful paintings. Many were altarpieces—large paintings that would be placed just above an altar in a church. El Greco painted scenes featuring Christ, the Blessed Mother, and other saints. He became known for painting figures who looked taller and longer than they would in real life. Can you imagine being painted to look like you were stretched a whole foot taller than you actually are? That's kind of what El Greco's artistic style looked like. He liked making the people in his paintings tall and graceful. He thought that color was very important, too.

El Greco's paintings were loved more and more in the years after he died in 1614. His work inspired other artists many years after his death. Some artists even recreated his paintings in their own style. Have you ever tried making your own version of a famous painting? Give it a try!

El Torcal

El Torcal is a small **mountain range** between the cities of Antequera and Málaga in **Spain**. El Torcal is known for its many fascinating rock formations made from a special kind of rock called limestone. Limestone is made of crushed seashells. This means that a very long time ago, these mountains were underwater!

Limestone can easily be shaped by the forces of nature. For example, when water freezes on the limestone, it can cause the rock to chip and break. When this happens enough times, the rocks can begin to take on interesting shapes. At El Torcal, some of these rock formations have been named after what they look like. For example, there are some large rocks with giant ridges along the sides that make them look like giant screws. Not surprisingly, this rock formation is called "the Screw." Other formations are called "the Jug," "the Camel," and even "the Sphinx," which is an ancient Egyptian legendary creature.

If you were to visit El Torcal, you might also see some interesting animals such as snakes, lizards, and Spanish ibex hopping along the rocks. Even more interesting are the plants that you might find. Most plants need soil to grow, but you can find flowers such as lilies, red peonies, and even three kinds of orchids growing from the rocks! The best time of year to visit is in the spring or autumn when the weather is very nice. Bring your hiking boots because there are three exciting trails that you can explore! They are long trails, but there are plenty of places to stop and look at the beautiful views.

The Elephant Festival is famous for the parade of elephants decorated with gold and colorful paint, scarves, and saddle cloths. People riding on the elephants throw colored powders on the elephants. The elephants also wear jingling ankle bracelets and have jewelry on their tusks. The most beautifully decorated elephant receives a prize, and there are games like tug-of-war, played between a strong elephant and a large group of people. There is also an elephant race! **Camels**, horses, and folk dancers can be part of the festival, too.

The festival honors the importance of elephants in Indian culture. Elephants have done many important jobs in India, including carrying heavy loads, uprooting trees, marching in the army, and hunting with humans. To Indians, elephants represent removing things that are in your way.

The Elephant Festival is a very popular event. If you stick around for the festival of Holi, which is introduced by the Elephant Festival, you will get colored powder thrown on you too, just like the elephants!

Elephant Festival

The Elephant Festival is a celebration that takes place in a city in **India** named Jaipur. It takes place the day before a larger Indian festival called Holi.

Emperor Penguin

The emperor penguin lives near the **ocean** in **Antarctica**. It is the largest of all penguins. An adult is about 4 feet tall and weighs 60 pounds or more. Are you bigger than this penguin?

There are many types of penguins. They are all birds, but none of them can fly. They can sure swim, though! Their wings are more like flippers, and they help the penguin swim fast enough to get away from their enemies: leopard seals and killer whales. If they're lucky, they can live up to 20 years.

The emperor penguin eats mostly fish, especially the Antarctic silverfish. Sometimes it will eat krill and squid. While hunting, it will dive deep down into the **sea**. It can hold its breath underwater for a very long time.

Emperor penguins are also very social birds. They do a lot of things together. Some of those things are hunting, diving, and swimming back up to the surface of the water (called surfacing).

Baby penguins are called chicks. Chicks have a way of talking that's different from the adult birds. The adults will call out loudly, but the chicks whistle.

Antarctica is so cold that humans can't really live there. So how do these birds stay warm? God gave them a dense coat of fine feathers. He also gave them a thick layer of fat just beneath their skin. What also keeps them warm is when they stand close together in a huddle. They slowly shuffle, giving each bird a turn on the inside.

Fun Fact:

- The daddy emperor penguin keeps the egg warm until it hatches. He balances it on his feet and covers it with his belly to keep it warm.

European Hedgehog

The European hedgehog lives throughout much of **Europe**, including the **United Kingdom**. European hedgehogs are often found in backyards, gardens, and parks, but they can also live in places like forests and meadows. The name "hedgehog" comes from the fact that they like to crawl under hedges and their snouts look a little like pig snouts. Hedgehogs even snuffle, squeal, and grunt like pigs, although their noises are much quieter and higher pitched.

The European hedgehog is covered with small spines that help protect it from predators like owls, **badgers**, and foxes. The spines are not poisonous or barbed, but they are very prickly and uncomfortable to touch. Hedgehogs can have up to 6,000 spines!

European hedgehogs are usually 6–12 inches long and weigh between 1–2 pounds. They like to live alone and are nocturnal, meaning they sleep during the day and are awake at night. Hedgehogs are omnivores, meaning that they eat both meat and plants. They will eat worms, insects, caterpillars, snails, and even frogs, snakes, and bird eggs. Hedgehogs can also hibernate (go into a deep sleep) to survive the winter. Before they go to sleep, they eat a lot and get fat so their bodies can stay warm while they sleep. Before hibernating, hedgehogs can weigh over four pounds—more than twice their usual weight!

Fun Facts:
- Hedgehogs are sometimes kept as pets.
- Hedgehogs were used for food in ancient Egypt and during the Middle Ages. They are still eaten today in some parts of the world.
- Hedgehogs are partly immune to the venom in snake bites, so they often survive if a snake bites them.

European Red Fox

The European red fox is native to **Europe**, **Asia**, North **Africa**, and **North America**. It is the largest and most well-known of all the foxes. It measures about 17 inches high, and it can weigh between 5–31 pounds.

When red foxes are born, they are brown or gray. In a month, a new coat of fur grows in. Usually it is a red coat, but sometimes it is golden, silver, or even black. A black fox would indeed be a sight to see!

A member of the dog family, the red fox is not only a great swimmer, but it can also jump over a six-foot high fence. Its hearing is so good that it can hear the squeaking of a mouse from 330 feet away.

The red fox feeds on mice, birds, rabbits, and other small animals. It usually hunts at night and will continue to hunt even when it is full. When the fox catches extra food, it will bury it. This food can be dug up later when other food is hard to find.

The red fox is a very clever animal. When it is being chased by a predator, it can outsmart it by playing dead. It can also dash into one of its well-hidden dens, safe from danger.

Foxes' dens are used for raising pups and storing food but not for sleeping. Instead, a fox sleeps curled in a ball just outside its den to protect its pups, or it even sleeps out in the open.

The winter can be very cold, so God gave the red fox a large bushy tail to cover itself for warmth. Its tail also helps it to blend in to its surroundings. This blending in is called camouflage. Camouflage is God's gift to His creatures for their protection. If the fox's enemies (bear, wolf, or **mountain lion**) cannot see it, then they cannot catch it by surprise and attack it while it is fast asleep, can they?

European Robin

The European robin is a small bird found in the **United Kingdom** and other parts of **Europe**. You might know this bird simply as a robin. It's an easy bird to recognize. It has brown feathers, a white belly, and a reddish-orange chest. It has a short, pointed beak that is perfect for catching its favorite food of insects, spiders, and earthworms.

Robins are actually very helpful birds to have around your garden because they can help catch and eat bugs that might try to hurt your plants. Robins are not easily scared of people and are friendly to gardeners. During the winter when bugs are hard to find, robins will hunt for wild berries and fruit to eat. They will even eat seeds that people leave out in bird feeders. If you're really patient, you might even find a robin that will eat seeds right out of your hand!

Robins normally make their nests out of moss, grass, leaves, and even feathers and hair to make it a warm place to lay their eggs. While robins usually build their nests in trees and bushes, others are very good at finding more interesting places to build their nests. Don't be surprised if you find a robin's nest hiding in watering cans, flowerpots, barbecue grills, and many other strange places. Robins are very clever birds!

Fallow Deer

Fallow deer are a kind of small deer that live in **Italy** and most of **Europe**. If you were to take a walk in the Italian countryside around sunset, you might see a fallow deer. They are about three feet tall, which is probably shorter than you are!

Fallow deer can be many different colors, from white to dark brown or gray. Male fallow deer have antlers that change as they grow. When they are younger, the antlers look like small, short spikes, and then when they get older, the antlers grow into a shape that looks like a shovel. In some places, fallow deer are even called "shovel deer" because of the shape of their antlers!

Fallow deer like to stick together in herds of up to 150 deer. They can run much faster than you or I—up to 30 miles per hour—and they can jump almost 6 feet high across gaps that are 17 feet long. Can you imagine jumping that far?

In Europe, fallow deer mainly live in forests, grassy areas, or near towns and gardens. If you really want to see some fallow deer, try to find a place where mushrooms or blueberries are growing. Fallow deer love to eat these tasty treats!

Fencing

Fencing is a sport that is quite popular in **France**. Fencing looks like two people fighting each other with swords, but it is much safer. It was first used as an exercise for soldiers, but in the eighteenth century, it became a sport. Schools of fencing started in **Italy**, but the French turned it into the sport we know today.

The rules of fencing are simple. Two players in a match each carry a metal sword that is long and thin but not sharp. The goal is to "tag" the other player with the sword to score a point. There are three different swords used in fencing, and how a player scores points depends on which sword they use:

The *foil* is the lightest sword. Players score points by tagging their opponent anywhere on the torso (the body between the neck and legs) with the tip of the foil.

The *sabre* is about as light as a foil. Players score points by tagging their opponent anywhere above the waist using any part of the sabre.

The *épée* is the heaviest sword, weighing about one and a half pounds. Players score points by tagging their opponent anywhere on their body with the tip of the épée.

Players wear special white uniforms and helmets with screens to protect themselves from being poked too hard by the swords.

The first fencing competition took place in 1880. Fencing became so popular that it even became part of the Summer Olympics. You can still watch these fencing competitions today!

Ferdinand and Isabella

Ferdinand and Isabella were the king and queen of **Spain** in the fifteenth and early sixteenth centuries. They unified the country in many ways, including building better roads and having everyone use the same type of money so business and trading were easier. After making the nobles less powerful, Ferdinand and Isabella made sure the common people were treated more fairly.

In 1492, the Moors, Muslims who had taken over southern Spain, were threatening the Catholic Faith and the people. Ferdinand and Isabella sent their army to free the city of Granada and chase the Moors out of Spain. Ferdinand and Isabella then required that anyone who wanted to stay had to convert to Christianity or leave.

After this victory, Isabella decided to pay for a voyage for **Christopher Columbus**. He thought he could find a shorter way to **Asia** by sailing west. Since the royal budget was tight, the queen offered to sell her crown jewels to pay for it, but the royal treasurer was able to find the money. Though Columbus didn't discover a shorter route, he did find **South America** and rediscover **North America**. Isabella kept her jewels and expanded the Spanish Empire and Christianity.

Because of their support and defense of the Church, Pope Alexander VI gifted Ferdinand and Isabella the title of the "Catholic King and Queen" in 1494.

They continued to rule for many more years and firmly established Spain as a great power in the world for their people and the Catholic Faith.

Fireworks

Fireworks are man-made devices that are built to explode for art and entertainment. Some of them make huge explosions in the air, and some make explosions on the ground. Fireworks make popping, banging, and whistling sounds. If they are not handled safely, they can cause fires or burns.

The first fireworks went off in **China** as far back as the seventh century. The Chinese made many different kinds of fireworks. To them, it was both an art and a science, not just something to do to pass the time. By the tenth century, many of the Chinese people, rich and poor alike, were buying fireworks at their local markets. Large fireworks were set off to entertain the emperor and his court.

A fancy word for fireworks is pyrotechnics, which means "fire arts" in Greek. Fireworks are not just noisy explosions but works of art. Many of them look like colorful flowers as they burst in the dark night sky. Others are meant to look like fish swimming away. The people who have the job of setting up the fireworks for a display are called pyrotechnicians. It can take a full day to set up a large fireworks show.

A display of fireworks can be an exciting way to celebrate or remember an event. In the United States, people like to set off big displays on days that are special to our country like Independence Day, also known as the Fourth of July. In China, they set off lots of fireworks to celebrate **Chinese New Year**.

Flamenco Dancing

Flamenco dancing began in southern **Spain** in the region of Andalusia. Flamenco song, music, and dance is an art form that has become a symbol of Spanish culture. It is now performed all over the world.

There are many different styles of flamenco dancing, but all of them are very expressive. Body motions, hand and finger positions, and the dancers' faces change a lot to show different emotions.

There is usually guitar music and a Spanish folk song being sung to go along with the dancing. Simply listening to the music gives a person a good idea of what the dance is like. The flamenco dance has both slow and fast parts. The last part of the dance is very exciting with fancy footwork going at lightning speed!

The dancers themselves add to the music when they stamp their heels and clap their hands. Often, they will hold small musical instruments called castanets. Castanets are like tiny wooden cymbals that are clacked together with the fingers.

The dancers wear traditional Spanish costumes. The man wears a suit with a flat hat, and the woman wears a long ruffled dress with high-heeled shoes. Sometimes she wears a shawl, carries a fan, and wears a rose behind her ear. As she dances, the ruffles of her dress make quite a show!

Flamingo

The flamingo is a large bird that is pink or red in color and has long, thin legs. There are six different kinds, or species, of flamingos in the world. There are two in **Africa**, **Europe**, and **Asia**, and four in **North** and **South America**.

Most flamingos live near water. They even live in the **rainforests** of South America. Like many other birds, they are good at flying. But unlike a lot of birds, they can also balance on one leg. Scientists still don't know why they do this, but some believe it helps them to keep warm.

The next time you come across a flamingo, pull out your binoculars. See if you can spot it feeding. As it walks on its long, stick-like legs through shallow water, watch its webbed feet stir up food from the bottom. Next, watch for it to dunk its curved bill upside-down into the water and move it back and forth. Then, it uses its large, rough tongue to take in water quickly and push it back out. It does this for hours, trapping its meal of tiny shrimp and algae. This is called filter-feeding.

Young flamingos have soft, furry, gray feathers. As they become adults, their color changes. They might be pale pink, peachy orange, or bright red. This coloring comes from something in their food called beta-carotene. Beta-carotene is what makes carrots orange, tomatoes red, and the salt in the **Camargue Salt Marshes** pink.

In the wild, a flamingo lives in a colony with thousands of other flamingos. The more birds there are, the better protection they have from predators. Flamingos are very social birds. At the zoo, have you ever seen just one pink bird all by itself? That would be a lonely bird indeed!

match lasts 90 minutes, with a 15-minute break halfway through the game.

Peru has had its own national football team since 1927. The team plays its home games in Peru's capital city, Lima. There is also a huge football competition known as the FIFA World Cup, which was created in 1930. It occurs every four years. Countries compete to see who has the best football team in the world. So far, Peru hasn't won the World Cup, but the country still loves football. With a lot of practice, maybe you could play in the FIFA World Cup!

Football (Soccer)

Football is a popular sport played in **Peru** and around the world. You might know of it by its other common name in the United States—soccer. The sport is played on a large field with two teams competing against each other. The object of the game is to kick the ball across the field and get it into the opposing team's goal net to score points.

Each team has 11 players on the field at a time. Ten of the players work together to kick the ball into the opposite team's net. The eleventh player is the goalkeeper. The goalkeeper's job is to keep the ball away from their team's net so that the other team can't score any points. Each game is called a match, and each

Forbidden City

The Forbidden City is a large palace in Beijing, **China**. It is very important to the history of China. It took 14 years to build and was completed in 1420. More than a million people helped to build this palace. The Forbidden City was the home and palace of the emperor of China for almost 500 years. It was rightly named, because people were not allowed to go in or out of the palace without the emperor's permission. Today, the Forbidden City is best known as the Palace Museum, which you can visit.

If you had lived in the Forbidden City, you would have had more than just one building to spend time in. The Forbidden City was actually a collection of nearly 1,000 buildings, temples, and beautiful gardens. The palace and its grounds were so large, you would have had nearly 10,000 exciting rooms to explore. You would almost certainly never get bored if you lived there!

Many of the buildings are made from a precious wood found in the **jungles** of China, blocks of marble mined from Beijing, and even specially made bricks for the main halls called "golden bricks." These bricks are not made of gold but from a special mud. They are made in such a way that if you knock on one, it makes a sound like metal. The rooms and halls of the Forbidden City have beautiful names, such as "The Hall of Supreme Harmony," "The Palace of Eternal Spring," and "The Palace of Heavenly Purity." If you could have named one of these halls or palaces, what would you have named it?

Francisco Pizarro

Francisco Pizarro was an explorer from **Spain**. He is best known for exploring **Peru** and defeating the Inca Empire.

Pizarro was born into a poor family in the year 1478, so there was no money to send him to school. In fact, he probably never learned to read or write. However, Pizarro still wanted to explore the New World, and in 1509, he set sail to explore the coasts of Central America and **South America**. Pizarro even became one of the first Europeans to see the Pacific Ocean from the Americas. He did this by crossing a narrow piece of land in Panama called the Isthmus of Panama, which separates the Pacific and Atlantic Oceans.

Later, the king and queen of Spain sent Pizarro to explore Peru. During this journey, Pizarro captured the leader of the **Incas**, Atahualpa. The Incas offered to give Pizarro a room full of gold to get their leader back, but Pizarro had him killed instead. After Atahualpa's death, there were many battles fought between the Spanish and the Incas. The Incas fought fiercely to defend their homeland. However, the Spanish had stronger weapons, and in the end, the Incas were defeated.

After the fall of the Inca Empire, Pizarro founded the city of Lima, where he governed for many years. He was killed in 1541 by some who did not agree with how he ruled.

French Revolution

The French Revolution happened in **France** in the late eighteenth century. Like the American revolutionaries, the people of France were tired of being ruled by a king and wanted to set up a country ruled by the people.

Before the revolution, there were many problems in France. King Louis XVI, the king of France, and the other people in the ruling class had lots of money and power and lived very good lives. But they didn't share with the lower classes, and many people in France were very poor. The ruling class also didn't let anyone else make decisions about how the country should be ruled. Many laws at the time were unjust, and the poor were treated unfairly.

In 1789, the people in the lower classes finally had enough. They attacked an important prison in Paris, the Bastille, where some poor people were punished unfairly. Actually, there were only seven prisoners in the Bastille at that time. This attack also set free some criminals who should have stayed in jail.

The motto of the revolution was "liberty, equality, fraternity." ("Fraternity" means "brotherhood.") The revolutionaries were led by a man named Maximilien Robespierre. They killed the king and his family with the guillotine, a machine that chopped off people's heads. The revolutionaries were so angry that they also killed thousands of people in the ruling class, whether or not they did anything wrong. This period of time was called the Reign of Terror. The revolutionaries were also angry at the Church because they were tired of being told what to do. They killed many priests, nuns, and other religious people. Many churches were destroyed or damaged.

The French Revolution lasted for 10 years. It ended when **Napoleon Bonaparte**, a French general, took over France in 1799. While the French Revolution's system of government did not last, it changed France forever. The French national anthem is still the *Marseillaise*, a song composed in 1792 praising the Revolution.

Frill-necked Lizard

The frill-necked lizard is a large lizard that gets its name from the frill around its neck. Its native home is northern **Australia** and southern New Guinea.

This kind of lizard spends most of its time in the trees, where it can hide from its enemies: eagles, owls, larger lizards, snakes, and **dingoes**. Sometimes it appears in **desert** areas, but it prefers humid climates like tropical woodlands.

The frill-necked lizard grows to be almost three feet long, including its tail. It feeds this large body with insects, spiders, smaller lizards, mice, moths, and butterflies. It usually eats a lot at one time, sometimes even hundreds or thousands of flying ants and termites in one sitting!

The frill around its neck usually stays folded against its body. That way it can look like tree bark and be camouflaged—hiding from its enemies. But watch out! If it gets frightened, its frills will pop out, showing bright orange and red scales. It becomes like a mini dragon to scare off its predators.

God gave this lizard a very unusual frilled neck so it can protect itself, and He also made it able to quickly run away to safety. Most lizards run on four legs, but the frill-necked lizard rears up on its two legs and runs like a human does!

Fur Traders

Animal fur has been used to make warm clothes and hats for thousands of years. In the sixteenth century, fishermen from **Europe** started trading fish, knives, and other things for **beaver** furs from native people in **Canada**. These beaver furs, called pelts, became very popular in Europe. Hatmakers in Europe found that they were perfect for making fancy felt hats. Soon, everyone wanted beaver felt hats.

Merchants from **France**, England, and the Dutch Republic began setting up trading posts all over northeastern **North America**. Trading posts were like forts where people could come and trade for items they needed. These merchants, or fur traders, traded beaver and other animal pelts with the natives in Canada and America. In return, the fur traders gave the natives metal tools and other goods they couldn't make for themselves. (If you're wondering why the Europeans had to go all the way to America to get beaver fur, it's because beavers in Europe had been hunted so much that there were almost none left!)

Over the years, the fur trade grew and grew. Countries even fought over the best places to trade. Native American Indian tribes also fought each other over who would get to trade with the Europeans. Beavers in North America were hunted so much that there were very few of them left.

Eventually, in the nineteenth century, clothing fashions changed and people didn't want beaver felt hats anymore. The fur trade became very small. Now, animals are still trapped and farmed for their fur in North America, but people must follow rules so that animals are treated properly.

Gavarnie Falls

Gavarnie Falls is a beautiful waterfall near the village of Gavarnie in the south of **France**. This waterfall pours down in two different levels, or steps. Think of a really tall wedding cake that has two levels. Now imagine a small waterfall pouring down the side of the wedding cake from the top layer and making its way down the sides to the bottom layer. This might give you a good idea of what Gavarnie Falls looks like with its two levels. Each waterfall level pours straight down onto the next, dropping from a total height of about 1,384 feet. That's about as high as some of the tallest skyscrapers in the United States!

Like any waterfall, the water at Gavarnie Falls needs to come from somewhere. This waterfall is fed by melting snow and a small **glacier** in **Spain**, which is very close to Gavarnie. The waterfall creates the beginning of a stream known as the Gave de Pau.

The waterfall may look different depending on the time of year that you decide to visit. During the winter, the weather can become so cold that the waterfall will sometimes freeze and stop flowing! But during the summer when the snow and ice are melting fast, the water pours down in great amounts. At its strongest, the waterfall pours more than 60 times the amount of water it normally pours. If the waterfall was a sink faucet, it would be opened all the way in the summer.

heads. The color of their fur helps them to blend into their surroundings.

Gazelles like to stay together in a large group, called a herd. There can be as many as 700 gazelles in a single herd. Can you imagine traveling around with that many friends every day? Gazelles stay together in large groups for good reason. When they are eating grass out in the open, gazelles will look for any signs of danger. In fact, gazelles have very good senses of sight, sound, and smell, which help them notice danger from far away long before it can get to them. Because gazelles are always looking out for one another, they can work together to keep the herd safe.

Gazelles are very graceful and fast when they run. They can reach speeds of up to 60 miles per hour! While it is impossible for them to outrun a **cheetah** (the main animal that hunts them), gazelles can sometimes escape by racing around in wild patterns and jumping up to 10 feet in the air. Sometimes gazelles look like they're flying!

Gazelle

The gazelle is a type of antelope found in the **deserts**, grasslands, and **savannas** of **Africa**. Gazelles look like deer and sometimes have a black stripe on their sides. Additionally, they have two long, curved horns on top of their

Geirangerfjord

One of the most famous **fjords** in the world is called Geirangerfjord. It is located in Norway, **Europe**. Fjords were created by **glaciers** years ago as they slowly moved through **mountains** and rocks, cutting the deep **valleys** we see today. Many fjords are found on the coasts of **Antarctica** and in the **Arctic**.

The beauty of Geirangerfjord makes it a place that many people like to visit. The fjord is nine miles long, and its water is dark blue. You'll see many waterfalls along the huge cliffs and mountains. The Seven Sisters are a group of waterfalls that jut out from the sides of the cliffs and drop more than 800 feet into the fjord! They create a spray of water that makes a curtain people can walk behind.

If you like the cold temperatures of winter, you'd probably enjoy visiting Geirangerfjord then, when the cliffs and mountains are covered in snow. Imagine this: you are on a boat, listening to stories of the fjord told by rangers. As you cruise through the cold, dark water, you breathe in the fresh winter air. Perhaps you do some fishing too. When you return to the town of Ålesund, you might decide to take a winter hike through part of the fjord, or maybe make a ski or snowshoe outing. You're sure to be ready for a cup of hot chocolate after your adventures!

The fjord is a great place to visit in the summer, too. Many people like to ride on rafts through the water of the fjord and enjoy swimming, hiking, and camping. From late June through early August, some parts of Norway experience what is called "midnight sun." During those months at Geirangerfjord, the nights never get fully dark. Can you imagine it being light out in the middle of the night?

Giant Panda

The giant panda is a kind of bear that lives in thick bamboo forests in the **mountain ranges** of central **China**. It has a thick, wooly, black and white coat to keep it warm, and it spends most of its time eating bamboo shoots and leaves. ("Shoot" is another word for a stem.) During the bamboo growing season, giant pandas eat for about 12 hours a day. Although they are diurnal, meaning they are usually awake during the day and asleep at night, they often get up for a midnight snack of more bamboo. These pandas really take eating seriously! They eat the shoots during this time and put on a lot of weight. Once all the shoots are gone, they eat the leaves.

Giant pandas sit for most of the day and rarely move quickly. They love to roll around. They look clumsy but are very good climbers. They can climb rocks and trees with ease. Giant pandas use their heads to help them climb because their legs are so short! They do not have a permanent den, and unlike other bears, they do not hibernate. Instead, during the winter, they move to warmer areas where they can find more bamboo to eat and take shelter in hollow trees.

Fun Facts:

- When a baby giant panda is born, it is pink and about as long as a pencil.

- Giant pandas are a national treasure in China and China's national symbol.

Giraffe

The giraffe is an amazing animal. No other mammal on earth has a neck as long as it does. It can be found in many different parts of **Africa** and lives on the **savanna** and open woodlands where the trees are smaller and spaced out.

Giraffes weigh between 1,000–4,000 pounds, and they can grow up to 18 feet tall. That's the height of three adults standing on top of each other! A baby giraffe is already six feet tall when it's born. A giraffe has only seven neck bones. That's as many as you and I have. So how can their necks be so much longer than ours? It's because each of their bones are much longer.

Some giraffes live alone, and some live in groups. When a giraffe talks to another giraffe, it makes all kinds of sounds. It will grunt, snort, hiss, whistle, cough loudly, or make strange flute-like sounds. But most of the time, it goes about its day without making a sound.

Lions are the giraffe's main predator. A giraffe isn't fast enough to outrun lions. So how does it protect itself? It uses its weight to keep from being knocked down and uses its strength to shake the lion off. The giraffe also uses its large, heavy hooves to kick at its predators.

One well-placed kick is powerful enough to take a lion's head off!

The giraffe eats grass, leaves, and sometimes fruit. It uses its 18-inch long tongue to grab the leaves and pull them into its mouth. Its mouth is so tough that sharp tree thorns don't even bother it. When the giraffe wants to drink from a **river**, it spreads its front legs wide apart and lowers itself. See if you can watch a giraffe drinking at the zoo. Doesn't it look a little silly?

Golden Gate Bridge

The Golden Gate Bridge crosses the San Francisco Bay, off the coast of California in the United States. Over a hundred thousand people use this bridge to travel to and from work every day. It reaches from the city of San Francisco north to Marin County.

Before the bridge was built, people loaded themselves and their cars onto a ferry, a floating raft that carried them across to the other side. They did this for over 100 years. But then, some smart builders and planners were asked to design the Golden Gate Bridge. They came up with a number of ideas and finally decided to build a suspension bridge.

There are many types of bridges, but a suspension bridge is often used over water that is wide and deep. The bridge hangs from towers at each end that hold up two huge metal cables (ropes). The bridge is attached to these cables, so it floats over the water. (If something is suspended, that means it is hanging or floating.) Isn't that an amazing way to build a bridge?

In 1937, after four years of work, all 9,000 feet of its length was completed. The 90-foot-wide bridge has three fog horns whose sounds guide ships safely through the fog. When the setting sun shines on the red-orange painted steel of the bridge, it really does look golden! The Golden Gate Bridge is a symbol of San Francisco and California, and many people think it is one of the top wonders of the modern world.

Golden Temple of Amritsar

The Golden Temple of Amritsar is a beautiful golden shrine in the city of Amritsar in Punjab, **India**. The building is also known as the Golden Gurdwara. (A *gurdwara* is a place of worship.) The Golden Temple was built in 1589 by Sri Guru Arjan. It has a square shape and stands two stories tall. It was originally built from bricks, but in the nineteenth century, the walls in the Golden Temple were covered in marble and gold foil was used to decorate the large dome. The Golden Temple sits in the center of a large square pool with a bridge that you can cross to get to the temple. Don't worry—the builders kept the pool dry and empty while the temple was being built!

The Golden Temple is considered a sacred place to followers of Sikhism, a religion from the Punjab region of India. In 1604, a copy of the Sikh holy book was placed inside the Golden Temple. Even the building's architecture reflects some of the beliefs of the Sikh religion. For example, the four walls of the Golden Temple each have an entrance to represent the four directions of north, south, east, and west. This symbolizes the Sikh religious belief of being open to all people, no matter who they are or where they're from.

If you are one of the nearly 100,000 people who visit the Golden Temple every day, you can see some of the designs made of mirrors in the ceiling and even watch traditional Sikh ceremonies inside the temple.

Grand Canal

The Grand Canal, also known as the Jing-Hang Grand Canal, is a large **canal** in **China**. The oldest parts of the canal were made in the fifth century BC, but more was added over the years. The Grand Canal is now the oldest and longest man-made canal in the world! It starts in the great city of Beijing, passes through several cities, and ends in the city of Hangzhou in eastern China. The canal stretches 1,104 miles long, connecting China's two longest **rivers**—the Yellow River and the Yangtze.

The Grand Canal was very helpful to the Chinese. It made travel easier between the north and the south. It was also easier and faster to trade goods between cities since people could travel by boat rather than walking or taking a horse-drawn cart.

One neat invention built into the Grand Canal was the pound lock system. It was added during the tenth century. The problem was that the water in the canal was lower in some sections and higher in others. For a boat to travel through the canal, it had to get from one water level to another, like going up or down a staircase. Before they had a lock system, boats had to be hauled up or down a ramp to enter the next canal section. Now, boats can enter a big box (called the "pound") blocking the canal. Then, people can add or drain the water in the box to match the water level where the boat is going. What an amazing invention! The canal is still used to this day.

Grand Canyon

The Grand Canyon in Arizona is the most

famous **canyon** in **North America**. The flowing water of the Colorado River created the canyon by wearing away rocks and soil over millions of years. It is called the Grand Canyon because of its size: it is 277 miles long, up to 18 miles wide in some places, and more than a mile deep!

About five million people visit the Grand Canyon each year. They enjoy hiking, camping, rafting on the **river**, riding donkeys on the trails, and even viewing the canyon from helicopters! Because it snows a lot there in the winter, the North Rim (edge or side) is open for visitors May through October. The South Rim is open year-round.

Thousands of different plants and animals are found there, including 22 kinds of bats and 41 kinds of reptiles. Temperatures range from more than 100°F in the summer to below zero on the rims during winter.

Many different types of rocks are found in the Grand Canyon, including igneous (melted rock originally found underground), sedimentary (small pieces of sand and mud stuck together in layers), and metamorphic (rocks that change because of great pressure or high heat). By studying these rock layers, scientists learn about the conditions that helped form the canyon.

Fun Fact:
The Grand Canyon has 12 kinds of plants that are only found in the canyon!

Great Barrier Reef

The Great Barrier Reef is a coral **reef** off the northeastern coast of **Australia**. Coral looks like a plant, but it is actually an animal! Many, many tiny animals called polyps grow on top of each other until a plant-like shape is formed. Most coral is found in tropical waters and in areas where the water isn't very deep. It grows very slowly and can't move. A coral reef is formed when a large number of corals grow in the same area.

A coral reef is called a barrier reef when it is near land but is separated from the coast by water. The Great Barrier Reef is the largest coral reef in the world! It is made up of almost 3,000 smaller coral reefs and includes over 600 **islands**.

The Great Barrier Reef is very important for **ocean** life. Many animals and plants can only live in coral reefs. In the reef, there are 1,500 different types of fish and many sea turtles, sharks, stingrays, sea snakes, eels, giant clams, snails, seahorses, seagrass, and dugongs, which are a type of sea cow. Many types of whales, dolphins, and porpoises are also found in and around the reef. The islands in the Great Barrier Reef are home to many plants and birds.

About two million tourists visit the Great Barrier Reef every year. Snorkeling, diving, and touring on glass-bottomed boats are great ways to view the beautiful coral and wildlife of the Great Barrier Reef.

Great Lakes

Have you ever heard of the Great Lakes? You might ask, "What makes them great?" These five **lakes** between **Canada** and the United States are called great because they are so large! Each one of the Great Lakes is so big that if you are standing on the shore, it feels like you are looking out at an **ocean**.

The names of the five Great Lakes are Superior, Michigan, Huron, Erie, and Ontario. These five lakes hold 90% of the United States' fresh water and 20% of the entire world's fresh water. They are also important because they make it possible to travel by boat from the middle part of **North America** to the Atlantic Ocean.

The lakes are home to many kinds of fish, including some you may have heard of: walleye, bass, steelhead **salmon**, and lake sturgeon.

Today, many people enjoy water sports on the Great Lakes, including kayaking, boating, and lake **surfing**. But many of the boats and ships on the lakes are not just for fun: they carry goods from one location to another that can then be sold in stores or used to make products. It is sometimes faster for those goods to be delivered by boat instead of by land. On many of the Great Lakes, goods are carried by ships that are 1,200 feet long!

Fun Fact:

The Great Lakes are so big that they can easily be seen from space.

Great Pyramids

The Great Pyramids border the city of Giza, Egypt in **Africa**. They are three of the most famous Egyptian pyramids and are called the Pyramid of Khufu, the Pyramid of Khafre, and the Pyramid of Menkaure. They were built as burial tombs for Egypt's kings around the twenty-sixth century BC—that's more than 5,000 years ago!

In ancient Egypt, kings were called pharaohs. As soon as a pharaoh began to rule, he would begin planning his pyramid so he could be buried there. It took thousands of men working 20 to 30 years to complete just one of these giant pyramids! Some pyramids were never finished because the king died before it was ready and the work completely stopped.

Inside of the pyramids are various items that ancient Egyptians thought the pharaoh would need in his afterlife, including grain, honey, wine, bread, meat, linen sheets, clothing, sandals, chariots, weapons, tables and chairs, perfume, and jewelry. An entire boat was found inside the Pyramid of Khufu!

Pyramids were shaped to look like rays coming from the sun. Many of them were coated with shining white limestone so that they would look as radiant as the sun when viewed from a distance.

Fun Facts:

- The Pyramid of Khufu is about 450 feet tall, the largest of all Egyptian pyramids.
- The **Great Sphinx** is also located near the Great Pyramids.
- There are over 100 Egyptian pyramids built on the West Bank of the **Nile River**. Most were built as tombs for pharaohs and their queens.

Great Sphinx

The Great Sphinx is a very large and ancient stone statue in Egypt, **Africa**. It is located in the city of Giza near the **Great Pyramids**, and it is one of the most famous sculptures in the world.

The Great Sphinx is very old. Archaeologists (people who practice **archaeology**) think it was built around 2500 BC for a pharaoh named Khafre. It is also very big—it is 200 feet long and 65 feet tall! The statue itself has the head of a man and the body of a **lion**, which is why we call it the Great Sphinx, after the mythological creature. In many stories about this creature, the sphinx gave people a riddle. If they couldn't answer the riddle, they would be eaten!

There is a granite tablet between the Great Sphinx's paws that tells a story. It says that one day, an Egyptian prince named Thutmose took a nap between the paws of the sphinx. At this time, the sphinx was mostly covered in sand. While he slept, Thutmose dreamed that the sphinx spoke to him. It asked the prince to free it from the sand, and in exchange, it would give him the throne of Egypt. What an exciting dream!

The Great Sphinx was made out of one very large piece of limestone. It used to be colorfully painted, but now the paint has worn away. Wind and sandstorms have slowly worn away the stone over thousands of years, and some misbehaving tourists used to chip off pieces of the statue to take home. The sphinx is even missing its nose! Even so, the sphinx continues to stand tall to this day. You can still visit the Great Sphinx—just don't try to take a piece of it home!

Great Wall of China

The Great Wall of China is an ancient wall in northern **China** made of cement, rocks, bricks, and earth. At about 13,000 miles long, it is the longest structure built by human hands. Millions of people worked on the wall. It was very hard and dangerous work. Almost half of the workers died from falling stones, exhaustion, sickness, animal attacks, and starvation. It took about 2,000 years for it to look the way it does today.

You might be thinking that the work began on one end and finished at the opposite end. But that is not how it came to be. This very, very long wall that is about 30 feet high is actually a series of walls built in sections over time. They are not all the same, either. These sections were later joined to form what the Chinese now call the "Long Fortress."

The wall was built to keep out invaders, primarily the **Mongols**, coming from the north. It has 7,000 watchtowers, houses for soldiers, and beacons to send smoke signals. Over the last several hundred years, China's enemies still managed to get through the fortress. It was weak in areas because some parts were only made of mud, straw, and twigs. Even today, the wall is not a continuous fortress because those weaker parts have disappeared back into the earth.

It stands today as a patriotic symbol to the Chinese people. Ten million people from all over the world visit the Great Wall each year. It is one of the New Seven Wonders of the World!

Grizzly Bear

The grizzly bear (also known as the brown bear) is a large mammal that lives in **North America**. Most of these bears live in Alaska and **Canada**. There are also some grizzlies in Yellowstone National Park in the United States. If you were to visit this park in Wyoming, you would probably get to see a few!

The bear cubs are born very small, weighing about one pound. They grow up fast, weighing 200–800 pounds as adults. Like a lot of other animals, the males weigh more than the females.

Grizzly bears will eat both animals and plants. A few of the things they like are berries, deer, clams, ladybugs, and salmon. It has been said that their powerful bite can crush a bowling ball!

After eating a lot of food, the bears hibernate (go into a deep sleep) in their dens for half the year during the coldest months. This is when the females have their bear cubs. Some grizzly bears don't hibernate because they live in warm climates.

Grizzlies have big paws with long claws. The claws can grow to be four inches long. They are used for things like digging up clams, turning over rocks in search of insects, and pinning down their prey. But watch out—just one swipe of this dangerous paw can kill. Although grizzlies don't normally attack people, we still need to be careful around them.

Fun Facts:

- Grizzly bears can walk upright on their two back legs.
- Though they are heavy, grizzly bears are good at climbing trees.
- Grizzly bears can live 20–30 years.
- You can't outrun a grizzly bear! They can run at almost 30 miles per hour.

Gypsies

Gypsies are people in **Spain** who once had a very different way of living from other Spanish people. Gypsies lived originally in **India**, but some people thought they came from Egypt, which is where they got their name. Many gypsies moved to Spain in the fifteenth century and have since spread to many other countries.

Today, they are called *Romani* in most countries, but in Spain, they are called *Gitanos*. They speak a language called *Calo* to each other but also speak Spanish. Historically, they moved around in horse-drawn carriages, traveling in groups called caravans. Some people considered them a little scary or suspicious because most families didn't travel around to make a living. Being called a "gypsy" was considered an insult since they were thought to be thieves. Many gypsies were abused in the countries they tried to live in, including being arrested just because they were gypsies.

Gypsies were very creative. They sold homemade goods and used herbs and plants they found. Many danced, wrote songs, played instruments, or told fortunes and gave palm-readings, which was frowned upon. Gypsies also knew a lot about animals and how to care for them.

Nowadays, gypsies live and work much like their neighbors. They have become a part of their communities. Even though gypsies are a nation without their own land, they are still very proud of their culture.

Hadrian's Wall

Hadrian's Wall was built by the Roman emperor Hadrian in what is now the **United Kingdom** in AD 122. Why did Hadrian need to build a wall? It separated the land in the south of Britain that belonged to the **Roman Empire** from the barbarian lands in the north. Usually, Romans conquered everyone they met, but the northern tribes living where Scotland is today were too fierce to control. So instead, Hadrian built a wall as protection against the Scottish tribes.

This wall was 80 miles long. Parts were made from stone and were 20 feet high, while others parts were made from piled-up dirt and grass and were only 11 feet high. The wall was probably originally covered with plaster and painted white so that it would shine in the sun and be seen from a long way away.

Forts called milecastles were built along the wall, each one being about a mile away from the next. Roman soldiers lived in these forts, which also had towers on them for watching and signaling. The milecastles allowed the soldiers to keep an eye on who came and went through the gates in the wall. It also allowed them to charge people a tax for entering Roman **territory**.

Large parts of Hadrian's Wall still stand, although in places it is almost gone because people took away the stones to build other things. If you go to the United Kingdom, you can follow the wall by walking along the Hadrian Wall Path.

Haflinger

The Haflinger is a kind of horse from Austria and northern **Italy**. It is a pony, which means it is a smaller horse. All Haflingers are chestnut colored and have a cream or white mane.

Haflingers have existed since the Middle Ages. Their name comes from the town of Hafling, or Avelengo, in northern Italy. Hafling is the way Germans say the name. So these horses are also known as Avelignese, after the Italian way of saying the town's name. These horses are tough enough to do well in the cold and on the rocky trails in the **mountains** of Austria and Italy.

During World War II, Haflingers were used to carry supplies for the army. People started breeding Haflingers to be shorter because this made it easier for them to carry heavy loads. The German and Austrian armies still use them for help in places where the ground isn't very flat! Sometimes in the mountains, it's better to have a horse than a car.

Today, Haflingers can have many different jobs: some carry and pull things, and some are therapy horses that disabled or mentally unwell people can ride to help them get better. Some Haflingers perform equestrian vaulting, which is something you might see at a circus. Gymnasts and dancers can do special jumps and moves on the backs of Haflingers!

Henry Hudson and Hudson Bay

Henry Hudson was an English explorer and navigator who traveled to **North** and **South America** in the seventeenth century. In **Canada**, Hudson discovered a very large bay (a bay is a large area of water with land on three sides). The bay he discovered, now called Hudson Bay, was named after him, and it is the second largest bay in the world!

Henry Hudson was a very good navigator. He was hired by an English trading company that wanted him to look for a way to sail from

England to **Asia**. At that time, many people thought there might be a way to get to Asia through the Americas. So Henry set out to the Americas to find this way, which was called the Northwest Passage.

Sailing northwest around the Americas meant going through the Arctic Ocean. This was very difficult because of the icy waters. Henry Hudson tried twice to find the Northwest Passage around America. During his second attempt in 1610, Henry found the Hudson Bay, but his ship got stuck in the ice. When spring came and the ice melted, Henry wanted to keep going, but the other sailors wanted to go home. They couldn't agree, so the other sailors left Henry, his son, and a few others behind, and sailed back to England without them! After this, Henry Hudson was never seen again.

Henry's explorations made it easier for other ships to look for the Northwest Passage. Also, Hudson Bay brought lots of trade to North America. For example, a huge fur trading business called Hudson's Bay Company set up trading posts in the bay and traded with Native American Indians for over two hundred years.

Henry VIII

Henry VIII was king of England, now part of the **United Kingdom**, between 1509–1547. He is best known for having six marriages and for separating the Church of England from the Roman Catholic Church.

Henry became king when he was 17 years old. He was charming and well educated, an author and a composer. He also loved power, which was a problem. Henry wanted a son to rule after him, but he and his wife Katherine only had a daughter. Henry banished Katherine from court and married another woman named Anne Boleyn. Although the pope never agreed that his marriage with Katherine was over, the Archbishop of Canterbury supported King Henry. When Anne Boleyn also only had a daughter, Henry wasn't happy. He accused Anne of being unfaithful and had her put to death. Henry finally had a son with his third wife, but she died soon after. He ended up marrying three more women!

Meanwhile, Henry began to dislike how much power the pope had and how the pope refused to end his first marriage. Henry wanted to do things his own way. So he declared himself Supreme Head of the Church in England. He closed all the monasteries and took their riches and land. Any money that would have gone to the Church in Rome now went straight to Henry. Henry did many cruel things with his power. He destroyed shrines. He martyred monks, **St. Thomas More** and **St. John Fisher**, and others who thought he shouldn't be in charge of the Church of England. Henry's actions helped start the Protestant Reformation in England.

Himalayas

The Himalayas are a **mountain range** in **Asia**. Starting in the country of Pakistan in the west, they go all the way to Tibet in the east, separating South Asia from the regions to the north and east. The Himalayas are home to 10 of the 13 highest **mountains** in the world, including the highest mountain on earth, **Mt. Everest**. Mt. Everest is more than 29,000 feet tall!

The word *Himalaya* comes from an old language called Sanskrit, and it means "house of snow." What clue does this name give you about the climate in the highest peaks of the Himalayas? Even though snow is almost always found in the highest parts of the Himalayas, there are a variety of climates found in other parts. At the bottom of the mountains, the weather is often humid and warm. On the Tibetan side of the mountain range, it is dry, cold, and very windy.

With different types of weather and plants in different areas, many types of animals live in the Himalayas. See if you can guess in what part of the mountain range each of these animal types are found: snow leopards, musk deer, **wild boar**, crocodiles, **Asian elephants**, and **Bengal tigers**. Blue sheep, also called *bharal*, are found in the higher parts of the mountains. Blue sheep got their name because the coloring of their fur helps them to blend in with their surroundings. This is called camouflage. If a predator like a

snow leopard gets close to them, they stay very still and hope they won't be seen. If they are seen, they quickly run up the steep cliffs.

Himeji Castle

Himeji Castle is a beautiful white castle in Japan, **Asia**. It was built in 1333 in the city of Himeji on the main **island** of Japan, Honshu. The castle is actually a large group of 83 wooden buildings that covers many acres.

Himeji Castle has one large main building called the keep, or *tenshu* in Japanese. During peacetime, the tenshu would have been used to store goods, and during wartime, the people would have defended this part of the castle the longest. Himeji Castle also has many strong walls, moats, storehouses, towers, passageways, and gates.

Like most castles, Himeji Castle was specially designed to help people defend it from enemies. The wooden buildings are covered with white plaster so that they do not catch fire as easily. There are also many loopholes, or small holes in the castle walls that allow you to shoot arrows at the enemy while staying protected. Many of the passageways are arranged like a maze with dead ends and hidden rooms to confuse the enemy. There are also narrow spaces where rocks or boiling oil could be thrown onto the enemy below.

It is amazing that the castle is so strong and so beautiful at the same time. The castle is sometimes called *Hakuro-jō*, meaning "White Egret Castle," because the white walls and curved roofs remind people of a white bird flying. Himeji Castle is Japan's largest and most visited castle.

Hippopotamus

The common hippopotamus (or hippo) is a large, heavy animal that lives in **Africa**, mostly south of the **Sahara Desert**. It can grow to be 15 feet long and weighs 7,000 pounds on average. It's one of the biggest mammals on earth—and one of the meanest!

Hippos have very strong mouths with two huge tusks inside them. Tusks are teeth that are sharper and longer than the other teeth. Hippos use their tusks to fight off crocodiles and **lions**. Hippos can be very dangerous to humans too. They think humans are just another predator that wants to attack their babies. They will do anything to protect their young, so be careful if you meet a hippopotamus.

Hippos live both in the water and on the land. As you know, it is very hot in Africa, so in the daytime, they keep cool by staying in the muddy waters of shallow **rivers** and **lakes**. When night comes and it is cooler, they go on land to eat plants. Hippos are herbivores and can eat around 88–110 pounds of grass in one night!

Fun Facts:
- Hippos can run faster than most people.
- Hippos have webbed feet but are not good swimmers and can't float.
- A hippo's nostrils, eyes, and ears are on top of its head so its body can be under the water while it watches for predators.
- Hippos can close their nostrils underwater and hold their breath for five minutes at a time.
- Hippopotamus means "river horse" in Greek.

Howler Monkey

The howler monkey can be found in **South America** and some parts of **North America**. It is the loudest monkey in the world. Its howl can be heard from as far as three miles away, and it sounds like a loud growl or a roar.

Howler monkeys live together in groups high in the trees of **rainforests**. They have a big bone in the front of their necks that enables them to howl so loudly. They howl to defend their **territory**, and sometimes groups of howler monkeys howl back and forth as a kind of discussion to decide where each group's territory ends.

The howler monkey is one of the largest monkeys in the Americas. It can grow up to three feet long. Its tail can be as long as its body, or even longer! Its tail is quite strong and can wrap around things, so howler monkeys often use it to hold onto branches and pick fruit from trees.

There are many different types of howler monkeys. Most are black or a deep reddish brown, but some are golden brown or black with reddish hands. They mostly eat leaves from trees, as well as flowers, buds, and fruits. Because leaves don't give them much energy, howler monkeys usually move slowly and spend a lot of time resting and sleeping. Howler monkeys are hunted by **jaguars** and other large cats, eagles, and large snakes. They can live for 15–20 years.

Huascaran

Huascaran is not only the tallest **mountain** in **Peru** but also the fourth-tallest mountain in all of the Americas. It is part of the **Andes mountain range**.

The Quechua people (the native people of Peru) have their own name for it. They call it *Mataraju*, which means "twin snow peaks." This is because Huascaran actually has two peaks, not one! (A peak is the pointed top of a mountain.) The taller peak is toward the south, so it is called Huascaran Sur. Its **summit** is 22,204 feet in **elevation**, the highest point in Peru. The shorter peak is called Huascaran Norte. It is pretty tall too, at 21,833 feet.

Huascaran is mostly covered in snow and ice. **Mountain climbing** can be a fun challenge on this mountain, but it can also be very dangerous. It takes five to seven days to climb to the top of Huascaran Sur, and sometimes there are **earthquakes** and avalanches. (An avalanche is when large amounts of snow, ice, and rocks fall down a mountain.) In 1970, an earthquake shook Huascaran and made a giant avalanche. The falling rocks and ice gathered mud as they slid all the way to the bottom of the mountain. An entire town and several villages were buried, and thousands of people died. An avalanche this large is very rare, but mountain climbers still have to watch out for smaller avalanches on Huascaran.

Visitors to Huascaran also hike, ski, and watch the amazing mountain wildlife, like the **Andean condor** and spectacled bear.

Humpback Whale

The humpback whale is a very large whale found in every **ocean**, but it is very commonly seen along the coasts of **North America**.

Humpbacks are a certain kind of whale called baleen whales. A baleen whale has thick, brushy bristles called baleen in its mouth instead of regular teeth. Baleen help catch very tiny **sea** creatures, such as plankton, for the whale to eat. Baleen are made of the same material as the hair on your head! Can you imagine making your hair into a net to catch tiny sea creatures?

Humpback whales are easy to recognize because of their long flippers and the large, knobby humps on their backs. These whales can grow to be around 60 feet long and can weigh as much as 88,000 pounds. That's heavier than three school buses! Even though humpback whales swim in the sea, they are actually mammals, not fish. This means that they need to breathe air like you do. On the tops of their heads, these whales have a large blowhole that acts as their nose. This makes it easy for them to breathe when they come to the surface of the water before diving again to find food.

If you ever go diving in the ocean, listen for the famous song of the humpback whale! Male humpbacks are known to sing beautiful songs that echo for miles in the open water. Even though we can only hear some of the sounds the whale can make, some of the lower sounds of the song can travel for more than 10,000 miles. Can you sing that loud?

Hundred Years' War

The Hundred Years' War was a series of battles fought between England and **France** in the Middle Ages. This long conflict actually lasted over 116 years—from 1337–1453.

The Hundred Years' War was fought because both England and France claimed land in present-day France. England thought it should have this land because when William the Conqueror conquered England in 1066, he gave land in France to English noblemen.

Neither side wanted to give up their land, so they kept fighting! This war changed many things. For example, by the end of this war, England and France had permanent armies instead of just having armies during wartime. Both countries became more patriotic during the war. Also, the Hundred Years' War was the last great time of chivalry (Christian knights and ladies who followed special rules for behavior).

Some of the most famous parts of this war are Henry V's invasion of France, which **Shakespeare** wrote about in his play *Henry V*, and **St. Joan of Arc** leading the French army to victory at the Siege of Orléans. Edward the Black Prince was also an important leader in this war.

The last big battle of the war was the Battle of Castillon. The English lost badly because the army's commander led his men to a French fort, thinking that the French were retreating.

They were not, and they used cannons to kill many English soldiers.

After this war, the English did not want to fight more long, expensive wars. The French felt better about it because they won. They are still very proud of winning the Hundred Years' War.

Iberian Lynx

The Iberian lynx is a medium-sized wild cat found mostly in **Spain**. The Iberian lynx is one of four species of lynx, which are smaller than other wild cats like **lions**, tigers, or leopards. The Iberian lynx has spotted brown fur, a white underbelly, and extra fur around the sides of its face that makes it look like it has a fluffy beard. The Iberian lynx also has large, sensitive whiskers and extra bits of fur on the tips of its large ears, which are very sensitive to sound. Iberian lynxes can run very fast, reaching speeds of 50 miles per hour.

The Iberian lynx is nocturnal, meaning that it sleeps during the day and hunts at night. Iberian lynxes like to hunt rabbits, but they will sometimes eat birds, deer, or wild sheep when there are not enough rabbits. Most males need to eat at least one rabbit per day, but a mother raising her kittens will eat up to three rabbits a day. If an Iberian lynx does not eat all of its food, it will bury the food and dig it up later when it is ready to eat again.

There are very few Iberian lynxes left in the world, making it one of the rarest cats found in the wild. With the help of wildlife experts, these cats have been saved from disappearing.

Ice Fishing

Ice fishing is catching fish that are under the ice of a frozen body of water, like a **lake**. This kind of fishing is done in parts of the world like **Canada** where winter temperatures are below freezing for a long time.

The surface of bodies of water freezes into a hard, thick sheet of ice. To get to the fish under the ice, fishermen use special tools to drill holes. They then use short fishing rods, or jigging rods, to catch the fish. The line, with a hook and bait attached at the end, is let down through the hole and quickly moved up and down. A lot of different things can be used for bait, like waxworms, minnows, corn, and salmon eggs.

When people go ice fishing, the temperatures are below zero, so it can be very dangerous. They must think of how they will keep warm. If they do not dress in warm clothing or take shelter in an ice shack, they can get frostbite.

Ice shacks are an important part of ice fishing in Canada. They are dragged onto the lake using a truck or snowmobile. Simple ice shacks can be made like a tent and used as protection from the cold and wind. Others are built to be sturdier and can have all the comforts of a home.

In Canada, ice fishing is often a social activity. Ice shacks can be rented by the day, and many fishermen spend their weekends out on the frozen lake all winter long. Where the fishing is good, there are so many ice shacks that it can look like a city on ice!

Ice Hockey

Ice hockey is the most popular sport in **Canada**. In 1875, the first organized game of hockey was played in Canada, but many children in Canada and the **United Kingdom** likely played a version of ice hockey before then.

Have you ever played ice hockey? Instead of using a ball like other games, this game uses a puck, which is a disk made of hard rubber that is about three inches across. The game is played by pushing the puck around the ice with a hockey stick. Like in soccer, both teams try to get the puck in the other team's goal net. The goaltender on each team tries to keep the puck from going in the net.

Both teams can have six skaters on the ice at the same time. Every goal is worth one point. The game is played over three 20-minute periods, and whichever team has more points at the end is the winner.

You'll need lots of equipment to protect yourself during the game—including shoulder pads, elbow pads, padded pants, leg guards, a helmet, a mouth guard to protect your teeth, and, of course, ice skates! If you play the position of goaltender, you'll need even heavier gear since you'll be blocking the puck from going into the goal.

Hockey is played in many places throughout the world and is part of the Winter Olympics. Ice hockey was officially named Canada's national winter sport in 1994.

Iguana

The common iguana is one of the largest lizards in **North** and **South America**. They can grow from five inches all the way up to six feet long! The iguana is native to the tropical areas of Mexico, Central America, South America, and the Caribbean. It can now also be found in the United States in some parts of Florida, Texas, Hawaii, Puerto Rico, and the US Virgin Islands.

The iguana is an herbivore, eating many kinds of leaves, flowers, and some fruits. It has a special liking for the wild plums of Panama. It likes to live in large trees, especially trees that hang over water. If the iguana is being hunted by a predator, it can easily dive into the water and escape. Its main predators are birds of prey, such as hawks and eagles.

Iguanas live to be up to 20 years old. This is partly due to how well they can hide from their predators. They hide using what is called camouflage. They can change the color of their skin to blend in to their surroundings. Male iguanas have a special flap of skin called the dewlap. If they feel like they are in danger, they will stretch out this dewlap and puff up their body while hissing and bobbing their head. If this doesn't scare off their enemy, iguanas will lash out with their tails, bite, and use their claws to protect themselves.

When iguanas want to talk with each other, they use their head bobs and dewlaps. A certain number of head bobs means one thing, while another number of head bobs means another thing. These giant lizards are amazing!

Iguazu Falls

The Iguazu Falls are a collection of almost 300 different waterfalls on the border of Brazil and Argentina in **South America**. They are some of the largest waterfalls in the world. The most impressive fall is called Devil's Throat, where the water falls over a gigantic U-shaped cliff. It is so impressive that a famous United States president's wife, Eleanor Roosevelt, said "My poor Niagara!" when she visited. Even though **Niagara Falls** is an amazing waterfall, she thought Iguazu Falls was even more amazing.

The falls are part of the Iguazu River. The word *iguazu* means "big water" in an old South American language. The falls are such an important site that there are national parks in both Brazil and Argentina so people can visit the falls in either country. Although the falls are the main attraction, the national parks are also home to many different plants and animals such as **toucans**, giant otters, and anteaters.

On the Brazilian side, you can walk along the lower base of Devil's Throat or take a helicopter ride. On the Argentinian side, you can take a train that will bring you to walking trails along the falls. You can also ride in an inflatable boat to get closer to the falls.

If you visit between December and

February, you'll see the falls at their best, with lots of water coming over the cliffs. But it's also the rainy season, so be sure to bring a raincoat!

Incas

The Incas were a native people in **Peru**. For many years, they lived in a very small kingdom around Cuzco (now spelled Cusco), their capital city. In 1438, the Inca ruler **Pachacuti** turned it into an empire that ruled many different peoples. The Inca Empire covered most of western **South America**, including parts of Colombia, Ecuador, Peru, Bolivia, Argentina, and Chile. It was the largest empire in the Americas!

The Incas spoke many different languages, but the official one was Quechua. This very old language is still spoken today. The Incas mostly farmed and raised herds of **llamas** and alpacas. Llamas were important for their wool, hide, meat, and more. Often, llama meat would be dried so it would not spoil. (Did you know the word "jerky" comes from the Quechua word for dried meat?) Most importantly, llamas were great pack animals. They are quite strong and can easily climb **mountain** paths. They are still sometimes used in Peru as pack animals.

The Incas built great walls, cities, temples, and palaces. Their roads were especially good, covering thousands of miles. The Incas were very rich in silver and gold, which they mined in the mountains. It's amazing that the Incas built such a large empire without knowing about the wheel or how to make iron and steel! They also didn't have a system of writing. Instead, they used knotted ropes to help them remember messages and stories.

The Incas worshiped many pagan gods. Sometimes they even practiced human sacrifice. Inca kings were often mummified after their deaths. In 1532, Spaniards led by **Francisco Pizarro** attacked the Incas and killed the Inca ruler Atahualpa. By 1572, the Inca Empire was defeated.

Indian Folk Dancing

Indian folk dancing is a kind of dance you can see throughout **India**. Indian folk dancing has been around since at least the Middle Ages. There are many different dance styles that come from different parts of India. Indian folk dances are performed for many special occasions, like weddings, festivals, and even changing seasons. Depending on the dance, men and women might perform separately or dance together. Indian folk dancers often sing while they are dancing, and musicians join them by playing instruments.

Most folk dances have special costumes with lots of designs on them. Some costumes help to tell a story, like the dance *Bagha Nacha*. In this dance, male dancers dress up like tigers, complete with a tail! Other dances use props, like clay pots balanced on the dancers' heads, or small swords that the dancers bite down on, kind of like a pirate. Still other dances might use small metal cymbals tied to the dancers' legs so that when they dance, you can hear the metal clinking of the cymbals.

Indian folk dance has inspired modern dance styles, many of which you can still watch today even if you're not visiting India. If you watch a Bollywood film, which is like the Indian version of Hollywood films, you will almost certainly see at least a few dancing scenes throughout the movie. See if you can dance along and learn some of the steps!

Indian Peacock

Something you may not know is that "peacock" is the name for a male peafowl, and female peafowl are called peahens. The male is one of the most beautiful birds in God's creation, but the female has gray-brown coloring and no train of long feathers behind it. But with her dull colors, the peahen can blend into the weeds and grasses around her. She is so well hidden that predators can't find her or her chicks.

Indian Peacocks, or peafowl, live in **India** and other parts of South **Asia**. Peafowl are omnivorous, so they like to eat grains, grasses, and veggies, as well as snai s, frogs, and small snakes. Leopards, Asian wild dogs, wolves, **lions**, **Bengal tigers**, and large birds of prey hunt peafowl. Staying in groups helps them stay safe because there are more eyes to keep watch. A group of peafowl is often called a muster. They can't fly very high, but they like to roost in trees at night.

Peafowl are the national bird of India. Indian peafowl, relatives of pheasants, are found in zoos all over the world. But if you were to travel to India or Sri Lanka, you would have the treat of seeing them in their native home. Find the dry forests there and listen for their calls. Peafowl make many different sounds. One of their calls sounds like a lady screaming!

Fun Facts:
- In the wild, peafowl can live for about 15 years.
- Peacocks are great dancers. They dance while displaying their feathers to the peahens!

Itaimbezinho Canyon

Itaimbezinho Canyon is the largest **canyon** in Brazil, **South America**. It is almost six miles long and almost half a mile deep. Itaimbezinho Canyon is part of the largest network of canyons in South America.

Many people like to visit Itaimbezinho Canyon to wonder at this amazing creation. The canyon was formed in a few different ways. At first, the volcanic rock of the canyon walls cracked in places where it was weak. Then, over a long period of time, water and wind wore away softer parts of the stone. This made the canyon wider and deeper.

Itaimbezinho Canyon has sharp, straight rock walls, and there are some beautiful waterfalls that flow into the canyon. The Rio do Boi River flows through the bottom of the canyon. During the rainy season, it can be dangerous to hike in the canyon because the **river** flows higher and stronger. After a hard rain, the river washes away anything that's not stuck to the ground.

If you visit this canyon, you can see evergreen trees, orchids, ferns, and palm trees. You might even see an azure jay, a red-bellied toad, or a Brazilian sand lizard. There are **mountain lions**, too, but let's hope you don't meet one!

Fun Fact:
Itaimbezinho Canyon gets its name from the word *itaimbe*, which means "cut rock" or "sharp rock."

Italian Wolf

The Italian wolf, also known as the Apennine wolf, lives in the Apennine **mountains** and also in the **Alps** in **Italy**.

Italian wolves look similar to other kinds of gray wolves (the species it is a part of), but their heads are a little rounder and their coats are slightly different in color. Italian wolves often stay together in small packs of up to seven wolves. Some packs will travel over 120 miles every day!

Italian wolves like to come out at night and hunt together for food. They eat mostly medium-sized animals like **wild boar** and deer. If those animals are hard to find, Italian wolves will hunt and eat smaller animals like rabbits. Sometimes they will even eat wild herbs and berries.

Wolves are special in Italy because they are part of the myth of how the Roman people and the great city of Rome began. In the myth, a wolf took care of two human baby brothers, Romulus and Remus, by giving them her milk. Romulus grew up to build the city of Rome. This story was told to show that Romans are tough and dangerous like wolves since the first Roman was raised by wolves.

Italian wolves almost died out in the twentieth century, but since the 1970s, they have been protected and are doing well again.

Jacques Cartier

Jacques Cartier was an explorer from **France**. He lived from 1491–1557 and sailed to **Canada** three times.

Cartier became an explorer because he was a good fisherman! The city he came from, Saint-Malo, was on the **ocean**. Many fishermen in Saint-Malo knew how to sail across the ocean to catch fish in the New World, the Americas. So King Francis I asked Cartier to sail to the New World and see if he could find some good land or riches for France.

On his first voyage, Cartier met Donnacona, a Native American Indian chief of the Iroquois people. He took Donnacona's sons back to France with him to teach them French and show them to King Francis. He brought them back to the New World, but then he captured Donnacona and took them all to France. Cartier wanted them to tell stories about America to help prove to the French that America was a rich land worth colonizing. Cartier also wanted to show that the Native American Indians would easily convert to Catholicism. Donnacona was probably baptized in France. They were treated well, but he and his sons died of illness soon after arriving. This was probably because their bodies were not used to the different diseases in **Europe**. Cartier started a French settlement in Canada, but the Native American Indians became less friendly toward the French. Eventually, the French had to leave.

Cartier was the first European to see many important places in Canada, including Prince Edward Island, the St. Lawrence River, and the Native American Indian village that became the city of Montreal. In all his explorations, he never lost a ship, and he entered and left at least 50 unexplored **harbors** without running his ship into anything too damaging. That's a pretty good record for an explorer!

Jaguar

Jaguars are the largest cat species in **South America**, and they are the third-largest cats in the world after **Bengal tigers** and **lions**. Jaguars are at the top of the food chain, which means no other creatures hunt them. Their fur has dark, rose-shaped spots that help them blend in with their surroundings in forests. This makes it easier for them to sneak up on their prey. Their jaws are so strong that they can bite through most things, even turtle shells and the tough scales of crocodiles!

Jaguars are very good swimmers and like water. They sometimes hunt in **rivers** to catch fish and turtles. Their favorite food, though, is **capybaras**. Jaguars can even climb trees to look for prey. They tend to hunt at night or at the beginning or end of the day when there isn't much light. Instead of chasing their prey, jaguars prefer to sneak up and then jump on them with a surprise attack. Once they have their prey, jaguars will take their food to a safe place to eat in peace.

Jaguars like to hunt alone rather than in groups, but jaguar mothers will stay close to their cubs. These amazing large cats talk to each other by growling and roaring so that other jaguars can hear them from far away. Can you imagine shouting so loudly that your friend across town could hear you?

Jog Falls

Jog Falls is a beautiful waterfall in southwest **India**. The Sharavati River drops down about 830 feet, creating Jog Falls. It is surrounded by beautiful green plants and forest. Something that makes Jog Falls different from other waterfalls is that it comes down as four individual waterfalls. These smaller waterfalls actually have their own names: Raja, Rani, Roarer, and Rocket. Each of these smaller waterfalls are like siblings, and they each have their own personality. The Rani waterfall looks like a soft sheet of foam as it falls over the rocky ledge, Rocket shoots down in jets of water, and Roarer and Raja come together to meet part of the way down.

During **monsoon** season when there is a lot of heavy rain, Jog Falls will turn into one giant waterfall that covers almost the entire mountainside like a huge wall of water! There is so much water pouring down every second that you might even see rainbows appear on the falls every now and then. If you like a good nature hike, Jog Falls is definitely the place for you to visit! There are 1,400 steps from the top of the waterfall down to the very bottom, so you can enjoy the waterfall from any view. Bring a camera so you can capture a rainbow!

Julius Caesar

Julius Caesar was a military leader and dictator in ancient Rome, where **Italy** is today. Caesar lived from 100–44 BC.

Before he ruled Rome, Caesar was an army general in the Roman Republic. He led Rome to victory in an eight-year war against the Gauls, a group of people in what is now Germany, **France**, Belgium, and Switzerland. He was very powerful after defeating them. Instead of continuing to work for the Republic, Caesar and his army marched on the city of Rome. At that time, it was illegal to bring an army or even weapons into the city of Rome because this would threaten the city's peace and the people's control over the government. Romans feared that whoever brought an army inside the city would take control of the government, which is exactly what Caesar did. He was made dictator for life—supreme ruler for as long as he lived. This meant that Rome was no longer a **republic** but rather a **dictatorship** because it was ruled by one man instead of by the people. Soon, under the next ruler, **Caesar Augustus**, Rome became the **Roman Empire**.

Some Romans didn't like Caesar being in charge. They wanted the Republic back. A group of senators (political leaders) secretly made plans to kill Caesar so that Rome could go back to the way it was. They succeeded in killing Caesar, but the common people were very upset. Rome was changed forever. After Caesar, only emperors ruled, not the people.

There are many famous lines said by Caesar or about Caesar:

"*Veni, vidi, vici*"—"I came, I saw, I conquered." Caesar said this after winning a battle quickly.

"*Et tu, Brute?*"—"You too, Brutus?" In **Shakespeare**'s play about Julius Caesar, Brutus is one of Caesar's friends who helps to kill him. This saying has come to mean, "You too, my friend, are betraying me?"

"Crossing the Rubicon." When Caesar crossed the Rubicon River with his army on his way into Rome, he knew a fight would follow. The Rubicon was Rome's boundary for armies: it was illegal for an army to cross this **river** and approach Rome. This saying now means "passing the point of no return."

● ● ●

Kangaroo

The kangaroo is a famous and very recognizable animal found in **Australia**. In fact, it is so famous that it even appears on the Australian one-dollar coin! Kangaroos live in wide-open places like **plains** and **savannas**.

Kangaroos are **marsupials**. Kangaroo mothers have a pouch made of skin below their chests where they carry their babies, which are called joeys.

When explorers from **Europe** first discovered kangaroos, they described them as furry creatures that had heads like deer, stood upright like people, and hopped like crows. If you had never seen a kangaroo before, that might have sounded crazy! While kangaroos do look kind of funny, they are pretty amazing creatures. Their big feet are very strong and can help them hop three times their height.

Using those big feet, kangaroos hop around wherever they go to find grass, shrubs, and other plants to eat. They usually travel around 12–16 miles per hour, but they can hop up to 43 miles per hour! When a kangaroo isn't hopping, it might go for a swim. Kangaroos are actually very good swimmers. They even use their large, long tail for speed and steering.

Fun Facts:
- A group of kangaroos is called a mob or a court.
- Kangaroos can't hop backward! This is because of their large tails.
- Kangaroos are the largest marsupials in the world.

King Arthur

King Arthur was a legendary king of medieval Britain (now the **United Kingdom**). So many amazing stories were told about him after his death that we're not sure which ones are true—although Arthur probably was a real person!

You may have heard some of these stories. It is said King Arthur was given an enchanted sword named Excalibur by a lady who lived in a **lake**. This sword proved that he was the true king of Britain. A mysterious magician named Merlin helped him become king. Arthur had knights, the Knights of the Round Table, who swore to help him keep the peace in England and defend everything good. Arthur was married to Queen Guinevere.

Before Arthur's time, Celtic people lived in Britain. They were ruled by the **Roman Empire** for a while, but in the fifth century AD, the Roman soldiers returned to Rome. This meant Britain was open to invaders. The Saxons (later known as the **Anglo-Saxons**), a group of people from central **Europe**, decided to invade Britain and settle there. But the Celts were not happy being ruled by the Saxons. The legend says that King Arthur defeated the Saxons in battle and made Britain into a free kingdom.

Many stories about Arthur say that he did not die. Instead, he fell into an enchanted sleep and will wake up when Britain needs him again. They say he will return to be a great king again.

King Cobra

Imagine that you are a farmer in **India**. The hot sun beats down on you, and you're dripping with sweat. Glancing down, you are surprised to see that you've almost stepped on a huge snake. It feels cornered, and it raises itself up off the ground so that it is as tall as you! Around its head is a hood decorated with stripes. It hisses to warn you that it will bite if you come any closer.

You've found a cobra—a king cobra, the largest type of cobra, in fact. King cobras can grow up to 18 feet long, about as long as a **giraffe**! King cobras live in tropical and **mountain** forests in South and Southeast **Asia**.

King cobras mostly eat other snakes, but they might also eat lizards, birds, and small mammals if they are hungry. They are hunted by mongooses, which are small, fast mammals that are not as weakened by cobra venom as most other animals. Other large snakes and birds of prey might also hunt king cobras. These cobras can live to be 20 years old in the wild, which is very old for a venomous (poisonous) snake.

Back to the farm in India, where you're facing down a king cobra; what do you do now? You can't do your farm work because the venom from a cobra bite is extremely poisonous. Without immediate medicine (called antivenom) from a doctor, one bite would kill you.

You decide to call a **snake charmer** from a local tribe called the Kalbelia. Snake charmers are very good at handling cobras, thanks to family secrets that have been passed down. Snake charmers used to make money in public performances where the snake charmer plays a special musical instrument called a pungi and waves it around to make his snake "dance." Owning a cobra to have snake charming performances is no longer allowed in India. However, snake charmers today still use their techniques to capture cobras and move them to a safer location. It's time to give one a call!

Klondike Gold Rush

The Klondike Gold Rush is also known as the Yukon Gold Rush. A gold rush happens when many people rush to a place where gold has been found. The Klondike Gold Rush took place from 1896–1899 in **Canada**. It began when the news spread that two men had found a gold nugget in Bonanza Creek, which flows from the Klondike River. Over 100,000 people rushed to the Yukon and Klondike Rivers.

The gold miners thought it would be easy to find gold. Most of the men left their families behind to "strike it rich." But many of them never found gold, and many died from illness. Throughout much of the year, ice and snow made it almost impossible to find gold, and it was very, very cold. Sometimes, the gold miners could not work at all because of the ice. Other times, they built fires to thaw the frozen ground.

Gold mining around the Yukon and Klondike Rivers brought many people to the area, but it also pushed out the natives. Many died because there were not enough wild animals, fish, and berries to feed everyone. Some of the miners found ways to work together with the natives, who were the best hunters and guides. Many of the miners would have starved to death if the natives had not helped them.

Koala

The koala is a furry gray animal found in the eastern and southern regions of **Australia**. These creatures may look a little bit like cuddly bears, but they are not actually bears. Their closest relative is the **wombat**.

Koalas are usually active at night, spending almost all of their time up in the trees. Their very favorite food is eucalyptus leaves. Unlike most animals, koalas don't usually drink water from **rivers** and ponds. Instead, they get their water from the eucalyptus leaves. The only problem is that eucalyptus leaves aren't very nutritious. Because of this, koalas aren't very active, and they sleep for up to 18 hours per day. This means that they are only awake for about six hours each day, spending most of that time eating! The only time that koalas will come down to the ground is when they want to climb up a different tree. When they are on the ground, they crawl on all fours.

Something really special about koala mothers is that they have pouches on the front of their bodies, like **kangaroos** do. After the koala mother gives birth to her baby, the little koala will crawl into its mother's pouch. The baby lives in the mother's pouch, and then on or near her, for about a year.

Fun Fact:

Koalas have fingerprints on their fingers just like you do! Even though human and koala fingers look different, the fingerprints are similar.

Komodo Dragon

The Komodo dragon lives on a few **islands** in Indonesia, **Asia**. It is a type of reptile called a monitor, which is a lizard with a long neck and strong tail and legs. Komodo dragons are the largest lizard, growing to be 8–10 feet long and up to 300 pounds. They live in grasslands, **savannas**, and tropical forests. They can live to be 50 years old.

Like other reptiles, Komodo dragons lay eggs and are cold-blooded. This means they have to lie in the sun to warm up and lie in the shade to cool down. They usually live by themselves. Komodo dragons are carnivores, eating many kinds of meat and even eggs. They swallow goats and smaller animals whole and use their sharp teeth to tear up larger animals, like deer and water buffalo, into smaller pieces. Sometimes, Komodo dragons even eat each other, so the young dragons have to be clever since they are smaller and weaker. They often sleep in trees where adult dragons can't reach them.

When a Komodo dragon is hunting and bites an animal, it leaves deadly poison and germs in the bite. Even if the animal gets away, it might still die. However, the Komodo dragon usually kills its prey right away. Scientists have made a medicine that kills germs based on the Komodo dragon's blood, which keeps the dragon safe from germs.

Komodo dragons are dangerous, but they don't attack people very often. There aren't very many of them living in the wild anymore, so now there are laws to protect Komodo dragons.

Kookaburra

The kookaburra is a large bird that lives in **Australia**. It can grow to be 11–17 inches long. Its big, boat-shaped beak is used to catch smaller animals like mice, snakes, and insects. In the wild, kookaburras like to live anywhere there are forests with big trees. They are very good hunters.

The kookaburra is probably best known for its very special birdcall. Its call sounds like a funny laugh. If you heard it, you might even mistake it for a group of monkeys! A kookaburra usually makes this call to tell other birds that this part of the forest is its home. It is a warning to other birds to keep out of its **territory**. If you visited the forests of Australia, you would hear whole groups of kookaburras calling out around sunrise and sunset. This is like a conversation that kookaburra families have to remember where everyone's space is. Have you ever wanted to have your own bedroom with a sign on the door that says "Keep Out"? That's what kookaburras do with their calls!

The kookaburra's call is so famous that it is often used as a sound effect in movies to set the mood for a tropical **jungle**. Next time you're watching a movie that takes place in a jungle, try listening for the sound of the kookaburra!

Korean Martyrs

The Korean Martyrs are brave men and women who gave their lives in Korea, **Asia** for believing in Jesus Christ and His Catholic Church. In the eighteenth and nineteenth centuries, 8,000-10,000 people were martyred, including some priests and missionaries. However, most of them were ordinary people like you.

For 100 years, Korea was strongly against anyone who believed in the love and mercy of Jesus. They did not let anyone build a church, teach others about Jesus, or even make the sign of the cross. Sadly, that is much how it is in North Korea today.

But some books about Christianity found their way to Korea. Those who could read studied them, became Catholics, and shared the Faith with those who could not read. Around 1800, there were about four thousand Catholics in Korea.

They longed to receive the sacraments but did not have any priests. Priests who entered the country would be in serious danger. Finally in 1836, a bishop and 10 missionaries secretly arrived in Korea from **France**. They had to stay in hiding during the day, but at night, they brought the sacraments to the grateful people.

Three years later, these brave men were put to death. During the decades that followed, thousands of Koreans were martyred for their faith. One of them, Fr. Andrew Kim Taegon, was the very first Korean priest. The Church celebrates the feast of the Korean Martyrs on September 20.

Kublai Khan

Kublai Khan was the grandson of Genghis Khan, the first ruler of the Mongol Empire in **Asia**. (*Khan* is an Asian word for "ruler.") Before Genghis Khan, there were many Mongol tribes and they often fought each other. But in 1206, Genghis brought all of the tribes together and made the Mongol Empire. Then he started attacking his neighbors and conquering them. His new empire spread far across Asia and the Middle East. His army was very bloodthirsty and killed millions of people. The Mongol army rode on sturdy horses and fought with bows and arrows. Genghis Khan is considered the founding father of Mongolia.

After Genghis Khan died, the Mongol Empire grew even more. It is the largest empire in history that was contiguous, meaning all its land was connected, not split up in different parts of the world. (The largest empire of any kind in history is the British Empire, but many of its **territories** were separated by **oceans**. The Mongol Empire is the second largest of all empires.) Genghis' grandson, Kublai Khan, is famous for conquering the rest of **China**. **Mongols** ruled China for almost one hundred years.

Kublai Khan was a smart, strong ruler. He built roads, schools, and **ports**. He also wrote Chinese poetry and encouraged the arts, sciences, and math in China. The famous explorer **Marco Polo** met Kublai Khan during his journeys in China. The Mongols controlled the **Silk Road** during this time. They made trade much easier across **Europe** and Asia.

Later, the Mongol Empire broke up. China even took over Mongolia and ruled it for a while. Today, Mongolia is pretty much the size of the Mongols' original homeland. But many Mongols still live in countries where the Mongol Empire once was.

Lake Garda

Lake Garda, also known as Benaco, is the largest **lake** in **Italy**. It is in the north of Italy near the **Alps**. This huge lake is surrounded by 26 different towns and is a favorite place for tourists to visit. It is big enough that there are five main **islands** in the lake. One of the islands has a medieval castle built on it—this island used to be a pirate's lair!

If you were to visit Lake Garda, you might go by bike. The lake is surrounded by miles of mountain-biking trails. After riding all that way, you'd probably be pretty tired and hot, so why not go to one of the many beaches and enjoy a swim? The vibrant blue water is nearly see-through. You can even scuba dive to explore the sunken shipwreck near the Island of Dreams or camp on the Island of Rabbits (guess what animal you might see there?).

After a swim, you might decide to take a hike through some of the beautiful hills surrounding the lake. Keep an eye out for the many types of plants that grow here, including cypress and olive trees, Canary Island date palm trees, and lemon trees. You can also find a monastery and some ancient Roman ruins to explore in the hills around the lake. Sometimes people paraglide from the top of the hills down to the shore.

Before you leave Lake Garda, be sure to have fun at some of its amusement parks! Gardaland, the first amusement park in Italy, features rides and fairy-tale fun. There are other theme parks, too, including one all about movies and one dedicated to medieval times that has duels between knights.

Lake Titicaca

Lake Titicaca is the largest **lake** in **Peru**. This lake also borders Bolivia, and it is one of the largest lakes in **South America**. The surface of this lake is 12,507 feet above **sea** level, making it the highest lake in the world that large ships can sail on. It is also very deep—up to 922 feet deep.

The lake has about 120 **islands**, which are home to the Uru people, also known as the Uros. But these are no ordinary islands. These islands are made from thick gold-colored reeds (lake plants). These plants can be

cut and bent. They can also float, so these are actually floating islands! The Uros cut and bend the reeds themselves to make their island homes.

The islands are usually big enough to hold a few small houses and sometimes even a watchtower. Most of the islands are about 50 feet long on each side, and the biggest ones are about half the size of a football field! If you lived on one of these islands, you would probably live with your family and a few relatives. You could do everything on the island: fishing, cooking, and even making a special reed flower tea. If you visit the Uros as a tourist, you can see their **reed boats**, but you'd probably ride in a motorboat to the floating reed islands.

Lascaux Cave Paintings

Lascaux Cave is a series of **caves** in the Vézère Valley in **France**. These caves are special because of what was found on their walls—prehistoric paintings! For thousands of years, nobody knew they were there until they were found by chance in 1940.

A teenage boy named Marcel Ravidat had a dog named Robot who fell into a hole. The boy went to get the help of his three friends. When they came to the hole where the dog fell, they discovered that it was part of a cave. Once inside, they found that the walls had over 600 paintings of animals and human figures!

Several years later, there were over a thousand people visiting the caves every day. That's a lot of people passing through! The moisture, the lights, and even people breathing on the paintings damaged them and made them less colorful. To preserve the paintings, the caves were closed to visitors in 1963.

Near-perfect copies were created by talented artists and set up in other caves nearby. These caves are known as Lascaux II and Lascaux III. After some time, the paintings were restored, but the original caves have to remain sealed so that they will not be damaged again.

Leaning Tower of Pisa

The Leaning Tower of Pisa is a famous bell tower located in Pisa, **Italy**. It is different from other buildings because it does not stand straight up—instead, it leans to one side! It was not always a leaning building, though. When the second floor of the tower was being built in 1173, something unusual happened. The building started to shift and lean. This is because the ground it was built on was very soft soil that kept sinking under the weight of the tower. Also, the tower was built on a small base. This made it unstable, like a cup that's big at the top and small at the bottom.

After the tower started leaning, construction had to stop for almost 100 years because the people of Pisa were at war. When construction started again, builders tried to build the tower taller on one side to help it lean back in the other direction. This gave the tower a slight curve—can you see it? In 1372, the tower was finished at eight stories tall, including a little room on top with bells. Later, the people of Pisa stopped ringing the biggest bells because they worried their movement might make the tower lean more.

In 1990, engineers began working to fix the building's lean so that it would not fall over. If you visit the tower today, you can still see it leaning a bit, but it is much safer now. You can even climb up its 294 steps. The tower is made of white marble. It stands over 180 feet tall and weighs almost 32 million pounds. No wonder it was such a challenge for builders to keep it from falling over!

Fun Facts:
- The tower leans slightly to the northwest.
- You can only go inside the tower if you are older than eight and are strong enough to climb 294 steps.

Leonardo da Vinci

Leonardo da Vinci was a very important artist from **Italy** who lived during the Renaissance. This was a time when people began to study the ancient world again and create beautiful art and poetry. He was born in 1452 in a town called Vinci. This is why he is called "Leonardo da Vinci," which means "Leonardo of Vinci." When he was young, he became a student of the artist Verocchio, who taught him how to paint, sculpt, and more. Leonardo learned quickly, and soon he became even better than his teacher.

Leonardo da Vinci's most famous paintings are called *The Last Supper* and the *Mona Lisa*. Leonardo also has other beautiful paintings that are loved by many. His way of painting with soft, "fuzzy" shadows changed the way many artists painted after him.

Leonardo was very smart and good at math, music, writing, and many types of science. He was also an inventor, engineer, and an architect. He had all kinds of ideas for building new things and liked to write about them in his notebooks.

Although most of Leonardo's ideas were never made, the notebooks he kept are very famous. He made many drawings of his ideas, some of which are very similar to modern-day inventions. He also made sketches for paintings he wanted to make, drawings of the world around him, and more. In all, there are almost 30,000 pages of Leonardo's notes and drawings!

Lion

Lions are large mammals of the cat family. They live in **Africa** south of the **Sahara Desert**, although a few live in **India**. Their natural **habitat** is **savannas**, **plains**, and open forests. Lions' fur blends into the tall, brownish grass found in these areas, giving them camouflage to help them hide from predators and sneak up on their prey. Lions weigh up to 570 pounds and live up to about 16 years in the wild or about 20 years in a zoo.

Lions are carnivores and scavengers. Half of what they eat is carrion, or dead animals that died from disease or that were killed by other animals. Lions also prey on animals like **zebras**, buffalo, and **giraffes**, eating around 150 pounds of meat a day. That's a lot of food—but if you weighed hundreds of pounds, I think you'd be hungry too!

The female lions, called lionesses, do most of the hunting, not the males. A lioness doesn't go out on her own to find prey. She knows that's the hard way. It's easier when several lionesses work together. That way they can corner their prey before going in for the attack.

Lions are nocturnal creatures, which means they do most of their hunting and scavenging at night. Unlike humans, they have good night vision. In fact, a lion's eyesight is five times better than ours! They have really good hearing, too. Can you hear things that are a mile away? Well, lions can. They can also leap a distance of up to 36 feet. These strengths help to keep them safe from their predators, like **spotted hyenas**, crocodiles, and leopards.

Fun Facts:
- Baby lions are called cubs.
- A group of lions is called a pride.
- A lion's roar is 25 times louder than a lawn mower and can be heard up to five miles away!

Llama

A llama is a mammal that lives in the **Andes mountains** of **Peru** and Ecuador in **South America**. You would surely see some of them if you were visiting the ancient ruins of **Machu Picchu**! Llamas are in the same family as **camels**, but they do not have any humps. They have soft, thick fur that keeps them very warm.

Llamas and alpacas look almost the same. This is how you can tell them apart: llamas are larger, have longer heads, and have banana-shaped ears. Another difference is that a llama's fur will usually be a few different colors, and an alpaca's fur is mostly one color.

A full-grown llama is almost six feet tall at the top of its head. It weighs between 300–450 pounds. Llamas live for 15–25 years and travel in herds. They take care of each other and are also good at guarding sheep.

When a llama is afraid or thinks it is in danger, it makes funny sounds. One sound is like a groan or a hum, and another noise sounds like "mwah." If you see a llama's ears folded back, that usually means it is uncomfortable or threatened. However, if you see its ears pointing to the sky, that means it is happy and would like to say hello to you.

Fun Facts:
- A baby llama is called a cria.
- Llamas are so friendly that they are used as therapy animals.
- Llamas are smart and can easily be trained to do simple tasks.

Loch Ness

Loch Ness is the largest body of freshwater in the **United Kingdom**. This long **loch** in the Highlands is one of Scotland's natural wonders.

It is almost two miles wide, 23 miles long, and 750 feet deep. That's a lot of water!

In 1933, Loch Ness became famous when someone said he saw a giant monster in the murky waters. They named this Loch Ness Monster "Nessie." Nobody knows the true story, but some scientists say it might have been a giant eel.

Loch Ness flows from southwest to northeast and has a lighthouse on each end. Cherry Island is at the south end. It's the loch's only **island** and is man-made. A long time ago, a castle stood on it, but nothing can be seen of that castle now.

Fifteen miles down the loch, though, are the ruins of Urquhart Castle. Hundreds of years ago, the crumbled walls were once a strong motte-and-bailey fortress. A motte is a mound of earth with a tower or castle on top, which is protected below by a bailey, or a walled courtyard. Urquhart Castle is one of the largest castles in Scotland.

God filled the Scottish Highlands with a lot of beauty. Scottish red deer, golden eagles, and brown trout are common wildlife. The nature surrounding Loch Ness is breathtaking.

bowl-shaped crater is thousands of feet wide and hundreds of feet deep. The **lake** itself is not very big. It is special because it was made by a giant space rock!

For a long time, scientists thought that this crater was formed like most crater lakes: a **volcano** erupts and then falls down into itself, which leaves a giant hole. But after studying the Lonar crater, scientists figured out that it was made by a huge rock from outer space! When this space rock hit the ground at high speed, it exploded. This left a giant hole surrounded by rocks that broke off the space rock. The rocks around the hole landed in an oval (stretched-out circle) pattern. Finding this pattern helped scientists figure out that the space rock hit the ground sideways rather than dropping straight down from the sky.

Try making your own Lonar crater. Throw a ball into a sandbox straight down and then from the side. Look at the shape made in the sand after each throw. Can you make an oval?

The hole made by the space rock filled with water from nearby streams. But the water is salty, like the **ocean**! The saltiness comes from the rocks and minerals deep inside the crater. If you were to visit the lake, you would also find medieval Hindu temples built near the lake, some inside the crater itself. This is because many people thought the crater was a sacred place, since it was created in such an incredible way.

Lonar Crater Lake

Lonar Crater Lake is a special lake in **India**. Its

● ● ●

London Eye

The London Eye, or Millennium Wheel, is a large metal Ferris wheel in the **United Kingdom**. It is one of the largest observation wheels in the world and one of the highest viewing points in London. It took seven years to build and opened in 2000, the year the world celebrated the new millennium (a period of a thousand years). Over three million visitors ride the wheel each year!

The London Eye was designed by a husband and wife team. It was supposed to be a temporary tourist attraction, but it was so popular that it is still there today! It looks like a huge bicycle wheel. The wheel was built in sections, and each section was floated up the Thames River on flatboats. The sections were assembled on platforms on the **river** before being gradually lifted until they were standing up.

There are 32 passenger capsules, which are air-conditioned and can hold up to 25 people each. When riding in the capsule, you can either walk around or sit. As the wheel rotates, you can see a full view of the city in all directions. You can see famous attractions such as **Big Ben**, the House of Parliament, **Buckingham Palace**, and the Thames River. It takes the wheel 30 minutes to make one full turn, so you'll have plenty of time to see everything! The wheel moves so slowly, in fact,

that it doesn't have to stop for people to get on and off.

If you find yourself in London, make sure to take a ride on this amazing observation wheel! You can even ride it at night when it's covered in glowing lights.

Louis Pasteur

Louis Pasteur was a famous scientist known for his research on germs, for his vaccine for rabies, and for creating a process called pasteurization. The specific type of science he studied was chemistry, which is the study of elements, atoms, molecules, and how they react together.

Louis Pasteur was born in Dole, **France**, in 1822. He was raised in a poor Catholic family in the town of Arbois. He studied hard in school and was able to finish college. After college, he taught chemistry at a university, where he met Marie Laurent. Louis married Marie, and they had five children. Sadly, three of them died from illness.

The loss of three of his children made him want to find cures for illnesses. He spent his life learning about harmful germs. He also helped doctors understand germs better. When doctors treat a patient, it is important that they wash their hands and tools well before caring for the next patient. If they do not, they can pass germs from person to person.

Pasteur made vaccines to help keep illnesses away. A very small amount of germs is put into a person so that the body becomes immune to them. Immunity is when someone's body is strong enough to fight off certain germs so the person doesn't get sick.

Pasteurization is a process that Louis Pasteur discovered to kill bad germs in milk, wine, and other food products. Usually, pasteurization is done by heating the food gently for up to 30 minutes. When this process is completed, the food can be stored much longer before going bad.

Louis was not alone in his work. His wife, Marie, did his paperwork and helped him with his discoveries. Together, they found ways to prevent diseases and save lives.

Louvre Museum

The Louvre Museum is a very famous art museum located in Paris, **France**. Some of the world's most famous paintings and sculptures are kept in this museum, including **Leonardo da Vinci**'s *Mona Lisa*. Did you know that there used to be a castle right where the Louvre stands today? Long ago, King Philip II of France built a large fortress to defend Paris against the English. This fortress was called the Louvre. Many years later, King Francis I and his successors built a beautiful palace where the castle was. This palace was also called the Louvre. The building changes did not stop there, though!

Did you know that at one time, the Louvre had the longest hall in **Europe**? At the beginning of the seventeenth century, a gallery called the *Grande Galerie* was added to the Louvre Palace to connect it to another nearby palace. This long hall was built along the banks of the Seine River, stretching for more than a quarter of a mile! If you had been an artist or a craftsman at the time, you might have received a royal invitation to live and work in the gallery's lower floors. Thanks to King Henry IV of France, this tradition lasted for about 200 years. It wasn't until after the **French Revolution** in 1789 that the Louvre became a museum for art.

Today, the Louvre museum has a special entrance that leads underground. You can find this entrance inside a large glass pyramid in the middle of the Louvre courtyard. The pyramid entrance was built in the 1980s because the original entrance had become too small to handle the large number of visitors who come every day. This glass pyramid is now a famous landmark in Paris. As many as 30,000 people visit the Louvre every day!

the male penguin cares for it. He protects it and helps to keep it warm while the female brings food to the chick every one or two days.

Macaroni penguins eat squid, fish, and crustaceans (animals with hard outer shells that live in the water). Krill is a special favorite on the macaroni penguin's menu. Like other penguins, they swallow small stones to help digest food with hard shells.

Macaroni penguins are easy to spot when they are on land, even from high up in an airplane, because thousands flock together in groups called colonies. They band together as a way of protecting themselves against predators. If a hungry seal invades the colony, most of the penguins will be able to escape it.

Macaroni Penguin

The macaroni penguin has a funny-sounding name, but it has nothing to do with pasta! In eighteenth-century England, "macaroni" was a slang word used for someone who dressed in a flashy, colorful way. When English sailors saw this penguin, it reminded them of a macaroni. So that's what they called it!

This flightless bird grows up to 28 inches tall and lives on **islands** near **Antarctica**, as well as on islands south of **Africa** and **North** and **South America**. They molt once a year, which means they shed their old feathers. This allows new feathers to grow in.

The male and female look so much alike that it is hard to tell the difference. But if you pay close attention, you can tell the two apart because the males are slightly larger and have larger bills (or beaks).

Macaroni penguins make their nests on the side of a cliff or a hill. After a new chick hatches,

Machu Picchu

Machu Picchu is an ancient city in **Peru**, **South America**. It was built in the fifteenth century by the Inca Empire. The **Incas** made houses, temples for worship, fountains, and even an observatory so they could study the stars. They carved terraces (flat areas of land) into the **mountains**, where they planted crops for food. The Incas built stone **aqueducts** to carry rain and spring water to the fountains.

Of all the structures in the city, these three were the most important to the Incas:

the Intihuatana, the Temple of the Sun (the observatory), and the Room of the Three Windows. The Inca emperor used these structures for religious ceremonies. The walls were made of polished stones, each carefully carved by hand to fit in its place. Most structures had roofs made with wood and thatch.

Machu Picchu is located high in the **Andes**. Because it was so difficult to reach, the Spanish never found the city when they invaded Peru. Over the next four hundred years, Machu Picchu became covered by **jungle**. Only the native people who lived in the area knew where the ruins stood.

In 1911, a man named Hiram Bingham discovered the "Lost City of the Incas." He uncovered thousands of artifacts that he shared with the world. Machu Picchu is now considered to be one of the great wonders of the world.

Magna Carta

The Magna Carta was an agreement between King John and the English people in the Middle Ages. *Magna Carta* is Latin for "Great Charter." A charter is a document that a king makes to give someone rights or privileges.

King John was an unjust king who had been treating the English people badly. He stole Church land and forced the people to pay lots of taxes. He ignored the rights of the common people, the bishops, and the barons (important men who owned land and served directly under the king). King John had also lost a lot of land to his enemies, which weakened his power and made him unpopular.

After all this, the barons rebelled. They met with King John at Runnymede, England, in 1215. They told him that he could either sign the Magna Carta or be removed from the throne. In signing the Magna Carta, King John promised to follow 63 rules that the barons demanded. The rules made sure that King John would respect the rights of the people and fix unjust parts of the government. For example, one rule states that no one could be arrested unjustly or punished without a trial. Another made sure that the people had a say in the taxes they would pay. These rules had been followed in England for many years, but this was the first time they had been written down. It was an important reminder that the king had to follow the law just like everyone else.

Although the Magna Carta was written many years ago, it is still very important in the **United Kingdom** and beyond. The rules written down in the Magna Carta have inspired just laws in countries around the world, including the United States.

Mahatma Gandhi

Mahatma Gandhi was an important leader born in **India** in 1869. At this time in history, India was ruled by another country, the **United Kingdom** (the British). India's people did not have control over their own land.

At the age of 18, Gandhi went to England to study law. He became good at writing, reading, speaking, and researching. After graduating, he looked for a job back home in India. But there was no work for him there, so he went to South Africa to work in a British colony.

In South Africa, a country in **Africa**, the law said that dark-skinned people shouldn't be treated the same as light-skinned people. That meant that there were people who treated Gandhi badly just because of his darker skin color. He gave up being a lawyer and spent several years helping the Indian people living in South Africa.

Gandhi's own country also needed his help. He became a powerful leader and wanted to help India become free from British rule. He taught that freedom from the British should not be won by violence, such as fighting and killing. Instead, he led peaceful protests, lived as a devout Hindu, helped millions of poor people, and showed others how to live in peace with their neighbors, even if they were different.

In 1947, India finally won its freedom. Not even a year later, Gandhi was killed by another Hindu who disagreed with his kindness to Muslims. He is now a symbol of peace to the world, the kind of peace won by truth and nonviolence.

Marble Caves

The Marble Caves are a beautiful group of **caves** found in Chile, **South America**. In Spanish, the language spoken in Chile, the Marble Caves are called *Cuevas de Marmol*. The stone in the caves has beautiful swirling patterns of white, gray, and blue. The stone also reflects the color of the water very well. Because of this, the caves seem to change color depending on the water level, time of year, and even the time of day.

The Marble Caves were formed by erosion, which means that the rock formations were naturally formed by water. Waves crashed against the rocks for more than 6,000 years, slowly carving the stone away. This means that what the caves look like today is totally different than how they looked 1,000 years ago, or how they will look 1,000 years from now!

The Marble Caves are located near a **lake** called Lake General Carrera. The only way to visit the caves is by boat. Visitors can kayak through the caves to see the many beautiful shapes that have been carved by the water. There is also a variety of wildlife to see in and around the caves, like fish, birds, and sea lions.

Marco Polo

Marco Polo was a famous Italian explorer who was one of the very first people to travel to **China** from the West. Born in 1254, he belonged to a family of rich jewel merchants. He traveled along the **Silk Road** that led from **Europe** to China.

When Marco Polo traveled to China, he met with the leader of the Mongol Empire, **Kublai Khan.** The khan became great friends with Polo and his family and trusted them to carry messages to other countries. One message he sent asked the pope to send him educated people to explain Christianity to him. Unfortunately, the two monks the pope sent were not able to complete the difficult journey to China. Polo stayed in China for nearly 17 years. Then he traveled to many other places. After 20 years, Marco Polo finally came home to **Italy** with many riches and treasures. He had traveled nearly 15,000 miles. That would be like walking more than halfway around the world!

Marco Polo told the Western world about his travels and the great riches of China. He became known as "the man with a million stories" and "Marco Millions" because of the many stories he had to tell. He wrote his many adventures and stories in his book called *The Travels of Marco Polo*. Many people did not believe his stories. As more people began to travel the trade routes from Europe to China, they discovered that everything Marco Polo had talked about was true!

Martial Arts

Martial arts are special kinds of fighting skills practiced mostly for sport and self-defense. Some people also learn martial arts for exercise, self-discipline, and even religious purposes. There are lots of different types of martial arts, and most types come from **Asia**.

There are so many different types of martial arts that talking about them all would take a very long time. However, some martial arts are well-known. You have probably heard of kung fu and karate, and you might have heard of jiujitsu or tae kwon do.

All martial arts focus on making use of a person's body. While each type of martial arts has its own special focus, all of them use moves like kicks, punches, and jabs. Some martial arts include weapons like swords, shields, and even fans!

If you were to practice martial arts, you

would be called a martial artist. As a beginner, you might be introduced to certain patterns of movement that look kind of like a dance. Each step is a beautiful pose of strength, balance, and control. These patterns are what some martial arts call *kata*, which means "form." Kata are used to help martial artists practice movements. Whatever style of martial arts you train in, if you practice hard enough and train for a long time, you could become a master!

Martyrs of Nagasaki

In the city of Nagasaki in Japan, Asia, 26 Catholics were killed for believing in Jesus and His Church. The group of brave men included missionaries and Japanese converts. Three of these converts were young altar boys. They were all strong in their faith and knew their catechism well. Their joy in serving Christ made others want to live like them and be baptized.

When the first missionaries came to Japan to spread the Good News, the rulers of Japan welcomed them. But much later, they decided the missionaries couldn't be trusted because they came from other countries. They were afraid that the other countries would come to rule Japan. So in 1597, the Japanese ruler,

Toyotomi Hideyoshi, had the martyrs arrested.

The men and young boys endured terrible suffering for the next 27 days. Before being crucified, they were made to march 620 miles, passing through village after village. During their slow journey in freezing weather, the martyrs encouraged each other to be brave. Louis, the youngest boy (age 12), was full of joy even on the cross, where he imagined flying from the cross into Heaven. Their feast day is February 6.

Michelangelo

Michelangelo was a very talented artist from Italy. He was born in 1475 during the famous Italian Renaissance. During this time, artists were inspired to do new and exciting things, but they were also inspired by the art of ancient Greece and Rome. Many great artists lived and worked during this period, and Michelangelo was one of the most famous and important of these Renaissance artists.

Michelangelo began studying art as a young boy, learning how to carve marble with a chisel and hammer. He was also very skilled at drawing and painting. He made copies of the very large wall paintings that he saw in the churches of Florence, Italy. He trained under master painters and was paid for his work when he was only 14 years old! He was even hired to create art for the Medici family, the richest and most powerful family in Florence. Michelangelo's work was said to look very similar to ancient Roman statues. He made many statues of Our Lord, Our Lady, and other people from the Bible. His most famous statue is his giant statue of David from the Bible story of David and Goliath. The marble statue is 17 feet tall. You can still see it in Florence today.

Pope Julius II learned about Michelangelo's work and invited him to come to Rome and work for him. The pope asked him to paint the ceiling of the Sistine Chapel in the Vatican. At first, Michelangelo didn't want to because he said he wasn't much of a painter. After the pope insisted, Michelangelo spent about four years painting scenes from the Bible telling the story of creation on the ceiling. You can still see these paintings today if you visit the Sistine Chapel. They look almost as colorful as when they were first made! Can you imagine painting such beautiful art on the ceiling, maybe while lying on your back?

Monastery of Our Lady of Montserrat

The Monastery of Our Lady of Montserrat is

an abbey of the Order of Saint Benedict and is located in Catalonia, **Spain**. It was built in the eleventh century on the edge of a **mountain**.

The 80 monks who live there follow the Benedictine rule of life: *ora et labora*, which means "pray and work." They assist at daily Mass, pray the Liturgy of the Hours, and have time for personal prayer. Their work may include studying history or philosophy and teaching. They may also work in the garden or the library. Some monks also teach songs to the *Escolania de Montserrat* choir, which is one of the oldest choirs in **Europe**.

The basilica of Montserrat has many statues, reliefs (wall carvings), mosaics, and paintings. Above the altar is a large dome gilded in gold. In addition to the main part of the basilica, there are several smaller chapels named for the paintings and sculptures featured within them, such as **St. Ignatius of Loyola**, **St. Benedict and St. Scholastica** (sister of St. Benedict), the Holy Family, and the Immaculate Conception. Our Lady of Montserrat is honored as the town's patroness, and a statue of her holding baby Jesus is located in the basilica.

Have you ever seen a serrated knife? Maybe your mom or dad uses one to cut slices of bread. *Montserrat* means "serrated mountain," because the mountain has jagged peaks just like a serrated knife has jagged edges.

Mongols

Mongols are a group of people native to Mongolia, a country in east **Asia** next to **China**. Today, Mongols also live in China, Afghanistan, and Russia. In fact, today there are many more Mongols living in China than in Mongolia itself!

The language Mongols speak is called Mongolian. The country of Mongolia includes the Gobi Desert and some **mountains**, but it is mostly **steppes**. Since there are no trees on a steppe and you have to travel far to find water, Mongols were often nomads. Nomads are people who move from place to place instead of living in one area.

Many Mongols live in tribes and raise sheep, goats, cows, and other animals. Many still travel by horse, **camel**, and yak and live in large tents called yurts or *gers*. These yurts are made with wooden poles arranged in a circle and then covered with thick wool felt. Yurts are perfect homes for nomads because they can easily be taken down and brought to a new place. Even today, many Mongols are nomads. They live in yurts and migrate (move) four times a year, when the seasons change, to find better pastures for their herds.

Although many Mongols live much like their ancestors lived, there are some modern they use sometimes: cars to help herd the animals and migrate, solar panels and satellite dishes on their yurts, . Some Mongols live in cities, and it is common for young Mongol adults to move to larger cities for a while to go to school or get a job.

Mongols have interesting traditions like wrestling, horseback riding, and folk art. Mongolian throat singing and horsehead fiddle music are very old traditions.

The most famous Mongols are Genghis Khan and his grandson **Kublai Khan**. Genghis Khan was the ruler who started the Mongol Empire. The Mongol Empire doesn't exist anymore, but it is the reason so many Mongols live in other countries. The most popular religion among Mongols is Buddhism, but there are also a few Catholics and Protestants. Christianity in Mongolia goes all the way back to the seventh century. The first pope ever to visit Mongolia was Pope Francis in 2023.

Monte Cassino

Monte Cassino is a monastery on top of a **mountain** near Cassino, **Italy**. A monastery is a building or a collection of buildings where monks live and pray together. Monte Cassino was founded by **St. Benedict** around AD 529, and it was the first community of Benedictine monks.

It was at Monte Cassino that St. Benedict

wrote his famous manual called *The Rule of St. Benedict*. This was the first time someone had written down instructions for how monks should live together. His instructions are more than just "dos and don'ts." The Rule teaches monks how to live and pray together in order to become holy.

The Rule of St. Benedict was used by many other monasteries soon after it was written. It became very important for the development of new religious orders, which are different groups of monks and nuns. It is also still followed by Benedictines today.

The monastery of Monte Cassino has been rebuilt a few times. Once, it fell down in an **earthquake**, and in World War II, it was destroyed by bombs. **St. Benedict and St. Scholastica** are both buried at Monte Cassino.

ice and snow has become **glaciers**. Glaciers can be dangerous for climbers to cross because of deep cracks in them. These are called crevasses. Climbers use ice axes and crampons (pointy shoe attachments) to keep from slipping on the ice. If they fall, they can get seriously hurt or even die. Because of this, they also use ropes to climb the difficult parts of the mountain. The glaciers on the *Cordillera Blanca* are one of the best places to practice ice climbing.

Mountain climbers face many other challenges. Some of these are avalanches (falling rocks and snow), dangerous storms, and freezing weather. Climbers can also get altitude sickness and become tired on very high mountains because of how thin the air is. Mountain climbing is a challenging sport. How do you think it feels to reach the top of a high mountain after days of climbing?

Mountain Climbing

Mountain climbing is a popular activity for visitors to **Peru**. The Cordillera Blanca is a **mountain range** with some of the best **mountains** for climbing. **Huascaran** is part of this mountain range, and there are dozens more to choose from. Mountain climbers in the Cordillera Blanca will see beautiful views wherever they go.

Many of the mountains in Peru are covered with ice and snow that never melt. A lot of this

Mountain Lion

The mountain lion is the biggest cat native to **North America**. It lives as far north as the Yukon Territory in northwestern **Canada** and as far south as the **Andes mountains**, which stretch to the bottom tip of **South America**.

The mountain lion's official name is *puma concolor*, which means "cat of uniform color." It is different from most other wildcats, which have stripes or spots. Mountain lions are also called cougars, pumas, and many other names.

Mountain lions are mostly tan, with some black and white markings on their faces. They are usually six to eight feet long, but sometimes they can reach nine feet. They have rounded ears that stick up, big paws with sharp claws, and long tails. Mountain lions are very strong. They can climb trees and even swim. They hiss, growl, chirp, purr, and scream. Even though they are larger than most kinds of cats, mountain lions are not considered to be big cats (like tigers and lions). They are considered small cats because they can't roar!

Mountain lions hunt at night because they see better in the dark. They hunt deer, **raccoons**, squirrels, foxes, rabbits, and skunks, but sometimes they eat other animals too. Mountain lions live alone unless they are raising cubs. Sometimes, though, they share food and visit with other mountain lions in their area.

Mountain lions live in wild places, far from people. But if you happen to meet one while hiking, stand still, raise your arms to look larger, and punch it in the nose if it tries to bite you.

the **Pyrenees** that borders **France** and Spain. For a long time, Monte Perdido was thought to be the highest peak in the area. But when Friedrich Parrot reached the top of another mountain in 1817, he realized Mt. Aneto was much higher! Both mountains were so tall that no one could determine the highest one from the ground. Aneto has a big **glacier** on its side. It is still the biggest glacier in the Pyrenees, but half of it has melted over the last 100 years. Eventually, it may melt all the way.

Mt. Aneto is one of the most popular mountains to climb in Spain. There are many cracks and dangerous areas near the top, so only the best climbers go all the way up. Because of the glacier, you have to climb through what one climber called "needles of ice"! But there are many easier climbs lower on the mountain that you could try.

When people visit the mountain, they often stop at a nearby town to buy food, supplies, and souvenirs. If you visit, you might want to try *olla*, a traditional Spanish stew, or some tasty cheese from the local sheep farms!

Mount Aneto

Mt. Aneto is the highest **mountain** in Aragon, **Spain**. It is a part of a **mountain range** called

Mount Ararat

Mt. Ararat is a **mountain** in Turkey, **Asia** that used to be a **volcano**. It is found in the part of Turkey that is close to Armenia and Iran. It actually has two **summits**, one larger and one smaller, called Greater Ararat and Little Ararat. Greater Ararat is the tallest mountain in Turkey. It is 16,945 feet tall. Greater Ararat also has an ice cap, a section of ice and snow at the very top, that never melts—even in the summer!

Mt. Ararat is very special for Christians. According to tradition, Mt. Ararat is where Noah's ark landed after the flood. Scripture says, "The ark came to rest upon the mountains of Ararat" (Genesis 8:4). Christians have honored Mt. Ararat for this reason for many hundreds of years.

Mt. Ararat is especially important to the Armenian people. Years ago, the country of Armenia used to be much bigger and included the area around Mt. Ararat. Ancient Armenians saw the mountain as sacred, and even today Armenians call it the "holy mountain." Armenians have a legend that says after the ark landed on Mt. Ararat, the Armenian people were founded by a descendant of Noah. Even though Mt. Ararat is now part of Turkey, Armenians see it as a symbol of their country. Sadly, many Armenians were killed by the Ottoman Empire, and they also lost the land where Mt. Ararat stands. To Armenians, Mt. Ararat is a reminder of the lands they lost long ago and injustices done to their people.

Fun Facts:

- Mt. Ararat was first summited, or climbed all the way to the summit, in 1829.
- Mt. Ararat with Noah's ark is pictured on Armenia's national coat of arms (a design painted on a shield).
- The last volcanic activity on Mt. Ararat was in 1840. Ten thousand people died from an **earthquake** and landslides near the volcano.

Mount Everest

Mt. Everest is the highest **mountain** on earth, located in a **mountain range** called the **Himalayas**. The highest point of Mt. Everest is on the border of Nepal and **China**. It is over five and a half miles high! If you were Sir George Everest, do you think you would be pretty proud to have the highest mountain in the world named after you? The mountain was named after Everest because he did the important work of mapping much of **India** and Nepal for the first time.

It is dangerous to climb Mt. Everest. The climate is extremely cold and snowy, with high-speed winds up to 200 miles per hour! July is the warmest time of the year, but it is still only around -10 °F. Snow covers the mountain all year round. **Glaciers** and avalanches make climbing even more dangerous. Because the mountain is so high, the air is very thin. Thin air is hard for humans to breathe. It can cause sickness and sometimes even death.

People often bring yaks up the mountain with them. Yaks are very strong animals and can carry up to 220 pounds. They are often used to transport many supplies needed for the dangerous climb.

In 1922, the first group of explorers tried to climb to the top of Mt. Everest, but they never

● ● ●

reached it. It was not until 1953 that Tenzing Norgay and Sir Edmund Hillary made it safely to the top. Imagine the view of the Himalayas that they saw! During their 81-day climb, they might have seen Himalayan tahrs (wild goats), snow leopards, Himalayan black bears, and **red pandas**.

Mount Kilimanjaro

Mt. Kilimanjaro is a very tall **mountain** in Tanzania, **Africa**. Its **elevation** is over 19,000 feet. It is the tallest mountain in Africa, and the tallest mountain in all the world that is not part of a **mountain range**. There are three peaks on Mt. Kilimanjaro. Mawenzi and Shira, the smaller **volcano** peaks, are extinct. The highest peak, Kibo, is not active, but it could erupt again.

The plants and weather change as you go up the mountain. The mountain is only 200 miles away from the **Equator**, but its top is as cold as the North Pole! At the bottom are warm, humid **rainforests**. As you climb, the temperature cools and the air becomes drier. The plants are replaced by rocks. At the **summit**, there are more rocks, cold, snow, and an amazing view of Africa.

There are seven major routes to climb up Mt. Kilimanjaro. Many people have made it to the top, but some don't make it because they get sick from being up so high. This is called altitude sickness. You don't need any special equipment, such as ropes or poles, to climb, but in some spots, you may need to crawl on your hands and knees. What you do need is a lot of time—it can take six days or more to reach the summit.

Mount Rushmore

Mt. Rushmore is a rocky **mountain** of granite in **North America** with four faces of presidents carved into it. Can you find Black Hills National Forest on a map of South Dakota? You will find it on the western border next to Wyoming. That's where the mountain is, in a beautiful forest.

From left to right, the presidents are George Washington, Thomas Jefferson, Theodore Roosevelt, and Abraham Lincoln. They stand for the first 150 years of American history. Each of the giant faces is 60 feet high—that's about as high as a five-story building!

It was 1927 when Gutzon Borglum and his son, Lincoln, began the work of carving the faces into the granite rock. Dynamite and drilling made tons of rock pile up beneath the faces. Even with hundreds of men at work, it took 14 years to finish.

One of the reasons for carving the presidents' faces into Mt. Rushmore was to get people to visit the state of South Dakota. Do you think the designers ever thought that over two million people would visit Mt. Rushmore each year?

Behind the face of President Lincoln, there is a 70-foot deep chamber, something like a **cave**. Lining the walls of this room are 16 panels describing the story of Mt. Rushmore, the history of the United States, and how our nation began as "one nation under God."

Mount Stromboli

Mt. Stromboli is a very large **volcano** found in the **Mediterranean Sea**, just off the coast of Sicily. It is one of the four active volcanoes belonging to **Italy** and is part of an archipelago, which is another name for a group of **islands** close together. The volcano's name, *Stromboli*, comes from an ancient Greek word meaning "round" because of its round, cone-like shape. The volcano is so big that it is its own island. The island stands 3,038 feet tall, but all that you can see of the island is just the top part of the volcano. If you were to measure the rest of the volcano, you would find that the rest of it stretches down 8,900 feet underwater. That is one giant volcano!

Mt. Stromboli is an active volcano, which means that it can erupt at times. Most of the eruptions are pretty small. Some eruptions are beautiful explosions of bright, glowing lava. Others are clouds of smoke and ash coming from the top of the volcano, kind of like smoke coming out of a chimney. Stromboli's volcanic eruptions can last for a few minutes or even a few hours. You can watch these eruptions from one of the nearby islands or on a boat. Because Stromboli has been constantly erupting for the past 2,000–5,000 years, people have given the volcano the nickname "the lighthouse of the Mediterranean."

Mount Teide

Mt. Teide is a **volcano** in Tenerife, one of the Canary Islands of **Spain**. The **summit** of this volcano is the highest point in all of Spain. Mt. Teide is also the third-tallest volcano in the world.

This **mountain** is considered to be an active volcano because its last eruption took place in 1909. Though that seems like a long time ago, for a volcano that has been around for thousands of years, that is not long at all. The pressure it takes for a volcano to actually erupt builds up over a long time.

Long ago, the native people of the **island**, named the Guanches, believed the mountain was very special. They thought it held up the sky and the sun. The Guanches were also afraid because they believed a giant black dog lived inside the mountain, an evil spirit like the devil. The Guanches called him Guayota. Whenever he was angry, he would make the earth shake or make the volcano erupt. When **Christopher Columbus** landed on Tenerife in 1492, his crew said they saw flames shoot out of Mt. Teide. He was one of the first to write down a record of an eruption there.

Mt. Teide and the surrounding area are called Mt. Teide National Park. It is the most visited natural wonder in Spain. On the slopes of the mountain is an observatory where people use special telescopes to watch the planets and stars. Mt. Teide is a place of interesting history and great beauty, and it's so tall that it also helps us to get a better look at space!

It might look and sound scary if you were to watch it erupt, but it would also be an amazing sight to see!

Mt. Vesuvius is an active volcano, which means it can still erupt. The last time it erupted was in 1944. Its most famous eruption was in AD 79, when it destroyed the Roman city of **Pompeii**. This town was built very close to the volcano. At the time, nobody knew that it was a volcano because it had not erupted for 600 years! The city was buried under 14–17 feet of ash and rock.

You can visit the volcano today and even hike up to see the crater at the top. It looks like any old **mountain** now, especially with trees growing on it. This is because the soil made by volcanic lava and ash has many minerals that help plants grow well. The fruit grown on Mt. Vesuvius is very tasty! No matter how many times a volcano erupts, new plant life will always grow back.

Fun Fact:
Mt. Vesuvius can grow taller every time it erupts.

Mount Vesuvius

Mt. Vesuvius is a large **volcano** on the coast of **Italy**, a few miles away from the city of Naples. It has a cone shape that has been built up from hardened lava, ash, and rock. This type of volcano can have very big eruptions.

Mute Swan

The mute swan is a bird that lives on the water and is found in the **United Kingdom**. It has white feathers and a long, graceful neck with an S shape. Adult mute swans are fairly large, measuring between four to five feet long. Their wings can spread nearly eight feet wide! The word "mute" means "silent," but that doesn't mean that this bird doesn't make any noise. Mute swans get their name from being much quieter than other swans, which honk and make calls that can sound like a trumpet. These swans mostly make little grunts, whistles, and snorts. They also sometimes make hissing sounds when another creature comes into their **territory**. One special sound the mute swan can make is by flapping its wings. Its wings are so powerful that this sound can be heard up to a mile away!

Baby swans are called cygnets. They are born with fluffy, gray baby feathers. Because they don't have regular feathers yet, they can't fly. But they can swim! They will sometimes ride on their parents' backs like a boat and hide under their wings if it starts raining. After four to five months, the cygnets start learning how to fly. A family of swans lives in a nest by a pond or **lake**, where they eat the plants that they find there. Mute swans in the United Kingdom don't migrate, as most other swans do. But when it gets very cold, they sometimes have to travel short distances to find a lake or pond that isn't frozen.

Napoleon Bonaparte

Napoleon Bonaparte was a great military leader from Corsica, **France**. He lived from 1769–1821. At nine years old, he went to a military academy and began his training to be an officer in the army.

Napoleon fought many battles. During the **French Revolution**, people turned against the king of France and took control of the country. At this time, France was also fighting Great Britain. Napoleon helped defeat the British. He was clever, hardworking, very organized, and good at winning battles. The French leaders liked what Napoleon had done, so they gave him more power.

Next, Napoleon fought and won many battles in Egypt, **Italy**, and other European countries. These battles were called the Napoleonic Wars. Napoleon formed a new government of France. Three leaders were to share control, but he wanted to be in charge. He crowned himself as the emperor of France and ruled the country like a **dictatorship**. He didn't even allow the pope to place the crown on his head—Napoleon put the crown on himself!

People began to dislike Napoleon when he started losing battles. He suffered his first big defeat when he tried to invade Russia in 1812. After that, he was defeated again and again. Napoleon was forced to step down as the emperor of France and was sent away to Elba, an **island** in the **Mediterranean Sea**. But Napoleon escaped Elba and took over France again, ruling for a hundred days. The rest of **Europe** was not happy! They fought Napoleon again in the Battle of Waterloo. Napoleon lost and was sent away once again so he couldn't be emperor anymore. This time, Napoleon was sent to Saint Helena, an island off the coast of **Africa**, too far away to cause any more trouble in France. He stayed there for six years until his death.

National Shrine of Our Lady of Lourdes, Scotland

Scotland's National Shrine of Our Lady of Lourdes, better known as Carfin Grotto,

opened in the **United Kingdom** in 1922. (A grotto is a carved-out area, like a small **cave**.) Monsignor Thomas Canon Taylor was the parish priest in the small village of Carfin. After visiting Lourdes, **France**, he wanted his village to have a similar shrine to honor the Blessed Mother, so he began to make one.

What began as a small shrine in a field was expanded over the years, thanks to the work of hundreds of volunteers. The main part of the grotto depicts Our Lady's appearance to St. Bernadette and has an altar for outdoor Mass. There is a beautiful glass chapel and life-sized statues of Jesus, Mary, and many saints. You can also visit a replica of the Holy Family's Loreto house and carpentry workshop, which are built inside a cave. (The real house is in the **Basilica of the Holy House of Loreto**.) You can pray the Stations of the Cross as you walk and stop at each life-sized station. There is also a statue honoring Our Lady, Star of the Sea, which even includes miniature **lakes**.

In addition to honoring the Blessed Mother, Fr. Taylor had a devotion to St. Thérèse, the Little Flower. St. Thérèse was beatified in 1923, and shortly after, Fr. Taylor had a statue of her added across from the statue of Our Lady of Lourdes. St. Thérèse is the secondary patroness of the shrine.

Today, the shrine welcomes more than 70,000 visitors each year from all across the world. It is open every day of the year.

Neuschwanstein Castle

Does this castle make you think of the one at Disneyland? If it does, it's because the Sleeping Beauty Castle was designed to look like this one! Now they are both famous and get countless visitors every year.

Neuschwanstein Castle is located in Bavaria, Germany in **Europe**. *Neuschwanstein* means "New Swan Stone." It was designed in 1869 by King Ludwig II, who wanted it as a private home.

The castle stands on a hilltop in the Bavarian **mountains**. It looks over the historic town of Füssen. Castles in the Middle Ages were built with tall towers and strong walls as a way of keeping enemies out. This castle looks like it came from the Middle Ages, but King Ludwig II did not need his castle for protection. He focused his attention on more modern details like telephones, running warm water, and flushing toilets. Many rooms in the castle are painted with scenes from Richard Wagner's **operas**.

The king's castle was never finished for two reasons. First, King Ludwig kept changing the plans for the castle, which meant that it took more time to build it. The second reason is that he died early at the age of 40. He had

spent more money than he could pay back and only lived in the castle for a short time: just 171 days.

Niagara Falls

Did you know that one of the world's most well-known waterfalls is in **North America**? Niagara Falls is on the border of **Canada** and the United States in New York State. There are actually three waterfalls that come together there: Horseshoe Falls, American Falls, and Bridal Veil Falls. After **glaciers** melted and formed the **Great Lakes**, some of that water carved the Niagara River. The **river** flows toward the Atlantic Ocean, creating Niagara Falls.

The cities closest to the falls on the United States side and the Canada side are both named Niagara Falls! Niagara Falls, New York and Niagara Falls, Ontario are connected by two bridges. You'll have a great view of the falls if you walk or drive over Rainbow Bridge. In the summer, you'll have lots of fellow visitors looking for great views of the falls. About 22 million people visit every year! The oldest and one of the most popular tourist attractions at Niagara Falls is the Maid of the Mist boat cruise. The cruise will take you so close to the falls that you can get splashed!

If you visit Niagara Falls by going through Niagara Falls State Park, there are lots of things to do. You might go to Goat Island to look at the falls. Goat Island also has a giant statue of Nikola Tesla, whose inventions helped make it possible to harness the energy made by the falls and turn it into electricity. From there, you can take an elevator down to the Cave of the Winds, which brings you to a point beneath Bridal Veil Falls.

Nile River

The Nile River is located in **Africa**. It is the longest **river** in the world. Some ancient texts, including the Bible, mention the Nile River. The Nile is more than 4,000 miles long, is usually 26–36 feet deep, and can be as wide as a little over 1.5 miles. It flows north, where it pours into the **Mediterranean Sea**. Before it reaches the **sea**, it crosses through 11 different countries in Africa, most famously through Egypt.

The Nile was very important to the ancient Egyptians since it was their only water source in a dry **desert**. Most of the water they used for drinking, cooking, washing, and even building came from the Nile. The Nile was especially important to farmers in ancient Egypt. Every year, the Nile would flood and grow wider. When it shrank back to its normal size, it would leave new layers of soil on the land. These new layers made the ground near the Nile a perfect place to grow crops like wheat, flax, and papyrus plants, which were used to make paper. The Egyptians traded their crops with other nearby countries, which helped them grow into a much richer and more powerful civilization. The civilization of ancient Egypt would not have existed without the Nile.

If you visit the Nile today, you can take a boat ride like the ancient Egyptians did. The river is now dammed in the south of Egypt, which means a barrier was built across it to control the water and stop it from flooding every year. Now, the river is the same size all year round. If you look carefully on your boat ride, you might even see animals that have made the Nile their home, including the **hippopotamus** and the crocodile. Just don't take a swim with them!

North American Martyrs

The Catholic Church has several different orders of priests. One of these is called the Society of Jesus, known as the Jesuits. Many of these priests and missionaries left **France** in the seventeenth century and went to **North America** so they could teach Native American Indians about Jesus and the Catholic Faith.

Some of these missionaries lived with a Native American Indian tribe called the Hurons. Many Hurons asked to be baptized, and the priests lived with them and gave them the sacraments. While many Hurons converted to Catholicism, there were still many who did not trust the Jesuits.

Another tribe called the Mohawks did not get along with the Hurons or the French. The Mohawks and the Hurons often fought, and sometimes the Jesuits were hurt as well. In 1642, the Mohawks captured Fr. Isaac Jogues and René Goupil (a missionary) and brought them back to their village. Sadly, they made the missionaries suffer and killed Goupil.

Months later, Fr. Jogues was ransomed by Dutch traders and eventually returned to France. But then he asked to go back to the Mohawk people. Can you imagine how brave he was to go back to the people who had hurt him so badly? Fr. Jogues loved Jesus and the people so much that he said he needed to go back. It was during this trip that some Mohawks killed Fr. Jogues and another missionary, Jean de Lalande.

Other Jesuit missionaries who were also killed by the Mohawks in following years were Antoine Daniel, Jean de Brébeuf, Noël Chabanel, Charles Garnier, and Gabriel Lalemant. These men are known as the Canadian Martyrs and also the North American Martyrs since they died for their faith. The feast day of the North American Martyrs is October 19 in the United States and September 26 in **Canada**.

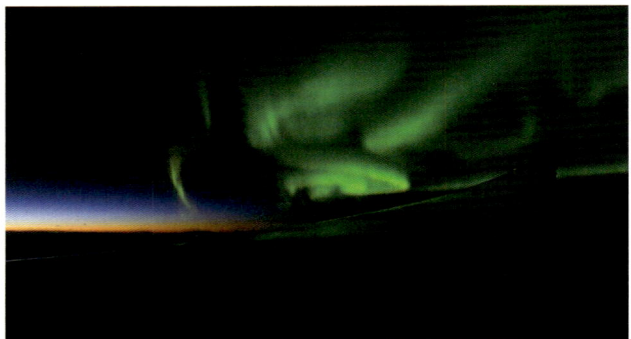

Northern Lights

The northern lights, also called the *aurora borealis*, are patterns of shimmering colored lights in the night sky. They can normally only be seen in northern parts of the world like **Canada**, Alaska, Greenland, Siberia, and northern parts of **Europe**. When auroras happen in the southern parts of the world like **Antarctica**, **Australia**, and parts of **South America** and **Africa**, they are called the southern lights, or the *aurora australis*.

Auroras often look like huge ribbons or curtains of brightly colored light. Sometimes the northern lights can move and dance across the sky. Other times they are just a quiet glow. Auroras are usually green, but they can also be red or blue.

Auroras happen when very small particles from the sun (called solar wind) hit the air far above our heads. Most of the time, these particles don't reach earth's atmosphere because of an invisible shield around earth called a magnetic field. But near the North and **South Poles**, some of the particles are able to get past the magnetic field and cause the lights we call auroras.

Auroras are harmless and very beautiful to look at. They can happen at any time of day or night, but they are too faint to see except at night. If you travel far north, look for the northern lights in the night sky!

Notre Dame Cathedral

Notre Dame Cathedral in Paris, **France**, is one of the most famous Catholic churches in the world. The name *Notre Dame* is French and means "Our Lady," a title honoring the Blessed Virgin Mary. Building of the cathedral began in 1163. It was not completed until 1345, almost 200 years later! Located on a small **island** on the Seine River, it is one of France's most famous landmarks.

While it is a cathedral, Notre Dame holds so many beautiful works of art that it is a popular place for people from all sorts of backgrounds to visit. Millions of people go there every year. If you visit, you can spend hours looking at the statues, paintings, and famous rose windows. These windows are very detailed and fancy, and they are huge! The name "rose" refers to the shape of the windows, which resemble the flower. Within each window are stained glass panels in many colors that show scenes from the Bible.

Some of the most extraordinary things kept in the cathedral are the relics of Jesus' Passion: the crown of thorns, a piece of the cross, and a nine-inch-long nail. **St. Louis IX** brought them from Jerusalem to Notre Dame in 1239. In 2019, the cathedral suffered great damage from a fire, but the relics were saved from harm. Repairs have been made, and the church was reopened in 2024.

Old Man of Hoy

The Old Man of Hoy is a land formation in the **United Kingdom**. It is located on the island of Hoy, which is one of the Orkney Islands. Depending on where you stand, it might look human-shaped. The Old Man of Hoy is not actually a man, but it is pretty old—almost 250 years old! That's old for a man, but young for a rock formation.

The Old Man of Hoy is made of red sandstone and is nearly 450 feet tall. Because it stands on its own away from the shore, it is a land formation known as a sea stack. It is one of the tallest sea stacks in the United Kingdom. Years of waves crashing against the rock have helped carve it into the shape it is today.

Probably, the **sea** first wore away the stone to create an arch, and eventually the arch collapsed to create the Old Man of Hoy.

If you like rock climbing, the Old Man of Hoy is a great place to put your skills to the test. It was first climbed in 1966 by three **mountain climbers**. Many other people have climbed it, including a pregnant woman, a blind man, and even an eight-year-old boy who climbed it in just under five hours! There is a plastic container buried under a small pile of stones at the top. In that container is a book with the names of all of the people who have climbed the Old Man of Hoy. If you make the climb one day, you can put your name on the list!

Opera

Opera is a performance with music that began in **Italy**. In an opera, a story is told by singers who act out their parts on stage while singing instead of talking. An orchestra plays along with the singers. Operas are amazing shows that will make you feel like you're in another world!

In an opera, the singers wear fancy costumes and act on a stage with a set—surroundings designed just for that opera. Seeing an opera is like watching a movie happen right in front of you. Most operas are performed in opera houses, big theaters designed just for operas.

Operas take a lot of work and skill to put on. In fact, the word *opera* means "work" in Italian! Of course, operas need good words, music, singers, and musicians. They also need carpenters to make the set, painters to paint it, seamstresses to make the costumes, backstage workers to move the set and change the lighting, and a director to tell everyone where to be at the right time. Can you imagine how many people work in an opera house?

The first opera was performed in Florence, Italy, at the end of the sixteenth century. It was so popular that soon, operas were being written and performed all over **Europe**. The first opera told the story of an ancient Greek myth, which became a popular kind of story in operas. Many operas also tell more modern stories that are funny or sad. Would you like to go to the opera?

Ostrich

The common ostrich is the largest bird in the world. You can find them in the flat, grassy **savannas** of **Africa**. Ostriches grow between 6–9 feet tall and can weigh over 300 pounds.

They also lay the largest eggs of any bird. A single ostrich egg is about the same size as 24 chicken eggs!

The ostrich has very small wings. It is too heavy to fly away from danger, but God gave it strong legs so it can run to safety. Ostriches are the world's fastest-running birds. If they're cornered, they will attack with powerful downward kicks. Each foot has only two toes, but they have very sharp nails that can be deadly.

The ostrich's eyes are very large and can spot predators nearly two miles away. Their eyes have long lashes that keep out the dust.

Ostriches mostly eat plants, though they will also eat insects, mice, and lizards. Like all birds, they do not have teeth, so they swallow their food whole. After they eat, you can see the food moving down their long throat!

If you went **bird-watching** in the African savannas, you would find ostriches in groups of 5–50 birds. You would find some that are black (male) and some that are brown (female). The brown females can be especially hard to spot. They hide themselves by lying on the ground with their necks stretched out in front. That way, they blend into the grassland. This helps them avoid their predators, including **lions**, **cheetahs**, and **spotted hyenas**.

If you listen carefully, you may even hear them talking to each other with chirps, honks, and grunts. Sometimes, the males make a booming sound, a little like a lion's roar. If you hear them hissing, it means stay away!

Our Lady of China

Our Lady of China is one of the many names of our Blessed Mother, Mary. It is believed that she appeared from Heaven to save the Catholics of a poor village called Donglu. Donglu is near Beijing, the capital of **China**.

In 1900, a group of 10,000 Chinese soldiers attacked Donglu, the village where 700–1000 Catholics lived. The local priest, Father Wu, prayed for Our Lady's help for his people. In answer to his prayer, the Blessed Virgin Mary appeared in the sky. The soldiers tried to shoot her down, but they could not harm her. Then, a man on a fiery horse came and chased them away. Some people think the man was St. Michael, a powerful archangel who defends us from evil.

The villagers built a beautiful church to thank Our Lady for her help, but it was destroyed by bombs during a war. Years later, a new church was built. In 1995, when thousands of people came to celebrate Our Lady's feast day, the Blessed Virgin Mary appeared once again. They even saw the sun dance in the sky! It was comforting to see their Mother Mary so close by.

But the Chinese government was not happy. They tried to keep the people from visiting the church by blocking the roads. Because the people would not obey, the shrine was destroyed. In China today, each time underground Catholics gather outside for Holy Mass, they are afraid of being found out. ("Underground" means they are not allowed to live their faith where people can see them.) When you pray the Rosary, remember your brothers and sisters in China who are suffering.

Our Lady of Fátima

The Blessed Virgin Mary appeared to three shepherd children in Fátima, Portugal in 1917. This apparition, called Our Lady of Fátima, was seen by 10-year-old Lucia dos Santos and her cousins, 9-year-old Francisco and 7-year-old Jacinta Marto.

The children reported seeing a woman "brighter than the sun, shedding rays of light." They said she held a rosary in her hand and urged them to devote themselves to the Holy Trinity and to pray the Rosary every day to bring peace to the world.

The children saw Our Lady six times between May and October. She urged them to pray the Rosary daily, and she told them about a miracle that would happen in October. She also asked them to pray and sacrifice much for sinners, saying that many souls are lost because they have no one to pray or make sacrifices for them.

The apparition on October 13 came to be known as the Miracle of the Sun because the sun seemed to move and dance in the sky. It was seen by about 70,000 people and was captured in photographs and recorded in newspapers. The crowd looked at the sun without it hurting their eyes. The three children said they saw the Holy Family, Our Lady of Sorrows with Jesus, Our Lady of Mount Carmel, and **St. Joseph** and Jesus blessing the people.

Francisco and Jacinta were canonized in 2017, and Lucia was declared venerable in 2023.

Our Lady of the Cape Shrine

Our Lady of the Cape Shrine is an old stone church in **Quebec**, **Canada**, that has an amazing history. It holds a very special statue of the Virgin Mary and is the site of a Marian miracle.

The church that later became a shrine to Mary opened for worship in 1720. It is the oldest church in Canada that celebrates Mass daily! Mary's special relationship with this church began when its new priest, Father Desilets, arrived. There had been no priest living there for 115 years. After so long, the people had forgotten to devote themselves to God and prayer. One day, Father Desilets found an escaped pig in the church chewing on a rosary that someone had dropped! This made him very sad. He consecrated himself to the Blessed Mother and encouraged people to pray the Rosary again.

More people came to church, and eventually they needed a bigger building. They planned to bring stone for the new church across the St. Lawrence River when it froze that winter. However, the winter of 1879 was very warm, and the **river** didn't freeze. What would they do? The people prayed all winter for Mary's intercession to freeze the river. Father Desilets promised Mary that instead of tearing down the old church, he would devote it to her if the river froze. What do you think happened? Huge chunks of ice floated down the river and formed a bridge just where they needed it.

Now, the old church is called the Shrine of Our Lady of the Cape. It has this name because it is built on a **cape** in Quebec formed by two rivers coming together. It holds a statue of Mary that is said to have opened its eyes in a miraculous way. Every year, many people pilgrimage to this shrine and to the nearby new church, which is now the Basilica of Our Lady of the Cape.

Our Lady of Walsingham

Our Lady of Walsingham is a title given to the Blessed Virgin Mary when she inspired a British noblewoman in 1061 to build a replica of the Holy Family's house. Lady Richeldis de Faverches lived in the tiny village of Walsingham in England, which is part of the **United Kingdom**.

Lady Richeldis had a special devotion to Mary and asked Mary to tell her if there was a special way to honor her. Richeldis did not see Mary with her eyes, but in her devout prayer, Mary led her to see Nazareth. Mary showed her the house where the Angel Gabriel had greeted Mary. Mary told Richeldis that she could honor her and the Holy Family by having a house made that looked just like their house in Nazareth so that people in England could visit it.

The replica house drew many people to make pilgrimages to it throughout the Middle Ages. The original statue and shrine were destroyed during the Protestant Reformation in 1538. Thankfully, in 1897, Pope Leo XIII announced that the sanctuary of Our Lady of Walsingham would be rebuilt, and it was renamed the Lady Chapel of the Catholic Church of the Annunciation.

The Little Sisters of Jesus have a community in Walsingham, and there is also a community of Carmelite nuns. The small village of Walsingham welcomes many visitors who want to see the replica of the Holy House of the Holy Family.

Pachacuti

Pachacuti was the ninth ruler of the **Incas** and the founder of the Inca Empire, centered in present-day **Peru**. Pachacuti was actually named Cusi Yupanqui when he was born. At first, Pachacuti's brother was going to be the next ruler. But then, Pachacuti won a huge victory in a battle against the Incas' biggest enemy, the Chancas. This showed the Incas what a good warrior and leader he was. Pachacuti defeated his brother and became the Inca ruler in 1438. He also changed his name to *Pachacuti* at that time, which means "Earth Changer."

Pachacuti first strengthened the city of Cuzco (the Incas' capital city). He rebuilt its temple, added warehouses (places where food and other supplies were kept), and created an army. Then he began to rule nearby nations, too. If any of them tried to fight back, he killed their rulers. His grown-up son helped him, and soon the empire was quite large. The Inca Empire grew even more after Pachacuti's death.

Pachacuti is also known for building **Machu Picchu**. This is a small city high in the **mountains** that is now a famous ruin. Pachacuti may have built it as a family home or summer retreat.

Pachacuti was a very strict ruler. Sometimes he forced thousands of his people to move to other areas of the empire. Pachacuti certainly "changed the earth" for the Incas and the people he conquered!

Pantheon

The Pantheon is an amazing ancient building in Rome, **Italy**. It was built around AD 126, which was almost 2,000 years ago! Do you think any of the buildings you visit will still be around in 2,000 years?

The Pantheon was built by Emperor Hadrian, but big letters carved on the front say it was built by a different emperor who lived over 100 years before him. Hadrian may have decided it should say this because the Romans liked old things.

The Pantheon has a dome roof, shaped like half of a ball. This dome is special because it is made of only concrete, without any metal or wood inside to make it strong. It is 19 feet thick at the bottom and just over 4 feet thick at the top. There's also a 30-foot wide hole at the top so you can see the sky. The Pantheon's dome is one of a kind—no one has ever made another like it!

Pantheon means "for all the gods," but it probably wasn't a temple. It was likely a place to look at the heavens through the hole in the ceiling. Since the seventh century, it has been a church dedicated to Mary and the martyrs. Many martyrs' bones are buried under the altar.

If you visit the Pantheon on the Feast of Pentecost, when we celebrate the Holy Spirit coming down from Heaven, you would see thousands of bright red rose petals dropping through the hole in the ceiling. They look like flames of fire from Heaven!

Fun Facts:

- The US Capitol building was modeled after the Pantheon.
- The painter Raphael and the composer Arcangelo Corelli are buried here.
- Roman firefighters throw the rose petals through the roof on Pentecost.

and Chile. Its name means "Flamingo Lake" in the Aymara language, which is spoken by a tribe near that area. Parinacota is a large dormant **volcano**. *Dormant* means that the volcano is "asleep": it has gone quiet and hasn't erupted in the past 10,000 years.

Parinacota has the familiar appearance of a volcano—a cone-shaped **mountain**. It was made from many layers of hardened lava and ash. Parinacota belongs to a group of volcanoes that are called the Payachata. There is even a volcano right next to Parinacota that is called Pomerape. Some legends call these volcanoes sisters!

Parinacota stands tall at 20,807 feet. The first people to climb this volcano were Carlos Teran and Joseph Prem in 1928. If you climb to the top of the volcano like they did, you can see a huge crater that looks like a large hole on the top. It is over half a mile wide and almost a thousand feet deep. The top of the volcano is often covered in snow, which makes it look quite beautiful. You can find many animals in the area surrounding the volcano, including certain kinds of deer, **mountain lions**, rodents, and yes—even **flamingoes**!

Parinacota Volcano

Parinacota is found near the western coast of **South America**. It is on the border of Bolivia

Parthenon

The Parthenon is an ancient building in Athens,

Greece. It is a temple that was designed and built in the fifth century BC by two famous Greek architects, Iktinos and Callicrates. It was built on top of the Acropolis of Athens, which is a rocky hill that was the center of ancient Athens. The Acropolis is where Greek kings lived and where the people would gather for religious worship.

The Parthenon is made of marble and is 45 feet tall, 228 feet long and 101 feet wide. It has 69 columns. The Parthenon took 15 years to build. It was dedicated to the ancient Greek goddess Athena, the goddess of wisdom.

The Parthenon is one of the best examples of ancient Greek buildings. Its design was so well thought out, it was made to survive **earthquakes**! Part of the trick is that the columns lean slightly inward instead of standing perfectly straight up. This makes the building sturdier.

Many beautiful sculptures were carved to decorate the Parthenon. You can still see stone carvings at the Parthenon, but many of the sculptures are now in museums. If you visit the British Museum, the **Louvre Museum**, or the Acropolis Museum in Athens, you can see many of these sculptures. Millions of people visit the Parthenon every year.

Fun Facts:

- At one point in the fifth century, the Parthenon was a church dedicated to the Virgin Mary!
- If the columns kept growing toward the sky, all of them would eventually touch about 1.5 miles over the Parthenon!

Perce Rock

Perce Rock is a very large land formation located in the water of the Gulf of St. Lawrence in **Quebec**, **Canada**. If you look out over the water in the **gulf**, you might mistake Perce Rock for a large ship because it is so big! As you approach Perce Rock, you'll find a huge hole in the rock. This opening creates a natural arch that is big enough for a sailboat to go through! This hole is what inspired its name "Perce," which means "pierced." It was named by the explorer **Samuel de Champlain** in 1607.

Perce Rock is part of a series of sea cliffs made of a special kind of rock called limestone. Limestone can be washed away very slowly over time by the splashing waves. The water has shaped Perce Rock and given it its arch. Hundreds of years ago, there was more than one arch. In 1760, Captain Harvey Smyth, an English Officer, drew a picture of Perce Rock. This drawing was important because it showed that there were two arches at the time. The waves eventually washed away one of the arches. We might never have known about the other arch if it wasn't for Captain Harvey's drawing. Who knew that a drawing would be so important!

When the tide is low, you can actually walk right up to Perce Rock from dry land. This is because there is a stretch of rock that connects

Perce Rock to the mainland, like a bridge attached to the earth. It is usually hidden just out of sight under the water. When the **ocean** tide is high, though, you will definitely need to take a boat to see Perce Rock up close.

Peruvian Weaving

Peruvian weaving is the making of cloth by the people of **Peru** in **South America**. They take two sets of threads, crossing them over and under on a loom until cloth is formed. Special shapes, patterns, and designs are woven into the cloth with the help of a tool called a shuttle. It is called a shuttle because of how it looks like a little boat taking the thread back and forth.

Wool and cotton threads are colored with dye from native plants. Peruvians use bright, bold colors like red, yellow, and orange. They are very good at this fine art of weaving. Local weavers have been doing it since the time of the **Incas**, over 800 years ago.

Peruvian weavers used to make padded cloth armor that was very strong and gave good protection. Now, weavers make articles of clothing, rugs, and purses. Woolen thread from **llamas** and alpacas makes warm ponchos and skirts.

Phumdis

Phumdis are floating **islands** on Lake Loktak in Manipur, **India**. The phumdis are huge mounds of tightly packed plants and dirt that float on top of the water. Most of the soil of a phumdi floats below the level of the water, much like an **iceberg**.

Local people build huts on the larger phumdis. There are about 4,000 people that live on the **lake** this way! Some of the phumdis are man-made. They are circular and used for fish farming. The largest phumdi on Loktak Lake is over 15 square miles and is a national park called the Keibul Lamjao National Park. It is the only national park in the world to be located on a floating island. It provides a home for a rare type of deer, the *sangai*. Sangai are also called Manipur brow-antlered deer or dancing deer. This name comes from the graceful way they walk, which has also inspired some movements of the local dance style. Sangai are only found in Manipur and have hooves that seem to be specially made for walking on the spongy ground of the phumdis.

Since Lake Loktak and its phumdis are very important to the people who live on and around them, the people want to keep Lake Loktak clean and unpolluted. There have been many projects to clean Lake Loktak and restore the water so that it can continue to be used for fishing, providing water for farmers' fields, and even generating electricity.

Pig-tailed Macaque

The pig-tailed macaque is a kind of monkey found in parts of **Asia**, including southern **China**, northeastern **India**, and Thailand. It is easy to spot with its fluffy fur and the thin red stripes at the outer edges of its eyes, almost like makeup. The pig-tailed macaque gets its funny name from the way its tail looks, rather like a pig's tail.

There are actually two different species of pig-tailed macaque: the northern and the southern. They look pretty similar, but northern pig-tailed macaques tend to be smaller than southern pig-tailed macaques. Pig-tailed macaques like to live in **rainforests** and spend their time in the trees. Small groups of these monkeys hang out together, and sometimes you can find more than 150 pig-tailed macaques together! That's a big group. How many siblings and cousins do you have? If you got them all together, would there be 150 of you?

Pig-tailed macaques like to eat fresh fruits, flowers, leaves, and other parts of plants. In the colder seasons when there isn't enough fruit, they eat insects, spiders, mushrooms, and tree bark. Sometimes they'll even eat lizards and squirrels.

Groups of pig-tailed macaques make plans about when to look around for food and when to settle down in a certain area. They make these plans based on the kinds and amounts of food in different areas. How clever!

Pine Marten

Pine martens live in most of **Europe**, but they are especially common in the **United Kingdom**.

Pine martens come from Scotland originally, but now they live as far away as Syria and Iraq. At one point, they were thought to have disappeared from England, but they have returned! They are about the size of a cat and related to otters, **badgers**, and weasels. Pine martens look cute and cuddly, but be careful if you are near one! They are shy and sneaky, but they also have fierce teeth and large claws.

Pine martens live in pine trees in forests. They are good climbers and can leap from tree to tree. Their long, bushy tails help them balance. They like to live alone and protect their **territory** from other animals. They make their dens in holes in pine trees or in old bird or squirrel nests.

Pine martens eat both plants and animals.

They like berries, eggs, fungi, insects, and small animals, like voles or rabbits. Even though they live in trees, they find most of their food on the ground. Pine martens usually come out at dusk to find their food. They do not hibernate in the winter, but they stay in their dens more than usual.

Fun Facts:
- Baby pine martens are called kits. They are born blind and deaf.
- Pine martens are fully grown at six months old.
- A group of pine martens is called a richness.
- Pine martens like to hide their food during summer and autumn so they have a stash ready for winter.

Poison Dart Frog

The poison dart frog is any one of many small, colorful frogs found in the **Amazon rainforest** of **South America**. These beautiful frogs are very small, sometimes as tiny as half an inch. The biggest ones can grow up to two inches long. On each toe, it has a suction cup pad to help it grip trees and rocks.

Poison dart frogs are different from most frogs. Unlike most frogs, poison dart frogs are active during the day. Their bright colors are a warning to other animals that they are not good to eat. But if an animal does try to catch and eat one, this little frog has a special defense. The frogs ooze a kind of poisonous sweat that sits on their skin. If an animal gets a poison dart frog in its mouth, it will be surprised by a very bad taste and let the frog go. The poison on the skin of some of these frogs can make animals very sick or even kill them.

These frogs are commonly called poison dart frogs because some native South Americans poison the tips of their blow darts by rubbing them on the backs of the more poisonous frogs.

Poison dart frogs cannot make their own poison. It is what they eat that makes them poisonous. These frogs can eat other poisonous animals, such as certain mites and ants. Although these little bugs have poison in their bodies, this poison doesn't hurt the frog at all. Instead, the frog can collect and reuse the poison for its own defense. The poison dart frogs you might see at the zoo are usually not very poisonous. This is because the food they eat there isn't as poisonous.

Polar Bear

The polar bear is found in the Arctic Circle. This includes Alaska, **Canada**, Russia, Greenland,

and Norway. As you know, the **Arctic** is very cold. One look at a polar bear tells us that it is well protected. Do you see that fluffy, thick fur? It is made of two layers that keep it very warm. The skin under the fur is black, which helps soak up the sunlight and add even more warmth.

The polar bear's fur looks creamy white, but it is not. It might surprise you to know that the fur is translucent, or clear. This helps it blend into its surroundings. In the daylight, the polar bear's fur looks as white as the snow. At night, you can hardly see a polar bear at all!

Polar bears are not social animals and mostly live by themselves. When two of them do meet, they greet each other in an interesting way. They circle around each other, making grunting noises. Finally, they get really close and touch their noses together.

They like to eat seals and fish that they find under the ice. Sometimes, they find berries to eat. A polar bear on the hunt for a tasty seal thrusts its head into a hole in the ice when it sees a seal come up for air. That must be why God gave them skinnier necks than other types of bears!

When cubs are born, they weigh only two pounds. During their young years, they wrestle in the snow to get strong and practice defending themselves with their paws and teeth. They also learn to hunt and swim. In 5–6 years, they are already 330 to 660 pounds. These huge bears are so strong that one swat of their paw can kill.

Pompeii

Pompeii was an ancient Roman city on the coast of **Italy**. It was a very wealthy city with many beautiful buildings and homes. There was one problem, though: it was built right next to an active **volcano**! The people of Pompeii thought that the volcano, which we know today as **Mt. Vesuvius**, was just another **mountain**. But in AD 79, the volcano suddenly erupted.

A Roman man named Pliny the Younger saw the eruption and wrote about it. He wrote that the eruption looked like a lamp lit in a dark room. This was because the volcano made very thick, black clouds of ash that stretched out for miles. These clouds blocked out the sun, making everything look like night in the middle of the day. The bright, hot lava coming from the volcano would have been the only source of light.

Pompeii was quickly buried in ash. Since it rained as the ash was falling, a layer of hardened ash covered the city for hundreds of years. Archaeologists (people who practice **archaeology**) dug through the ash to uncover Pompeii's history. You can visit the city today, walk the same streets, and enter the same buildings that the Pompeiians did. You can see some very beautiful homes called villas where the richest people lived. Homes like this would have had a beautiful garden or courtyard at the center of the house—like having a backyard inside the house. You can also see many amazing works of art that were painted on the walls. You might even see wheel marks that carts made in the old streets of Pompeii!

Pont du Gard

The Pont du Gard is part of a **Roman aqueduct** in southern **France**. It was built in the first century AD, and it helped supply the city of Nîmes with water.

The name *Pont du Gard* means "bridge over the Gard." This part of the **aqueduct** crosses the Gardon River. There are three rows of arches. Originally, there were 64 arches, but now there are 52 left because it is so old.

The Pont du Gard is one of the best examples of Roman architecture to be seen today. The builders didn't use any mortar or cement to stick the stones together. Instead, they cut and fitted the stones so carefully that the aqueduct is still standing today. Do you think you could build a stone wall that lasts that long?

Even more amazing is the very gradual tilt of the aqueduct. It had to be lower toward one end so that the water would flow in that direction. The Roman engineers who built it made it work with hardly any tilt at all. The end of the aqueduct is only 41 feet lower than

the beginning, even though it is over 30 miles away!

The aqueduct was used until the fourth century AD, when the water stopped flowing all the way through. The water channel had become too clogged by mineral deposits and other things because it wasn't cleaned often enough. The Pont du Gard was still used as a bridge, though.

If you want to explore the Pont du Gard, you can take a walk along the top of the aqueduct. It is a very popular spot for tourists to visit in France.

Prado Art Museum

The Prado Museum is **Spain's** main national art museum. It is located in Madrid, Spain's capital city. Its name means "meadow" in Spanish, probably because of the large grassy area where it was built.

The Prado Museum was founded in 1819 as a museum for paintings and statues, but it has other kinds of art, too. The first collection of art was the Spanish Royal Collection, which was owned by Spain's royal family. The museum has mostly European art, especially by Spanish and Italian artists. If you visit it, you can see paintings by famous artists including Francisco Goya, Hieronymous Bosch, **El Greco**, Peter Paul

Rubens, Titian, and Diego Velásquez.

The Prado Museum has an interesting history. King Charles (Carlos) III of Spain started building the museum in 1785 to house his natural history collection. But before the museum could be finished, **Napoleon Bonaparte** invaded Spain. Napoleon's horse soldiers used the Prado Museum as their headquarters, storing their gunpowder there. When Napoleon was finally defeated, the new king of Spain—Ferdinand VII, Charles III's grandson—decided to make the Prado an art museum.

The Prado Museum's most famous painting is *Las Meninas* by Diego Velásquez. The title of the painting means "The Ladies-in-Waiting," talking about the women of the court who served women in the royal family or other women with a high position. The painting shows a young princess, Margarita Teresa, with her ladies-in-waiting, a dog, and other people. About two and a half million people visit the museum every year to see this painting and other works of art. The Prado has over 21,000 works of art. It would take weeks for you to see them all!

Pyrenees

The Pyrenees are an amazing **mountain range** in **France**. They make a natural border between France and **Spain**, stretching over 270 miles between the **Mediterranean Sea** and the Atlantic Ocean.

The weather in the Pyrenees can be different depending on where you are. The wet air from the Atlantic Ocean causes more snow and rain in the western Pyrenees. You can usually see snow on the mountaintops from October until April, so those would be great times to go **skiing**!

The eastern Pyrenees have warmer weather. During the warmer months, hiking and rock climbing are great activities. You can drive or hike around the foothills, but you can only hike up the tall peaks. Many of the mountains are difficult to hike and require very good hiking skills. If you are brave enough to hike to the **summit** of a mountain, you will probably see tall cliffs, icy **lakes**, and snow.

There are some beautiful landscapes in the Pyrenees, like winding **valleys**, high peaks, and lively wildlife. There are also incredible landmarks such as the Cirque de Gavarnie. A *cirque* is a bowl-shaped valley that is very tall on one side. A steep rock wall surrounds the Cirque de Gavarnie. This cirque also has waterfalls. One waterfall, known as the Grande Cascade de Gavarnie, is the second-highest waterfall in **Europe**.

If you like adventure and the outdoors, the Pyrenees are the place to visit. You will find many hidden paths and secret valleys to explore!

Fun Fact:
Over 17 million insects migrate annually through the Pyrenees. Make sure to bring your bug spray!

Python

Pythons are large snakes that are not poisonous. Instead, they kill their prey by wrapping around them and squeezing very hard until they cannot breathe.

At least two kinds of pythons live in **Africa**, south of the **Sahara Desert**. The Central African rock python is Africa's largest snake, with adults measuring between 9 and 20 feet long. These pythons can weigh up to 200 pounds!

Different kinds of pythons have different patterns of brown, white, black, and orange on their skins. They have long forked tongues and very sharp teeth. They have scales around their mouths that sense heat, which helps them find prey even in the dark. They also have see-through scales that cover their eyes as they sleep. They don't have any ears, but they use vibrations to "feel" sounds in their jawbones.

Pythons like to live near water, but they can also live in forests, **savannas**, rocky areas, and even near **deserts**. They sleep underground or in other shelters like tree branches, under logs and rocks, or in **caves**. They hatch their young from eggs, which they protect in their shelters. During the dry season of the year, they spend most of their time sleeping. They sometimes come out to drink water, but they won't eat until the dry season is over.

A python first catches its prey by biting it. Then the python squeezes it strongly before opening its mouth and slowly swallowing the prey whole. Pythons can open their mouths much wider than most snakes—they eat animals up to the size of antelope and can even eat crocodiles! Sometimes crocodiles eat pythons, though.

Quebec

Quebec is a **province** of **Canada**. It is different from all the other Canadian provinces, though, because the people there speak French!

Originally, Quebec was a French colony, which is why almost everyone there speaks French. Later, Quebec became part of the British Commonwealth, meaning that it is ruled by the king or queen of the **United Kingdom**. Even though the rest of Canada has two official languages—French and English—Quebec's only official language is French.

Quebec is a large province. It is almost three times the size of Texas or **France**. It has lots of fresh water—there are over half a million **lakes**! Quebec is almost completely surrounded by water, too. This water is partly salty from the **ocean** and partly fresh from all the **rivers** nearby. Because of all this water, Quebec produces and sells a lot of hydroelectricity (electricity made from water power). The climate is very cold up north, but in the south, you will find hot, humid summers.

Quebec is known for its maple syrup and for making **ice hockey** popular in Canada. The biggest city is Montreal, which is home to several hockey teams. The city also hosts the world's largest jazz music festival, a comedy festival, the Canadian Grand Prix, and a French music festival.

Most Quebecois (people of Quebec) are Roman Catholic, and overall, they are more religious than the rest of Canada. If you visit, be sure to see Notre-Dame de Quebec Cathedral!

Raccoon

The raccoon is a common mammal found in **North America**. It has also spread to some parts of **Europe** and **Asia**. It is about the size of a large cat and has a bushy striped tail. The black and white fur on its face makes it look like it is wearing a bandit's mask. Raccoons are nocturnal, meaning that they sleep during the day and come out at night. Some people think that the black fur helps it see better in the dark because the color black doesn't reflect much light, so there is less glare. Or maybe its black and white patches help raccoons recognize each other in the dark!

Raccoons can live in a few different areas, including forests, **marshes**, and even cities. Raccoons are very clever and have learned to live alongside humans. You may have seen one looking through your garbage at night. They are omnivorous, which means that they eat both meat and plants. They like to eat lots of different foods, including insects, worms, fish, crabs, frogs, eggs, fruit, and nuts.

Raccoons use their front paws for many things. They often catch and hold their food with their front paws. Their paws are very sensitive. This means raccoons can tell a lot about objects by feeling them with their paws. Raccoons are known for washing their food in water before eating it. However, water softens the skin on their paws and makes their sense of touch better. Raccoons may be just trying to get a better sense of their food when they seem to be washing it!

Red Panda

Red pandas are mammals that live in southern **China**, Nepal, and the **Himalayas**. The Chinese name for the red panda means "fire fox" because of their small size and red fur. Red pandas look like a mixture of a cat and a bear. Red pandas share their name with **giant pandas**, but besides eating bamboo, the two are not very similar.

Red pandas sleep in trees, and they are awake at dawn and dusk. They usually take a long nap during the middle of the day. They do not eat any meat at all. Instead, red pandas mainly eat bamboo. They also like fruits, roots, acorns, flowers, berries, bird eggs, and insects.

Red pandas are less than 2 feet long and

weigh between 6 and 12 pounds. They don't live in large groups. Instead, they enjoy being alone.

When they're in danger, red pandas may run up a tree to escape or stand on their back legs and raise their front paws to try to look bigger. They also use their claws and teeth against attackers. Snow leopards, **badgers**, weasels, and other predators hunt red pandas.

Reed Boats

Reed boats, or boats made from reed stalks (stems), are one of the oldest types of boats. One of the few places in the world where people still make reed boats is **Lake Titicaca** on the border of **Peru** and Bolivia in **South America**. The native people around Lake Titicaca, called the Uros, used reed boats to catch fish and to travel between **islands** on the **lake**.

Reed boats are made by tying bundles of reeds together very tightly and then coating the underside of the boat with tar. (Tar is a sticky black liquid that has long been used to make something waterproof.) The reed boats of the Uros are very strong and can last up to one year. They can be as small as a canoe or as large as a small ship, nearly 100 feet long. Reed boats can be strong enough to cross **oceans**!

Drawings of reed boats from thousands of years ago have been found in Egypt and other countries. Do you remember how Moses' mother hid him in a bulrush basket and set it in the **river** (Exodus 2:3)? This was probably just like the reed boats that were being made in Egypt at the time. Egyptians and Ethiopians used papyrus reeds to make their boats. Native American Indians in California also made reed boats, using the tule reeds that grow across **North America**. The Uros around Lake Titicaca use totora reeds for their reed boats. (The famous floating islands of the Uros are also made from totora reeds!)

Rhinoceros

The rhinoceros lives mostly in **Asia** and some parts of **Africa**. The name "rhinoceros" comes from Greek words meaning "nose" and "horn of an animal." It has one or two horns on its face. It's called a "rhino" for short. It is one of the largest animals in the world. It can weigh over 5,000 pounds and be over 6 feet tall!

Rhinos eat a lot of food. They have to because they are so large. For them, a good hearty meal is usually grass—or leaves, bushes, and branches. If they can't reach the branches, sometimes they will even knock down small trees! They have long, pointed upper lips that help them grab food. They use the flat teeth in the backs of their mouths to grind it up.

Some rhinos have wart-like bumps, some have skin that looks like armor, and some only have one horn. Did you know that they like to play in the mud, too? One of their favorite places to be is deep in a mudhole. That's how they keep cool and protect their skin from the sun. The mud works the way sunscreen does for us.

No animal is brave enough to come after rhinos. Sometimes they fight with each other, though. When fighting, they use their sharp front teeth—and of course their horns come in handy, too!

Whether they are living deep in the **rainforest** or out on the **plains**, most rhinos live alone. But some rhinos do live in groups. A group of rhinos is called a crash.

Fun Facts:
- Rhinos can smell and hear really well, but their eyesight is poor.
- Rhinos only have three toes on each foot.
- Rhino horns have been used in Chinese medicine.

Rice Production

Rice is a delicious grain that is grown for food. In **China**, **Africa**, and many other countries, rice is a staple food, which means it is one of the most important foods in that country. Did you know that rice comes from grass? Well, not the type of grass growing in your lawn! Rice is a cereal grain, which means that it is a grass plant with seeds that are good to eat. ("Cereal" doesn't always mean you eat it in a bowl with milk!) Wheat, corn, and oats are other examples of cereal grains.

Rice is best grown in a **rice paddy**. In the past, water buffalo (animals from **Asia** that are like oxen) were used to plow rice paddies. Now, modern plows and other farm machinery are more common. When the rice is ready to be harvested, the water is drained out of the rice paddy.

Sometimes fish or ducks are raised in rice paddies while the rice is growing. The fish and ducks eat bugs and other pests in the paddy, and their droppings fertilize the rice plants. In places where the land has too many hills to make regular rice paddies, rice terraces can be built into the hills and **mountains**. Rice terraces look like huge flat steps going up the mountainside.

How many foods can you think of that are made with rice? In China, there is fried rice (stir-fried rice with vegetables, egg, and seafood or meat), rice noodles, rice cakes, rice dumplings, rice porridge, rice wine, and much more.

Rock of Gibraltar

The Rock of Gibraltar is a **mountain** of limestone

rock that stands 1,398 feet high. It is in Gibraltar, which is the place where **Spain** and **Africa** meet. Gibraltar is a **territory** that belongs to the **United Kingdom**.

The rock is very old, and it has all kinds of fossils and **caves**. There is even a castle on it where the Moors (Muslims from Africa) once ruled for over 700 years. The plants and animals are protected so that nothing disturbs them. A type of monkey called the Barbary macaque lives there. Twice a year, migrating birds rest on the rock before going further on their journey.

The land of Gibraltar and its rock are very important because of their location. They guard the main entrance to the **Mediterranean Sea**. Ships travel past the Rock of Gibraltar all the time, and it is a natural fortress for protection against enemy ships.

Many, many battles have been fought over Gibraltar. The Spanish took it from the Moors, and the British took it from the Spanish. When Spain wanted to take it back, they surrounded Gibraltar with their ships, cutting off help from outside. This was called the Great Siege of Gibraltar. Although they were greatly outnumbered, the British soldiers did not give up. They fought hard and fired cannons at the enemy ships from high up in the rock. After three and a half years, the British won.

Today, visitors are welcome to explore the famous Rock of Gibraltar. Deep inside are long tunnels and passageways once used during the Great Siege. By the end of the eighteenth century, British soldiers had built almost 4,000 feet of tunnels! These included caverns, called galleries, where the cannons were placed.

Roman Aqueduct

In the lands they conquered, the **Roman Empire** built many **aqueducts** to carry water to cities. Since the Romans were such good builders, many of these aqueducts still exist. Ruins can be seen across **Italy**, Germany, **Spain**, **France**, Turkey, and even parts of **Africa**. Two of the best are the Aqueduct of Segovia (Spain) and the **Pont du Gard** (southern France).

An aqueduct works by sending water through a channel across many miles toward a town or city. The water is then used for farms, fountains, houses, gardens, and more. Often, Roman aqueducts started in the **mountains** where there was a spring of water. The Romans built the aqueduct to slowly slope downward across the land. When the water channel had to cross a **river** or **valley**, a bridge was built. These bridges have many rounded arches that carry the water channel across the top. A rounded arch, often called a Roman arch, is when the gap between two pillars is rounded on top, like part of a circle.

These aqueducts with Roman arches are very famous. The Aqueduct of Segovia and the Pont du Gard have more than one row of Roman arches stacked on top of each other! The Aqueduct of Segovia was probably built in the first or second century AD and is very well preserved. It is over 9 miles long and 93 feet tall at its highest point. It was used to bring water from the mountains to the city of Segovia, Spain.

Roman Empire

The Roman Empire, the largest empire in the ancient world, was centered in **Italy**, with Rome as the capital. The Roman Empire ruled **Europe**, North **Africa**, and the **Mediterranean Sea** for over 400 years, from 27 BC to AD 476. It reached from present-day Saudi Arabia to northern England. Known for its strong army and its discipline, Rome conquered and controlled many new lands. For a long time, the people from these different lands lived together in the Roman Empire without fighting. This was called the *Pax Romana*: the Roman peace.

The Roman Empire is also known for the many advanced and handy things they created. For example, they made very long, straight roads so people could travel easily. They also made heated floors in some houses and baths, and they had running water in cities from **Roman aqueducts**. If you were part of the Roman Empire, you would probably get a nice public bath, a place to exercise, and some fun festivals and sports events to attend.

Part of the reason for the Roman Empire's

● ● ●

success was due to education. Many people could use the Latin language to talk to each other. Learning was even important for children in ancient Rome. Boys were taught reading, writing, and basic math by their fathers or tutors. Girls were usually taught how to run a home by their mothers. Children as young as six years old worked! Some worked in trades such as pottery or metalworking. Children also played games like marbles and spinning tops. They even enjoyed watching theatre and chariot races.

Over time, the empire became so large that it was hard to govern. The rulers of the empire were not always good people or good leaders. There was fighting within the empire, and in AD 395, it split into two: the Eastern Roman Empire and the Western Roman Empire. The Eastern Roman Empire continued on for more than 1,000 years and became the Byzantine Empire. The Western Roman Empire only lasted for 80 years after this split.

Roman Forum

The Roman Forum is a large open space in the city of Rome, **Italy**. It was the center of business and politics in ancient Rome, and it was surrounded by many of the most important buildings at that time.

The Forum was originally a marketplace where people would go to buy and sell food and other goods. It also became the place to make a speech, have a parade to celebrate when the Roman army won a battle, hold trials for criminals, and even watch some gladiator matches.

In the middle of the Forum is a stone called the *Rostra*, which speakers stood on to deliver important messages. Mark Antony, a general, stood on this stone to deliver a famous speech at **Julius Caesar's** funeral. (When you are older, you might read **Shakespeare**'s version of this speech in the play *Julius Caesar*.)

Around the Forum, you can still see the ruins of many important ancient buildings. You can find many beautiful temples, a courthouse, the Senate house, and offices for public officials. There is a mysterious old shrine protecting a black stone called the *Lapis Niger* that is so old even the ancient Romans did not remember why it was important! There is also a triumphal arch—a beautiful carved stone arch that generals would march through after winning a victory for Rome.

Today, if you walk through the Roman Forum, you will have to imagine the market booths with all their smells and sounds. But do you know what you won't have to imagine? Hundreds of people packed into the Forum, as they were in ancient Rome! About 4.5 million tourists visit the Forum every year. Can you imagine all those tourists wearing white robes, like the togas ancient Romans used to wear?

Rough-Skinned Green Tree Frog

The rough-skinned green tree frog is a small frog found in **Peru** and nearby countries in **South America**. It is also called the Demerara Falls tree frog.

This frog is small enough to sit in your hand and still leave some space for its friend. You can tell it apart from other frogs by checking if it has blue circles around its eyes. If you gently rub your finger down its back, you'll discover why it has its name: its skin will feel rough and bumpy. If you hold the frog up to the sun, you may notice that you can see inside the frog! This is because the frog's skin is partly see-through. That's how it got its other nickname, glass frog. Its skin is almost as crystal-clear as glass.

Try to guess where rough-skinned green tree frogs like to live. If you guessed trees, you'd be right! However, they also enjoy moist, tropical places that have plenty of water, like forests, swamps, **rivers**, and freshwater **marshes**. They like to eat insects, and they are hunted by snakes, birds, and larger frogs. When they are young, they also have to watch out for fish. At night, especially near **lakes** or other bodies of water, you may hear the males make a kind of chirping sound. The best time to hear them is during the summer rainy season in South America, from December to March.

Royal Canadian Mounted Police (Mounties)

The Royal Canadian Mounted Police, also known as Mounties, is the national police force of **Canada**. Their name comes from the fact that they used to do their job mounted on horses!

The Mounties began in 1920. At that time, a horse was one of the best ways to travel. There were cars in 1920, but they weren't as reliable or affordable as they are today. Also, what happens if you're chasing a criminal and your car breaks down or the criminal runs through fields with no road? Sometimes a horse is the best way to go!

Mounties have done a lot of important things throughout Canada's history, including going undercover in the Mafia (a criminal organization) to catch criminals. Traditionally, Mounties have done many different jobs. You can find Mounties everywhere in Canada except the **provinces** of Ontario and **Quebec**, which have their own police forces.

Today, Mounties are similar to police officers in the United States. Mounties carry pistols and make sure people are safe and following the law. They drive ordinary cars, except when there is a big parade. Then, you can see Mounties in their traditional uniforms riding their horses. The Mounties have a special farm where they breed beautiful black horses! In 1939, the Mounties started breeding black horses because the black looks nice next to their red uniforms.

Every year, some Mounties who are specially trained tour Canada and beyond on what is called the Musical Ride. The Musical Ride is a horse show with music where the Mounties show off their riding skills and horses.

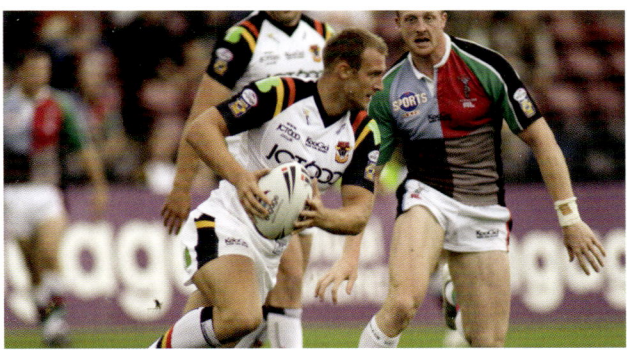

Rugby

Rugby is a sport very similar to football that began in England, part of the **United Kingdom**. It is named after the Rugby School in Rugby, England, where it started.

Legend says that in 1823, a student at the Rugby School playing soccer decided to run toward the goal carrying the ball instead of kicking it. This change to the game became popular, and it became one of the official rules of rugby.

Rugby is played on an outdoor field by two teams of 13 or 15 people. It uses an oval ball, like an American football. The players' goal is to get more points than the other team during the 80-minute game. Players earn points by scoring tries (getting the ball into the goal area) or kicking goals. The field has H-shaped goals at each end, and a goal is scored by throwing or kicking the ball through the top of the H.

There are different kinds of rugby with slightly different rules. Rugby union is the most popular form, and it is the national sport in New Zealand, Wales, Fiji, Samoa, Tonga, and Madagascar. Rugby league is very popular in England, **Australia**, Ireland, and New Zealand. The Rugby World Cup, the rugby union international tournament, is a major sporting event that happens every four years.

Ruins of Saint Paul's

The Ruins of St. Paul's are in Macau, a tiny region on the coast of **China**. Jesuit missionaries built a college there in 1594 called St. Paul's College. In 1637, they built a church for the college called the Church of St. Paul, which was also known as *Mater Dei*, the church of the "Mother of God."

The church was made in a style that is partly European and partly Asian. The facade (front wall) is covered with beautiful statues and stone carvings made by Japanese Christians. This was because Christians had been banned from Japan, and many skilled Japanese Christian craftsmen took refuge in Macau, where they helped to build the church. In 1835, the college and church were both destroyed in a fire that started during a **typhoon**. Today, only the front wall of the church with all of the carvings is standing. It is called the Ruins of St. Paul's.

St. Paul's College was founded by Father Alessandro Valignano, who was in charge of the Jesuit missions in **Asia**. The college was very important because it was the first place where missionaries could go to learn Chinese. (One of the missionaries who studied there was **Ven. Matteo Ricci**.) St. Paul's was also the largest seminary in eastern Asia. It was sometimes called "a seminary of martyrs" because of the brave Christians who gave their lives for Christ. The relics of many Japanese and **Vietnamese martyrs** can still be seen at the Ruins of St. Paul's. They are kept in a special underground room called a crypt.

Sagrada Família

Sagrada Família is a magnificent Catholic church in Barcelona, **Spain**. *Sagrada Família* means "Holy Family" in Spanish. The church is 300 feet long and 200 feet wide, and it can seat 9,000 people. It has 18 spires that represent Jesus, Mary, the four Evangelists, and the twelve apostles. When completed, the tallest spire will be a towering 560 feet tall, making it the tallest church building in the world.

Construction on the church began in 1882. It was designed by architect Antoni Gaudí. He worked on the church until he died in 1926. Gaudí is actually buried in a crypt inside the church. The Spanish Civil War in 1936 slowed construction. There was even a fire that destroyed some of the original building plans. It has taken a long time to build this church, but it is supposed to be finished soon.

The design of Sagrada Família is inspired by two art styles. The first is Gothic architecture, which uses pointed arches and many beautiful decorations. The second style is Art Nouveau, which is a decorative style inspired by flowers and plants. You can see this style in the tall spires and the extremely detailed designs inside and outside the church. The stone carvings on the outside of the church show the Nativity, the Passion, and the Glory (the soul's final journey to God). The inside of the church has tall columns that are made to look like trees and branches. It also has brightly colored stained glass windows that make the church glow with color.

More than three million people visit Sagrada Família every year. It is one of the most visited sites in Spain.

Sahara Desert

The Sahara Desert, one of the world's largest **deserts**, is in North **Africa**. It is almost as large as the whole United States! The weather is hot and windy with very little rain. In the summer, it gets very hot. At night, it can get very cold very quickly.

In the Sahara, there are 500-foot **dunes**. There are sand "seas" filled with sand and flat **plains** covered with sand and gravel. The northern part, which is closer to the **Mediterranean Sea**, has some grasslands and small plants. The plants grow low to the ground, have long roots that search for water, and store water in their thick stems. The middle of the desert is very dry and has few plants. The southern part is a **plain** that has no trees.

Many animals call this desert home, including antelopes, **gazelles**, **cheetahs**, fennec foxes, **camels**, lizards, cobras, raptors, **ostriches**, scorpions, ants, and beetles. Some of these animals can go for a long time without water.

People called nomads have lived in the Sahara Desert for a long time, living in tents and moving around to find water. People used camels to carry things to trade, such as gold, salt, cloth, and ivory. Today, about 2 million people live in the Sahara Desert, not counting the people in the **Nile River** Valley. Some are nomads, and some live in cities near the Atlantic Ocean.

Fun Facts:

- *Sahara* is the Arabic word for "desert."
- Eleven different countries are a part of the Sahara desert.
- Emi Koussi, an extinct **volcano** in Chad, is the highest point in the desert with an **elevation** of over 11,000 feet.

Saint Alberto Hurtado

St. Alberto Hurtado was a **South American**

priest from Chile. He was born in 1901 and died in 1952. He is called Father Hurtado not only because he was a priest, but also because he was a true father to everyone who came to him—and to everyone he went to.

Alberto and his brother had loving parents and lived in a nice house with plenty of food. But when Alberto was four years old, their father died. They were sad and missed him very much. Then, the small family also lost all their money and became very poor. But God brought good from it.

Alberto learned what it was like to not have all he needed or wanted. So when he became a Jesuit priest, he opened a home for poor children called the Home of Christ. He bought a green truck and would go around the streets finding children who needed a place to sleep and food to eat. Hundreds of thousands of children were helped, all because Father Hurtado knew what it felt like to be in need.

Fr. Hurtado spent many years studying. He was actually a lawyer before becoming a priest. He used his knowledge to defend workers who were not being treated well. He even wrote books and articles about Catholic social teaching, something you will learn about in high school.

Wherever he went, Fr. Hurtado brought joy with his warm smile. Do you know where he got this joy? From his devotion to Jesus and the Blessed Mother. He was heard to say, "I am happy, Lord, I am happy," even while he was dying from cancer. St. Alberto Hurtado's feast day is celebrated on August 18.

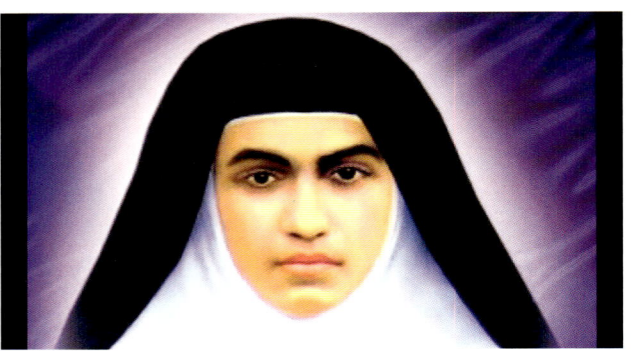

Saint Alphonsa of the Immaculate Conception

St. Alphonsa of the Immaculate Conception was a Poor Clare sister from Kerala, **India**. She lived from 1910–1946. St. Alphonsa is a special saint because she is the first Indian woman to be canonized.

Before becoming a sister, Alphonsa's name was Annakutty. Annakutty never knew her mother because she died when Annakutty was still a baby. She had four older brothers and sisters. They learned their catechism and lives of the saints from their grandmother. At age five, Annakutty could lead the family in their evening prayers. Maybe you can do that too?

Her aunt taught her how to be a good housewife so she could be married. But Annakutty did not want to get married. Since her First Communion, she was sure that Jesus wanted her to be a religious sister. Around this time, an accident happened and she burned her feet badly, which left her disabled for the rest of her life.

When she was 17, Annakutty entered the Franciscan Clarist Congregation. Then she was called Sr. Alphonsa and became a schoolteacher. But she suffered many serious illnesses, and most of the time, she was too sick to teach her students.

One night, a thief came to the convent and stumbled into her room. It shocked and surprised Sr. Alphonsa so much that she lost her memory for a whole year! She couldn't even remember how to read or write, although she had had beautiful handwriting before.

When Alphonsa was 35 years old, a painful tumor spread all through her body. One of her favorite saints was St. Thérèse of Lisieux, who had just been canonized. Sr. Alphonsa offered all of her pain to Jesus, just like St. Thérèse did. She died on July 28, which is the day we celebrate her feast.

Saint Amandina

St. Amandina of Schakkebroek was a missionary who lived from 1872–1900. She was one of the **Chinese Martyrs** who were killed for being Christians. St. Amandina came from the country of Belgium in **Europe**. I know you can find **China** on your map, but can you find Belgium? Hint: look near **France**.

Sr. Amandina's baptismal name was Pauline. Her family was not wealthy, but they were blessed with nine beautiful children. Pauline's mother died when she was only seven years old. This changed Pauline's life. The family had

to move, and she was taken care of by a kind neighbor.

When one of Pauline's sisters went to **India** as a missionary, she decided that she wanted to become a missionary too. She joined the Franciscan Missionaries of Mary and took the name Sr. Marie Amandina.

Did you know that **St. Francis** was a very joyful saint? Amandina, now a Franciscan, was just like him. She was always singing and full of joy. Before being sent to China, she was a nurse in France. Her joy made her sick patients happier.

In China, the people there called Amandina "the sister who is always singing." She helped put smiles on 200 orphans' faces and took care of the sick in their little hospital.

Later, she and many others were put into prison for believing in Jesus. But she kept smiling and singing. This helped the other prisoners to be brave. Sr. Marie Amandina was martyred at age 28. We celebrate her feast day on July 9.

Saint André Bessette

St. André Bessette was a religious brother who lived in Montreal, **Canada**. He had a strong devotion to St. Joseph, who was his close guide and friend throughout his 91 years. Brother André is perhaps best known for founding **St. Joseph's Oratory of Mount Royal** and the miraculous cures obtained through his intercession.

Alfred Bessette was born in 1845 in **Quebec**, Canada. He was 9 years old when his father died in a logging accident and 12 years old when his mother died of tuberculosis. From that time on, Alfred lived with relatives and had to work, which kept him from going to school.

Alfred joined the Congregation of Holy Cross at age 25 and took the name Brother André. Because he was not well educated, he was given the job of being the doorkeeper of Notre Dame College. He always greeted visitors with great kindness, took care of their needs, and prayed for them. In 1904, St. Joseph's Oratory was completed. Brother André became the caretaker of this shrine to his favorite saint.

Brother André suffered from poor health and stomach problems all his life. This helped him to show compassion toward the thousands of sick people who came to him for healing. Today, people still receive the grace of healings through his intercession. The Oratory of St. Joseph is now a basilica that attracts over two million visitors a year. St. André Bessette's feast day is celebrated on January 6.

Saint Anthony of Padua

St. Anthony of Padua is one of the most popular saints in the Catholic Church. He was a Franciscan priest in **Italy** with a brilliant mind and the gift of preaching. People often pray for his intercession when they have lost something.

He was born in 1195 and given the name Fernando at baptism. Fernando was raised in a rich family in Lisbon, Portugal. When he was only 15 years old, he felt that he could serve God best by giving up the life of a rich person and becoming an Augustinian monk. His relatives and friends made it difficult, though. They would visit him so much that he was not able to pray or study well. So Fernando asked to be sent away to a different city where he would not be so distracted.

After 10 years, Fernando decided to leave the Augustinian order and instead join the order of St. Francis of Assisi, the Order of Friars Minor. Fernando then took the name Anthony. He longed with all his heart to die for Jesus, so he was sent to preach in the land of the Saracens in Morocco, **Africa**. But before he could begin sharing God's Word, Anthony became very sick and had to leave Morocco as soon as he was able. This was a hard thing for Anthony to accept, but he trusted that God had better plans for him.

When **St. Francis** discovered that Anthony was so well educated, he gave him the task of teaching the other friars. After a time of teaching, he began preaching in Padua, Italy. It was there that God began working many miracles through him, and people flocked to hear him preach.

A serious illness caused Anthony's early death. He was only 35 years old and was canonized the following year. In 1946, he was proclaimed a Doctor of the Church. His feast day is June 13.

Saint Anthony the Great

St. Anthony the Great is an important Christian saint who lived in Egypt in the third and fourth centuries AD. He is often called St. Anthony of the Desert or St. Anthony of Egypt. He is also known as the father of Christian monasticism. This is because he spent most of his life as a hermit, which is someone who gives away most of his things, never marries, and lives by himself away from other people in order to pray without distractions.

When he was 20 years old, St. Anthony was inspired by the words of the Gospel to "go and sell all you have." He became a hermit and lived in a **cave** outside his village. Stories about St. Anthony's life say that he received many temptations there and fought with demons in the shape of wild animals.

Later in life, St. Anthony went even deeper into the wilderness, and no one saw him for 20 years. Other people were inspired by St. Anthony's dedication to God, and other hermits came to him, asking him to teach them. St. Anthony became one of the first people to lead a group of hermits, teaching them to live holy lives as well. These hermits lived alone in little huts in the wilderness and only came together for Mass.

St. Anthony had a gentle and cheerful nature and many virtues. He died around AD 356 and became known as the father of Christian monasticism because of the way he lived his life. Many monks, hermits, and other religious people have learned from his example. His feast day is January 17.

Saint Athanasius

Has anyone ever lied to you? Did it upset you? If your answer is yes, you have something in common with St. Athanasius, a bishop of the early Church in **Africa**, who was also lied to. The liar was Emperor Constantine, who told lies about Jesus, saying that Jesus wasn't God!

Even worse, he wanted Athanasius to lie about Jesus too! Athanasius refused to lie and instead ran into the **desert** so that he could pray and write the truth about Jesus. He gives us a good example of turning away from people tempting us to sin and instead choosing to pray and do something good.

Athanasius wasn't the only holy person in the wilderness. **St. Anthony the Great**, a hermit, fought the devil in the desert. Anthony was a real hero! Athanasius wanted to make sure that everyone knew the inspiring story of how Anthony fought for Jesus, and so he wrote a book, *The Life of St. Anthony*. People loved the story. Lots of people still read it today.

Athanasius wrote lots of other good books, so many that he became a Church Father. This is a special way of saying he helped a lot of people. All of his books told the truth about Jesus and the people who followed Him. Because Athanasius loved Jesus so much, many people came to know the truth that Jesus is God and that He became a man because He loves us.

We celebrate his feast day on May 2.

Saint Auguste Chapdelaine

St. Auguste Chapdelaine was born in 1814 and

was raised on a farm in **France**. Auguste was one of nine children. He left school early to work on the family farm. Because he was very strong, he was able to work hard.

Auguste began thinking about becoming a priest. His parents wanted him to keep helping on the farm, so they did not encourage him. But later, his parents understood that it was more important for Auguste to be a priest. They let him leave the farm to study for the priesthood.

After many years of studying, Fr. Auguste was ordained a priest and became a missionary. When he was sent to **China**, he traveled from France to Singapore, then from Singapore to the Guangxi **province** in southern China. It was a long, hard journey. He was even robbed once by bandits!

At the time, it was very dangerous to be a missionary in China. The Chinese rulers did not want their people to learn about God. Fr. Auguste was thrown into prison only 10 days after he got there! After his time in prison, he spent the next two years baptizing hundreds of people. But he had to be careful not to get arrested again.

Soon, Fr. Auguste was captured with some other Catholics. He was treated very badly for teaching people about God. After terrible suffering, he died in 1856 and is now one of the 120 **Chinese Martyrs** whose feast day is July 9.

● ● ●

Saint Augustine

St. Augustine lived in North **Africa**. As a young man, he liked to brag, show off, and think only about himself. However, holy people such as his mother, **St. Monica**, and the great preacher St. Ambrose helped him realize he needed to stop being so selfish and instead follow Jesus. It was so hard to be good after being so bad! But by God's grace, he did turn away from sin and follow Jesus. He even became a bishop. He wrote his life story, *Confessions*, to show how God helped him to change his life.

As bishop, St. Augustine wrote a lot of other books too, many of them about his new faith. He really wanted to understand it well! He even wrote a book about God as Trinity: Father, Son, and Holy Spirit. According to a legend, as he was writing it, he took a walk along the seaside. He saw a little boy scooping up water from the **sea** and dropping it in a hole on the beach. The boy was trying to move the whole sea into the hole! When St. Augustine told him he could never move the whole sea, the boy looked at him and said that St. Augustine would never be able to understand everything about the Trinity either, and then he disappeared. St. Augustine realized that the child was Jesus and that the message for him was to be humble when writing about the mysteries of God. He finished his book on the

Trinity with great humility, as the riches of God are far deeper than the deepest sea.

We celebrate St. Augustine's feast day on August 28.

Saint Augustine of Canterbury

St. Augustine of Canterbury was an archbishop who we call the Apostle to the English. Usually, "apostle" means someone who followed Christ while he lived on earth, but someone who teaches others about Jesus for the first time is also called an apostle. In the sixth century AD, Augustine taught the pagans in England, now the **United Kingdom**, about Jesus. A pagan is one who believes in many different gods.

Nobody knows what Augustine's childhood was like. We don't even know who his parents were or the year he was born. But we do know that he came from Rome, **Italy**.

When Augustine was a young man, he became a monk in the Benedictine order. The abbot (the monk in charge of a monastery) was Pope Gregory the Great. Because he was busy, he put Augustine in charge of the monks.

Some years later, Pope Gregory decided it was time to evangelize England. He wanted its people to know about God and turn away from their pagan ways. But he could not go himself—he needed to stay in Rome. He knew he had to send someone who could be in charge of a mission like this.

Who do you think he sent to England? You're right, it was Augustine! Off Augustine went with 40 other monks to bring the Gospel of Jesus Christ to the pagans. They were welcomed in Kent by the king of the **Anglo-Saxons**, Aethelberht, and his Catholic wife, Bertha. Soon, the king was baptized, and thousands of pagans in his kingdom followed his example.

Now as the Archbishop of Canterbury, Augustine replaced the pagan temples with Catholic churches. He replaced pagan feast days with feasts of Christian martyrs, and now he has his own feast day, May 27.

Saint Basil's Cathedral

In the center of Moscow, Russia, there is a famous city square called the Red Square. At one end of the Red Square is a colorful church called St. Basil's Cathedral. This church is part of the Eastern Orthodox Church. Eastern Orthodoxy is a form of Christianity common in Russia, Ukraine, Greece, and other countries in eastern **Europe**.

St. Basil's Cathedral was built in 1555 when Ivan the Terrible was the *czar*, or ruler, of Russia. The church was dedicated to the Intercession of Most Holy Theotokos, so sometimes it is just called Intercession Church. (*Theotokos* is the Orthodox name for the Blessed Virgin Mary.)

Later, a saint named Basil Fool for Christ was buried in the church, which is how it became known as St. Basil's Cathedral. In the 1600s, the church was made larger and the bright colors were added to the outside.

St. Basil's Cathedral is actually a group of eight tiny chapels around a center church, which was supposed to remind people of the Heavenly Jerusalem. Each of these nine chapels is topped by an onion dome. An onion dome is a special roof that has a bulging shape and comes to a point, like an onion or garlic. Some say the onion domes make the church look like a giant bonfire. What do you think?

Saint Benedict and Saint Scholastica

St. Benedict and St. Scholastica were brother and sister (possibly even twins) born in **Italy** around AD 480. They were both devoted to God from a very young age.

Benedict is most well-known for *The Rule of St. Benedict*, which is a set of guidelines he wrote for his monks to follow. The motto of *ora et labora*, meaning "pray and work," still guides Benedictine monks today. They devote about eight hours each to prayer, sleep, and work (manual work, acts of charity, and sacred reading). Do you think you could follow a rule like this in your life?

Benedict founded 12 communities for monks in Lazio, Italy, but then he moved to the rocky **mountains** of **Monte Cassino**. It was here that Scholastica founded the first convent of Benedictine nuns.

In one famous story about the siblings, Benedict visited Scholastica. The two spent all day worshiping God and discussing the Bible and the Catholic Faith. When it was time for Benedict to go home, Scholastica asked him to stay. Benedict refused, as he was trying to follow his own rule (can you remember his rule?). Scholastica prayed, and then a strong storm began that made travel impossible. Benedict said, "What have you done?" and she replied, "I asked you and you would not listen. So I asked my God and He did listen." Three days later, Benedict saw his sister's soul leaving earth and rising to Heaven in the form of a white dove.

St. Scholastica is the patron saint of Benedictines, education, children, and protection against storms and rain. Her feast day is February 10.

St. Benedict is the patron saint of many, including farmers, monks, students, and the dying. His feast day is July 11.

Saint Bernard Dogs

St. Bernard dogs are large dogs that are gentle, loyal, and friendly. About 1,000 years ago, they were bred to rescue people who were lost in the snowy **mountains** of the **Alps**. Their keen sense of smell made them the perfect search and rescue animal.

Between Switzerland and **Italy**, there is a place for travelers to stay named Great St. Bernard Hospice. It was built to house people who were making their way on foot over the Great St. Bernard Pass in the western Alps. Many of them were pilgrims on their way to Rome or the Holy Land. The pass, the hospice, and the dogs were named for St. Bernard of Montjoux, a tenth-century missionary and founder of the hospice.

The most famous St. Bernard dog to save people at the pass was named Barry, who saved between 40 and 100 lives. Another famous dog was named Rutor, the faithful companion of Abbot Pierre Chanoux. The classic St. Bernard dog looked very different from St. Bernards you can see today. They were smaller in size, more like a German Shepherd dog. St. Bernards are larger dogs now because they were bred with Newfoundland dogs.

Today, St. Bernard dogs are no longer used for rescues in the Alps. Roads and tunnels keep travelers from getting lost. When the roads are covered in snow, the pass can be crossed by airplane!

Saint Charles de Foucauld

St. Charles de Foucauld was born in **France** in 1858. His parents died when he was young, and his grandfather raised him from the age of six. Like many children, Charles loved reading and learning new things. He had always loved God, but sadly, as a teenager, he stopped living a Christian life.

After becoming a soldier and spending years as a military officer, Charles decided to leave the military and travel in the country of Morocco in **Africa** for several years. Europeans were forbidden to go there at that time, so this was a dangerous trip. Charles had to disguise himself as he traveled. He wrote many note-books about his experiences there. Afterward, he returned to France and worked on publishing a book about his adventures. It was then that he started to feel God speaking quietly to his heart. After a few years, Charles knew God was calling him to become a monk. He joined the Trappists in 1890 and was ordained as a priest in 1901.

Charles was sent to Nazareth to serve a group of Poor Clare nuns. After that, he was sent to Algeria in North Africa. It was there that he learned about the horrors of slavery, and he made sure to care for slaves, the poor, the sick, and anyone in need. He spent much of his time in prayer and adoration of the Blessed Sacrament and made it his life's mission to show the love of Jesus to each person he met. Charles was killed by bandits on December 1, 1916. His feast day is December 1.

Saint Charles Lwanga

St. Charles Lwanga is a saint who was martyred as a young man in **Africa**. Missionary priests brought the Catholic Faith to his village and baptized him. Charles was so happy to belong to God. He told everyone about the true God and how they could become Christians too.

Charles was the head servant to King Mwanga. He was in charge of the king's other servants. Sadly, this king did not believe in God and did not want to obey God's laws. Instead, he beat people who angered him and arrested and killed Christians.

Most of the king's servants believed in God and did not want to disobey His laws. The king would get very angry at them, but Charles protected the other servants. Some were only 13 years old. Charles was like a big brother to these young servants.

King Mwanga did not like his servants obeying God instead of him. So he ordered the death of every servant who would not give up his belief in Jesus Christ. Charles and 25 other Christians refused. They were tied up and marched for long miles to a place where they were to be killed. Charles was burned alive on June 3, 1886. He was 26 years old. Every year, the Church celebrates St. Charles and his companions' feast day on June 3.

Saint Devasahayam

St. Devasahayam was the first layman (non-ordained church member) from **India** to be martyred. He lived from 1712–1752. He was from the Kingdom of Travancore, which used to be located at the southern tip of India.

Before Devasahayam became Catholic, his name was Nilam. His family was very wealthy. Just like other boys in the kingdom, he was taught to fight and use weapons. As a young man, he joined the king's army. The king thought highly of him.

Devasahayam had a good friend whose name was Eustache De Lannoy. They talked together about many different things. One day, Eustache noticed that Devasahayam was sad and worried. Devasahayam told him that he was having a lot of bad luck. Eustache was Catholic, so he told Devasahayam about God. He told him the story of Job from the Bible. After that, Devasahayam was curious about Catholicism.

Devasahayam grew to love Catholicism and was baptized with the name Devasahayam, which is the name Lazarus in the local language. (Lazarus means "Help of God.") Devasahayam told his wife about God, and she was baptized, too. She was his first convert.

Devasahayam's conversion from Hinduism to Christianity made everyone very angry, especially the king. People thought Devasahayam was dangerous to the kingdom. The king said that if he didn't deny his faith, he would be put in prison and killed.

Devasahayam did not give up his faith. He was chained and imprisoned for three years, and finally he was killed. We celebrate his feast day on January 14.

Saint Dominic

St. Dominic was born in **Spain** around the year 1170. At age 14, he was sent to a monastery to study, and he continued studying the arts and theology for another 10 years.

In 1191, a famine was causing much suffering in Spain. Dominic gave away his money and sold almost all of his possessions (even his favorite books!) to feed people who were starving.

At the age of 24, Dominic was ordained as a priest. In 1215, Dominic and six others founded a house that would include education and monastic rules. The next year, Dominic was given permission by Pope Honorius III to form the Order of Preachers, also called the Dominican Order. The Dominican Order is made up of priests, cloistered nuns (nuns who do not leave their convent but work and pray behind its walls), sisters, and friars. There is also a special order for laypeople (those not called to religious life). The four pillars, or main guides, of Dominican life are prayer, study, community, and preaching. This is lived out through preaching the Gospel, working in parishes, teaching, and social work.

Dominic had a special devotion to the Blessed Virgin Mary. He had a vision of her in which she gave him the Rosary. From then on, he told everyone about the Rosary, as did his fellow priests. The Rosary is one of the most well-known devotions in the Catholic Faith, and it is at the heart of the Dominican order. Do you know how to pray the Rosary?

St. Dominic was a mystic (someone to whom God gives special visions). He is the patron saint of astronomers (scientists who study stars and planets) and natural scientists. His feast day is August 8.

Saint Edmund Campion

St. Edmund Campion was a Jesuit priest who was martyred in England, now the **United Kingdom**. He lived from 1540–1581. In his day, there were no Catholic schools or churches in England. Catholics had to practice their faith in secret.

Edmund was born in London. He was an excellent student and became very well educated. Eventually, he taught at the University of Oxford, a world-famous college in Oxford, England.

Edmund could have done many important jobs. He was even honored by the queen of England! But in his hours of prayer, he felt God was calling him to become a Catholic priest. He knew that meant he would have to leave the country because there weren't any Catholic seminaries in England. So he said goodbye to the country he loved and left for **France**.

Eight years later, Fr. Edmund secretly returned to England as a Catholic priest. The joyful news spread that a priest had come to bring the sacraments. He was the shepherd the hungry sheep had been praying for!

Fr. Edmund had to be careful, though. Priest hunters were trying to catch him. Sometimes he had to disguise himself or hide in what was called a priest hole. It was a secret place inside someone's home made for a priest to hide in.

Later, Fr. Edmund was arrested by a spy. He was taken to the **Tower of London** and imprisoned for over four months, then put on trial and killed. St. Edmund Campion's feast day is celebrated on December 1.

Saint Elizabeth of Hungary

St. Elizabeth of Hungary, also known as St. Elizabeth of Thuringia, was born in 1207 to the king of Hungary, a country in **Europe**. As a child, St. Elizabeth loved God dearly and prayed to Him often. When she grew up, she married Louis IV, the new ruler of Thuringia. St. Elizabeth and Louis were very happy and had three children.

St. Elizabeth loved helping the poor and the sick. When Louis was away, St. Elizabeth would visit the villagers to bring them food, clothing, and other things they needed. When there was a plague (a sickness that many people catch at the same time), she built a hospital next to the castle and cared for the sick herself. When Louis returned, he was happy his wife acted unselfishly and cared for their people so well.

Unfortunately, Louis died when St. Elizabeth was only 20 years old. This made her very sad, but she never stopped trusting God and continued to care for the poor. After Louis' death, she met **St. Francis** of Assisi and became one of the first Franciscan Tertiaries. This means that she joined the Third Order of St. Francis, which is made up of laypeople who follow the example of St. Francis. After making sure her children were looked after, St. Elizabeth gave away most of her money. She spent the rest of her life taking care of the sick.

St. Elizabeth died when she was only 24 years old. Despite dying so young, she cared for many people and changed many lives. She is considered the patron saint of bakers, beggars, charity, and more. Her feast day is November 17.

Saint Frances Cabrini

St. Frances Cabrini founded a religious order of sisters to help poor Italian immigrants in **North America**. Immigrants are people who have left their homes to find a better life in another country. In her 67 years, she helped to start a total of 67 orphanages, schools, and hospitals.

They spread across the **continents** of **Europe** and North and **South America**.

Frances was the thirteenth child born to her farming parents in 1850. She and her family lived in **Italy**. She did very well in school, getting excellent grades. Frances tried to join two different religious orders, but they would not let her because of her poor health. She didn't give up but bravely kept praying and seeking God's will.

At age 24, she was asked to take charge of an orphanage. She had the heart of a mother, so she was very willing. Soon, other young women joined her work, and the bishop asked them to form a new religious order. That is how the Missionary Sisters of the Sacred Heart of Jesus was founded.

After many years of caring for the poor in Italy, she asked the pope to allow her to serve in **China**. This had been her dream since she was a girl. But he wanted her to go west to help the Italian immigrants in the United States. Wanting only to do God's will, she did as the pope asked.

For the next 28 years, Mother Frances Cabrini served the poor and orphaned from New York to California, back to Europe in **France** and **Spain**, in Nicaragua in North America, and across the **Andes** to Brazil and Argentina in South America. Everywhere she went, she spread the love of Jesus' Sacred Heart. The Church in the United States celebrates her feast day on November 13.

Saint Francis and Saint Clare

St. Francis and St. Clare were both born in Assisi, **Italy**. They are wonderful examples of how to become holy.

Born in 1181 or 1182, Francis' given name was Giovanni di Pietro di Bernardone. After a wild life as a young soldier, Francis was eventually inspired to become a friar. From then on, he lived a life of poverty. He founded the men's Order of Friars Minor, the women's Order of St. Clare with St. Clare, the Third Order of St. Francis, and the Custody of the Holy Land.

In 1223 in Greccio, Italy, Francis arranged the first nativity scene as part of a Christmas celebration. His love for animals makes him a popular patron of animal lovers. Many churches hold ceremonies to bless animals on his feast day of October 4. For several years before he died in 1226, Francis had the *stigmata*, which are the wounds Jesus bore on the cross (bleeding from the hands and feet, wound in the side, and pain from the crown of thorns). He had a great devotion to the Eucharist and is also the patron saint of Italy.

St. Clare of Assisi was named Chiara Offreduccio at her birth in 1194. She became one of St. Francis' first followers. With St. Francis, she began a religious order for women called the

Order of Poor Ladies (after she died, it was re-named the Order of St. Clare or the Poor Clares). She was the first woman to write a rule of life for a community, which details their goals and how to live their lives. Parts of their rule included not wearing shoes, sleeping on the ground, not eating meat, and being almost completely silent.

St. Clare's feast day is August 11. She is the patroness of many people and things, including laundry, workers, television, eye disease, bicycle messengers, and needleworkers.

Saint Francis Xavier

St. Francis Xavier is a saint who was born in 1506 in **Spain**. The son of a powerful noble family, Francis studied at the University of Paris. He was known as a good athlete.

In 1529, a new student, Ignatius, started sharing a room with Francis. Francis began studying theology and became a priest some years later. In 1539, Ignatius, who we know as **St. Ignatius of Loyola**, created guidelines for a new religious order, the Society of Jesus (also known as the Jesuits). The new order was approved by Pope Paul III the next year. Francis helped to start the order. He was one of the first seven Jesuits who took vows.

Several Jesuits were to go to the East Indies in **Asia** to teach people about Jesus. At the last moment, one of them became seriously ill and could not go. Ignatius asked Francis to go instead. Though he became a missionary because of what appeared to be an accident, it quickly became clear he was meant for missionary work.

Over his years of travels to **India**, Japan, and beyond, Francis encountered many difficulties and hardships, but he never gave up. He helped build almost 40 churches in India and converted many people to Catholicism throughout Asia.

St. Francis Xavier is considered one of the greatest missionaries since St. Paul the Apostle. Along with St. Thérèse of Lisieux, he was named co-patron of all foreign missions by Pope Pius XI in 1927. St. Francis Xavier's feast day is December 3.

Saint Francisco Solano

St. Francisco Solano was a brave missionary priest who lived over 400 years ago. He spent 20 years in what is now Argentina, Bolivia, and Paraguay in **South America**. He showed thousands of people the way to God and His Church.

Francisco was born into a noble family in

Spain. They taught Francisco to pray well and do his best at school. After his years of schooling, he decided to give his life to God by becoming a Franciscan friar.

He had a special gift of reaching people's hearts by his preaching, and he was loved by all. When he prayed for people to be healed, many were cured. Soon, everyone began calling him a wonderworker. He did not like people giving him the attention that they should be giving to God, the true Wonderworker. He decided to ask to be sent on a mission to North Africa.

At that time, missionaries were being killed in North Africa for teaching people about Jesus. Father Francisco had a strong desire to go there, but missionaries were needed in the New World, so he was sent to South America instead. He did not complain but prepared for the long journey by ship and learned the language of the natives in a very short time.

Father Francisco was once again loved by all the people. He preached the love of God with kindness and even cheered the sick by playing the violin for them. After 20 years, he was sent to Lima, Peru, where he died in 1610. His feast day is celebrated on July 14.

Magenta, Italy. She was a pediatrician, which is a doctor who takes care of children.

Gianna and her husband, Pietro, had four children: Pierluigi, Mariolina, Laura, and Gianna Emanuela. Sadly, Mariolina died at the age of six, but as of 2025, Gianna's other children are all still alive!

When she was pregnant with her daughter Gianna Emanuela, Gianna developed a health problem that was dangerous for both her and her unborn baby. The doctors wanted to perform a surgery that would save Gianna's life, but it meant that her baby would die.

The Molla family knew that they would never have a surgery that would cause the death of their baby. Instead, they asked the doctors to perform a different type of surgery. This surgery would not injure their unborn baby, but they knew that it might not make Gianna well. Gianna told her doctors that her unborn child's life was more important than her own. On Holy Saturday, 1962, Gianna's baby Gianna Emanuela was born. Sadly, Gianna died one week later.

Gianna Emanuela became a doctor, just like her mother was. Pietro and his children were all at the ceremony when St. Gianna was canonized in 2004. It was the first time a husband had ever witnessed his wife's canonization.

St. Gianna's courageous actions and love for her unborn baby remind us that life is a beautiful gift from God. She is the patroness of mothers, wives, families, doctors, and unborn babies.

Saint Gianna Molla

St. Gianna Beretta Molla is a modern saint from

Saint Ignatius of Loyola

St. Ignatius of Loyola came from a very rich family. He was even born in a castle, in the year 1491. The castle was in a place called Loyola, which is in the far north of **Spain**.

As a young man, Ignatius was a knight. During the Battle of Pamplona, a cannonball almost killed him. Instead, it went between his legs. Both of his legs were hurt badly. He suffered a lot and had to stay in bed for a long time.

To help pass the time, he wanted to read. Ignatius asked for books, but the ones he asked for were the kind that are not good for people to read. At that time, he was not living for God but for his own glory. By God's grace, there were no books of that kind. So he read what was given to him: the life of Christ and a book about saints' lives.

He compared his life with the lives of the saints. He was ashamed of how he had only been thinking about himself. He knew he needed to change his ways and become the person God created him to be. After his legs were healed, he studied many long years and became a priest. This time, he would be a knight for God's glory!

At that time, there were many lies going around about Jesus Christ and His Church. People needed to be told the truth. Fr. Ignatius,

along with six young men, saw the need and wanted to help. That is how the Society of Jesus (the Jesuit order) was founded. For over 400 years, there have been Jesuit priests all over the world who preach, teach, and care for the sick. St. Ignatius of Loyola's feast day is on July 31.

Saint Isaac Jogues

St. Isaac Jogues was one of the brave **North American Martyrs** in **Canada**. He was a Jesuit priest who sacrificed his life, like Jesus did, to save the souls of his people. His people were the Native American Indian tribes in **North America**. Among those tribes were the Hurons, the Sioux, the Iroquois, and the Mohawks.

Born in Orléans, **France**, in 1607, he joined the Jesuits at age 17. After years of study, he was ordained as a priest and was sent to Canada as a missionary to the Native American Indians. He was 29 years old.

He worked long, hard years with the Hurons and other tribes. They were spread out from **Quebec** to the **Great Lakes**. He was the first missionary to go as far as present-day Sault Ste. Marie, Michigan. He would have gone as far as the headwaters of the Mississippi River to convert the Sioux tribe, but he was captured by the Iroquois. They made him a slave in a Mohawk village in present-day Albany, New

York. But he didn't get discouraged. Instead, he saw this as a chance to convert the Mohawks. He baptized 70 of them before escaping and returning to France.

Did he stay in France where he was finally safe? No, Fr. Isaac Jogues understood that a priest is another Christ, so he chose to do what Christ would have done. He returned to Canada, putting his life in danger again. In present-day Auriesville, New York, he was captured again and killed. Five other priests and two brothers were canonized with him as the North American Martyrs. We celebrate their feast day on October 19.

Saint Joan of Arc

St. Joan of Arc was a young teenager who freed her country, **France**, from being conquered. At that time, France was involved in a long war with England, the **Hundred Years' War**. There was a story going around that said a maid (a young, unmarried woman) would save France. People believed Joan was that maid, so they called her "The Maid of Orléans." (Orléans was one of the cities she set free.)

Joan grew up in the little farming village of Domremy in France. She had three brothers and a sister. As a young girl, she did household chores, spun wool, and helped her father in the fields. Her mother taught her to say her

prayers and to listen to God's voice.

When Joan was 12 or 13, she started having visions of three saints (St. Michael, St. Catherine, and St. Margaret). At first, they encouraged her to grow in holiness. Later, they told her God wanted her to leave her family to lead an army to save France. This was a strange message, wasn't it? Men were soldiers and men led battles, not young women. She was afraid.

But war was raging in France. The city of Orléans was surrounded by enemies—the English and a Germanic tribe known as the Burgundians. So Joan put her trust in God, and He showed her what to do. She was only 16, but she learned to fight and led men to win many battles. With God's help, she drove out the English and Burgundians and saw Charles VII crowned as the king of France.

In 1430, Joan of Arc was captured by the English, put in prison, and then burned at the stake. Her feast day is celebrated on May 30.

Saint John Bosco

St. John Bosco was a priest who lived from 1815–1888 in Turin, **Italy**. He took care of homeless boys in Turin and is called the Father and Teacher of Youth.

John was born in a small village in northern **Italy**. He had two older brothers. His father died when John was just two years old. His mother and brothers worked very hard on a farm. John worked as a shepherd and learned not to be afraid of hard work.

When he was young, he loved watching the traveling circus that visited his village. He learned their tricks and then put on his own shows! He juggled, did magic tricks, walked a tightrope, played the violin, sang songs, and told stories. He liked to use his shows to help people think about God. For example, he would end with a prayer or a hymn.

When he grew up, he became a priest. Fr. John Bosco would play with the boys and teach them their catechism. He taught them that sin is ugly and virtue is beautiful. They often heard him say, "Do the best you can! God and Our Lady will do the rest!"

Later, he began to work with boys who had no homes and nobody to care for them or love them. Father Bosco opened places for them to live and found work for them to do. They were so happy to be loved and cared for.

By the time he died, he was caring for and finding shelter for 800 boys at a time. His feast day is on January 31.

Saint John Fisher

St. John Fisher was a cardinal of the Catholic Church who was martyred with **St. Thomas More** in 1535 for standing up against **King Henry VIII**. His diocese, or the area that he was in charge of, was Rochester, which is east of London, England in what is now the **United Kingdom**.

John was the oldest son of a merchant who sold beautiful cloth, like silks. Sadly, his father died while he was still a young boy. His mother remarried and had more children—nine all together. Throughout his life, John remained close with his family.

John was very smart and was an excellent student. He studied for many years and became a priest and bishop. He wrote a lot of books in his lifetime. He even taught Prince Henry, the future King Henry VIII!

When he was king, Henry VIII wanted to divorce his wife Katherine and marry a different woman named Anne. Bishop Fisher told him that he was not allowed to divorce her. The king was so angry that he decided not to obey the Catholic Church anymore. Henry wrongly married Anne and then told everyone that he was now in charge of the Church in England instead of the pope.

Bishop Fisher was very sad about this, and he was also sad that his fellow bishops agreed with the king. But he bravely refused to agree that King Henry VIII was the head of the English church. The king was angry with him, so he put him in prison. Over a year later, the king had him beheaded. Before his death, the pope made St. John Fisher a cardinal. His feast day is June 22, the same as St. Thomas More's.

Saint John Henry Newman

St. John Henry Newman is a saint from England in the **United Kingdom**. He was born in London in 1801 and died in 1890.

Newman grew up in a Christian family and studied the Bible well. When he was young, he joined the Evangelical movement, which was leading a revival in England. Then he became an Anglican priest (Anglicans are members of the Church of England). He taught at Oxford University, a famous university in England, and studied the Church Fathers. He preached so well that people began traveling from all around to hear him.

In 1833, John became very ill. While he was sick, he had a mystical experience that led him to begin a big change in the English Church. He taught, preached, and wrote essays encouraging this change. His work began a movement of reform (change) known as the Oxford Movement.

John began to believe that the Roman Catholic Church was the truest form of Christianity. He joined the Catholic Church in 1845 and went to study in Rome. He became a Catholic priest in 1847. Then, he returned to England as a religious leader. In 1879, he was ordained as a cardinal by Pope Leo XIII for his services to the Catholic Church, but he asked to remain in England to continue to serve the Church there. It was very unusual for the pope to ordain a cardinal who had never served in Rome, but the pope wanted to show his approval of John.

John was also a writer and poet. He wrote the famous hymn "Lead Kindly Light," and his theological writings were also very important. He is beloved by the English people. He was canonized in 2019, and his feast day is October 9.

Saint John Neumann

St. John Neumann was a bishop in Philadelphia, Pennsylvania who lived from 1811–1860. During that time period, Philadelphia was the second- and then third-largest city in the United States and one of the largest cities in all of **North America**. He is known for starting the first Catholic school system in the United States. He was also the first American man to be declared a saint.

John was born and raised in Bohemia (now Czechia, a country in **Europe**). In school, he loved to read books. His parents thought that one day he could become a doctor or even a priest. After school, he would play the guitar or make pictures with a pantograph—a fun tool to research in your free time!

When he was a young man, he decided to study to become a priest. But after five years, he was told there were already enough priests in Europe. He was sent home.

He was so disappointed. He prayed, asking God what he should do. Maybe God wanted him to be a missionary priest in the United States. Yes! He would go and help the immigrants who needed more priests. He knew eight different languages, so he was just right for the job.

He said goodbye to his beloved family and set off on the long journey to America. Once there, he was ordained as a priest and began teaching catechism, visiting the immigrants, and starting Catholic schools.

Eventually, he became the bishop of Philadelphia. He was a good bishop. He brought sisters to teach in his Catholic schools, wrote catechisms, and stood up for the rights of the immigrants.

Bishop John Neumann died from a stroke at the age of 48. His feast day is on January 5.

Saint John Paul II

Chances are you have heard of St. John Paul II, a modern pope from Poland in **Europe**. He is often called the Mercy Pope for his love and promotion of the message of Divine Mercy. His great love for Mary and the Rosary led to him choosing *Totus Tuus* (meaning "Totally Yours") as his papal motto.

Named Karol Józef Wojtyła, he was born in 1920. As a child, he enjoyed playing soccer and being in theater as an actor and a writer of plays. During World War II, Karol worked many jobs to avoid being sent to Germany because many young Polish men were being forced to join the Nazi army. Karol became a priest in 1946. Twelve years later, he became the youngest bishop in Poland. In 1978, he was chosen to be the pope. He was the first non-Italian pope in 455 years!

St. John Paul II loved to learn and understood 13 languages. He visited 129 countries during his papacy and was the first pope to ever visit the White House. In 1984, he held the first World Youth Day in Rome, a gathering encouraging teenagers and young adults to be faithful to God. Now, World Youth Day is held in a different country each year, and millions of people have attended. Do you think you would like to go to World Youth Day when you are older?

Pope John Paul II was pope for 27 years, the second-longest serving pope in history. In the years close to his death, he suffered from Parkinson's disease and had many struggles, yet he always pointed to God's mercy and goodness. He spoke his final words, "Let me depart to the house of the Father," on the eve of Divine Mercy Sunday in 2005.

The feast day of St. John Paul II is October 22.

Saint John Vianney

St. John Vianney was a parish priest in Ars, **France** who lived from 1786–1859. He is the patron saint of parish priests.

John was one of six children born to devout Catholic parents. The **French Revolution** was going on while he was a boy. There were so many bad things happening. Priests were even hunted down and killed. When the day came for John to receive his First Holy Communion, the Mass had to be said secretly in a neighbor's kitchen.

When he grew up, things had become better in France. He decided to become a priest like the brave ones he knew as a boy. But since he couldn't get much schooling during the French Revolution, he struggled with his classes, especially with Latin. A kind priest helped him, though. He was ordained and sent to a parish in Ars.

He soon discovered that the people were not going to Mass on Sundays and they hardly knew their catechism. He had a lot of work to do, so he put the future in the hands of the Blessed Virgin Mary and his favorite saint, St. Philomena. After some time, people started coming to hear his sermons, and their hearts were converted. They were sorry for their sins and made good confessions.

Slowly, people all over the world heard how wonderful and holy Fr. Vianney was. Thousands of people traveled to Ars to have their confessions heard. During the last 10 years of his life, he was in the confessional for 16 to 18 hours a day! He died at the age of 73. We celebrate his feast day on August 4.

Saint Josemaría Escrivá

St. Josemaría Escrivá was a priest who lived from 1902–1975 and founded the Catholic group *Opus Dei*, which means "Work of God" in Latin. He is known as the Saint of Ordinary Life.

Josemaría and his family were from Huesca, **Spain**. He loved his parents, brother, and sisters very much. When his father died, he took good care of them. They needed money to live on, so he earned it by teaching classes about the law. He had been studying law for a while, and it came in handy.

When he was ordained a priest, he was sent to Madrid where he took care of the poor and sick in the slums (poor neighborhoods) and hospitals. Madrid is the capital of Spain— find it on your map! But he wasn't sure that's what God wanted him to be doing. So he went on a retreat, taking time to pray for a few days. That's when the Holy Spirit gave him the idea to begin Opus Dei.

Opus Dei would be a special group of ordinary people and priests. They would teach people that they can reach Heaven by living an ordinary life and doing ordinary things. Ordinary actions become holy when they are done for God. Did you know that brushing your teeth can get you closer to Heaven? Now you know why St. Josemaría is called the Saint of Ordinary Life.

Throughout his adult life, he suffered from diabetes. But he still worked tirelessly to build up Opus Dei. He had a great sense of humor that made others want to listen to him and learn about his work.

Fr. Josemaría Escrivá passed away from a heart attack in his office. Today, there are tens of thousands of members across the world who continue the work he started. St. Josemaría Escrivá's feast day is June 26.

Saint Joseph

St. Joseph was the husband of Mary, the Mother of God, and the foster father of Jesus Christ, the Son of God. He was a Jewish carpenter from Bethlehem in Judea, part of the country of Israel in **Asia** today. King David was his ancestor.

St. Joseph was a man who obeyed God. He did what God wanted when he took Mary to be his wife and when they traveled the long journey from Nazareth to Bethlehem where Jesus was born. He obeyed God when he protected the baby Jesus from King Herod and when he brought Him safely back to Nazareth from Egypt.

Joseph was always listening to God so he would know what God wanted him to do. He listened when God spoke to him through angels and people in his life, like the Magi (the kings from the East who came to worship Jesus). He listened to the needs of Mary and Jesus, too. They were a poor family, but Joseph worked hard to give them shelter, food, and clothing.

Joseph taught Jesus many things. He showed him how to be a just and honest man and how to be a carpenter. He also brought Jesus to the synagogue, the Jewish place of worship, and taught Him His prayers.

St. Joseph is the patron of the Universal Church. We call the Catholic Church "universal" because God's love is for all peoples all over the world. Just as St. Joseph protected Mary and Jesus, he now protects the Church and each one of us!

The month of March is dedicated to St. Joseph. He has two feast days, March 19 and May 1.

Saint Josephine Bakhita

St. Josephine Bakhita is a saint who is called

the Flower of Africa. She was born in 1869 in a small village in Darfur, in what is now western Sudan, **Africa**. She had a wonderful, happy childhood. She loved her family, obeyed her parents, and was kind to her three brothers and three sisters. Bakhita did not know what it meant to suffer.

But when she was eight or nine years old, she was kidnapped and separated from her family forever. This experience caused such terrible fear and shock that she no longer knew her own name. The kidnappers named her *Bakhita*, which means "lucky" or "fortunate."

Bakhita suffered terrible pain at the hands of her captors and was not treated as a human being but as an object. She was a slave, sold and bought five times.

When an Italian bought Bakhita, she was finally treated with kindness. This Italian gave her to Augusto Michieli and his wife. They were also very kind to her. Bakhita cared for their daughter, Mimmina, and was a special friend to her. Children loved Bakhita, and she loved them.

In 1890, she became a Catholic. Six years later, she took her vows as a Canossian Daughter of Charity in Venice, **Italy**. Sr. Josephine Bakhita served her community as a cook, seamstress, doorkeeper, and more. She was gentle, calm, always smiling, and became well-known as the "little brown sister" or "black mother." She forgave the people who had enslaved her, saying that they didn't know how much they had hurt her; and that if she hadn't been enslaved, she would never have become a Christian.

She died in 1947 after long, painful years of sickness. Each year on February 8, we honor St. Josephine Bakhita for her bravery, her forgiveness, and her gratitude to God.

Saint Joseph's Oratory of Mount Royal

If you visit Montreal, **Quebec**, be sure to stop by St. Joseph's Oratory of Mount Royal. It is one of **Canada's** National Historic Sites and Canada's largest church. This national shrine has one of the largest domes in the whole world! It was founded in 1904 by **St. André Bessette** in honor of his patron saint, **St. Joseph**.

More commonly known as Brother André, Bessette was a monk and member of the Congregation of the Holy Cross. He was very holy and became known around the world as a miracle healer. The original chapel he built to honor St. Joseph was about 15 feet by 18 feet. It still stands today, though it was moved from its original place in order to build the new shrine. The oratory has several chapels, and the main shrine is big enough for 10,000 people. Something you'll notice right away when you walk inside is a very large statue honoring St. Joseph.

The inside of the basilica features bright colors, stained glass, and many arches. Construction work took many years, with the basilica finally being completed in 1967. More than two million people visit the shrine each year.

Work is being done on the inside of the dome and observatory, and eventually there will be space for people to enjoy the beautiful view from the top of the dome. From there, you can see the entire city of Montreal!

Saint Juan Diego

St. Juan Diego was a native of Mexico in **North America** who lived in Cuautlitlán, which is now part of Mexico City. He was born in 1474 as a member of the Chichimeca people and is believed to have been a farmer. When Franciscan missionaries came, Juan Diego and his wife, María Lucía, were among the first to be baptized.

On December 9, when Juan Diego was about 57, the Blessed Virgin Mary appeared to him on Tepeyac Hill. She told him she was the Mother of God and asked him to bring a message to the bishop. In her message, she asked the bishop to have a church built there. Juan Diego delivered the message, but the bishop did not believe that the Mother of God had appeared to him. The bishop wanted some proof.

Two days later, Juan Diego woke to find his uncle sick and close to death. He loved his uncle very much and set off to find a priest to give him the Sacrament of Anointing of the Sick. On his way, he was stopped by Our Lady. She told him not to worry about his uncle—he was cured!

Juan Diego thanked her and told her that the bishop wanted some proof that she was really the Mother of God. She had him gather roses that were miraculously blooming in the middle of winter. He carried them in his cloak and showed them to the bishop. When he opened his cloak, letting the flowers fall to the floor, the bishop was amazed to see an image of Our Lady of Guadalupe on the cloak! There was his proof.

The church was built, and for the next 17 years, Juan Diego spent his time praying, caring for the church, and telling the many visitors about Our Lady of Guadalupe. We celebrate his feast day on December 9.

Saint Kateri Tekakwitha

St. Kateri Tekakwitha was a Native American Indian who lived about 370 years ago in what is now New York. She is called the Lily of the Mohawks because her heart and mind were as beautiful and pure as a white lily.

When Kateri was four years old, her Christian Algonquin mother, Mohawk father, and baby brother died of smallpox. Kateri survived the sickness, but it left ugly marks on her face. The sickness also hurt her eyes so she couldn't see very well. Kateri had an uncle who was chief of the Turtle Clan. This Mohawk chief and her aunts adopted little Kateri. While she was still very young, her aunts tried forcing her to marry. She did not want to marry. Instead, she wanted to become a Christian and give her heart to God alone.

When Kateri was a young woman, she received baptism from the missionary priest, Father Jacques de Lamberville. This made the entire village angry. Her people made her life very difficult. Kateri never stopped praying or being kind toward those who made her suffer. She offered everything to God in union with Jesus' suffering on the cross.

Kateri finally escaped across 200 miles of wilderness into Montreal, **Canada**, where she was free to live her faith without persecution (being mistreated because of her faith). When she died at age 24, the scars on her face miraculously disappeared. St. Kateri Tekakwitha is the first Native American Indian to be canonized a saint. Her feast day is celebrated on July 14.

Saint Katharine Drexel

Born in 1858, St. Katharine Drexel was the

second American-born person to be declared a saint. Katherine was born to a rich banking family in **North America** and had two sisters. Her parents gave their daughters a loving home and strong faith. The Drexel family opened up their home three days a week to give food and clothes to the poor, so Katharine was taught to serve others from a young age. Katharine began teaching Sunday school as she grew older. During this time, a local pastor, Reverend James O'Connor, became her friend and guide in the Catholic Faith. When Katharine was 25 years old, her beloved stepmother died; two years later, her father died as well. Katharine inherited most of the family's wealth.

Katharine wanted to become a cloistered nun, which is a nun who spends her time praying and does not leave her monastery. God had different plans for Katharine! Reverend James O'Connor suggested she start a new religious order to help serve Native American Indians and black Americans. At first, Katharine didn't know if she could do this, but she took a leap of faith, trusted God, and started a new order called the Sisters of the Blessed Sacrament.

St. Katharine put her wealth to good use by helping people in need. Katharine founded more than 60 schools and missions all throughout the United States to help spread the love of God. St. Katharine Drexel died on March 3, 1955 at the age of 96. We celebrate her feast day on March 3.

Saint Kinga's Chapel in Wieliczka Salt Mine

St. Kinga's Chapel in Wieliczka Salt Mine is located in the town of Wieliczka in the country of Poland, **Europe**. An underground mine is a group of tunnels deep in the earth where miners dig for resources like coal, metal, and—yes—salt! People first started mining for salt in Wieliczka Salt Mine in the early thirteenth century.

The Polish miners wanted places to pray and hear Mass when they were down in the dark mines. So they carved a chapel right into the rock salt! In fact, they made dozens of underground chapels. The most famous is St. Kinga's Chapel. St. Kinga is a patron saint of Poland and of salt miners. St. Kinga's Chapel is made entirely out of rock salt. The Polish miners carved salt statues, salt floors, a salt altar, and even a salt chandelier! This chandelier is a large, fancy lamp hanging from the ceiling. It is decorated with glittering salt crystals.

One of the beautiful salt sculptures in the chapel is of the Last Supper. Another is a large salt statue of Pope **St. John Paul II**, who visited the mine before he became pope. Relics of both St. Kinga and St. John Paul II are kept in the main altar of the chapel. (A relic is an object that was very close to the saint, such as a piece of clothing or a lock of hair.)

Many visitors come to Wieliczka Salt Mine just to see St. Kinga's Chapel and be inspired by the faith of these Polish miners. You can attend Holy Mass on Sunday 330 feet underground!

Saint Kuriakose Elias Chavara

St. Kuriakose Elias Chavara was a priest from Kerala, **India**. He helped to start the first religious order in the Eastern Catholic Church in India. He is the first Indian-born male to be canonized.

Kuriakose and his family belonged to a community known as the **St. Thomas Christians**. While growing up, he went to the village school and learned languages and basic sciences. He began studying for the priesthood at a very early age.

After his ordination, he and two older priests decided to found a Carmelite monastery. As soon as they had permission from their bishop, they were ready to begin. The first stone of the monastery was laid in the city of Mannanam, and it was dedicated to St. Joseph. Sadly, the two older priests died before the monastery was finished.

Fr. Kuriakose and 10 other men finally became the Carmelites of the Immaculate Heart 24 years later. Fr. Kuriakose was named the prior and was put in charge of the religious order. He even has a mango named after him called the Prior mango. This is because he took care of mango trees and shared their fruits with others.

As a Syriac Christian, he had a higher social status, which means that people thought he was an important person. But he knew that everyone is important in God's eyes. So he acted in a kind and humble way toward everyone.

He started schools for poor people and helped the "untouchables," those who had the lowest social status and were treated unkindly. He started St. Joseph Press to print newspapers. He taught people that it is important to talk with God in prayer.

He died in 1871, at age 65. His feast day is February 18.

Saint Louis IX

St. Louis IX was a saint who was also king of **France** in the thirteenth century. He is the only

king of France to be declared a saint.

Louis became king when he was only 12 years old. Can you imagine being responsible for a whole country at 12 years of age? Fortunately, Louis' mother ruled for him while he was growing up. He learned to be a good king and a strong Catholic, and when he was older, he began to rule. When he became king, he invited a hundred poor people to eat in his palace every day. Often, Louis would even serve the food himself.

When Louis was 20 years old, he married Margaret, a woman who was just as pious as he was. They became good friends and enjoyed riding horses, reading, and listening to music together.

Louis was king for almost 45 years. This was a good time for France. Louis made better laws and helped the country prosper. For example, Louis created a system where people who hadn't received justice in court could come talk to the king about it. He was a wise king, and other kings asked him for advice.

Louis led two Crusades to the Holy Land, spending most of his time fighting the Muslim rulers in **Africa**, especially Egypt and Tunisia— the Seventh and Eighth Crusades. Sadly, Louis became sick on the Eighth Crusade and died. He is still remembered as a good king and a holy man. His feast day is August 25.

Saint Margaret Clitherow

St. Margaret Clitherow lived in northeast England in a place called York. She was a beautiful young wife and mother who was brave and courageous. Margaret became known as the Pearl of York.

Three years after being married, Margaret became a Catholic. It was in the year 1574, at a time when Catholics in England were being ill-treated for their beliefs. People were looking for priests in order to kill them. Margaret loved the Catholic Church and wanted to help, so she decided to hide priests in her own home.

In a secret room, the priests were free to offer Mass and give Holy Communion to the people. It brought the priests joy to be able to serve God through the sacraments. They were very brave because if they were caught, they would be put to death.

What Margaret was doing was not legal. It was against the law to hide and protect priests. Because of this, she was arrested and jailed many times, sometimes for two years at a time. But her husband was a wealthy butcher who would often pay to get her out of prison.

Finally, she was arrested and sent to the castle prison. This time, her husband could not help her. Margaret had known priests who had

been killed before her. Like them, she would lay down her life for Jesus, who she loved so much. She was martyred on Good Friday at the age of 30. Her feast day is on March 26.

Saint Margaret Mary Alacoque

St. Margaret Mary Alacoque was a Catholic nun who lived in France. She always had a great love for Jesus in the Blessed Sacrament. As a child, she became very sick and was in bed for a long time. During that time, she promised the Blessed Mother she would become a nun. To remind herself of her promise, Margaret added Mary to her name.

When she was older, Margaret's family wanted her to marry. Margaret thought her promise was no longer needed, so she went to dances to find a husband. But one night after a dance, Jesus appeared before her. Jesus told Margaret that He was sad she had forgotten Him, even though He had shown His love to her so clearly. It was then that Margaret entered a convent and became a nun.

At the convent, Margaret had more visions of Jesus and His Sacred Heart. Jesus wanted Margaret to share His great love and mercy with people. But many people didn't believe her visions were real. Margaret faced many problems but remained kind, honest, and patient as she shared Jesus' message of mercy.

Saint Margaret Mary gave her life to the love of the Sacred Heart of Jesus. She shared that love with many people. After her death, Margaret's practice of Devotion to the Sacred Heart of Jesus became a common tradition. Saint Margaret Mary Alacoque is the patron saint of people devoted to the Sacred Heart of Jesus, people who have lost parents, and people with polio. Her feast day is celebrated on October 16.

Saint Marguerite Bourgeoys

St. Marguerite Bourgeoys was a religious sister in **Canada**. She started one of the first uncloistered religious orders in the Catholic Church. ("Uncloistered" means that the sisters are allowed to work outside the convent.)

Marguerite was born in Troyes, **France**. She came from a large Catholic family of 13 children. When she was about 15 years old, she decided she would join a group of women who taught poor young girls.

Some years later, she was asked to leave France and serve the French immigrants living in Montreal, Canada. For seven difficult months, the ship, called *Saint Nicholas*, carried her and 100 other passengers across the North Atlantic Ocean. Finally, she arrived in Montreal! At that time, it was called the City of Mary.

Marguerite soon noticed that the community was missing a real church. So she gathered a group of workmen to start building one. Then, she was given a stable, which she turned into the first schoolhouse in Montreal. It was the first of many schools she began.

A couple of her schools were for young women. They learned how to manage their homes and be good wives and mothers. She also set up a small school for the Catholic Native American children in the mission village.

Eventually, the life and work of Marguerite Bourgeoys and her companions became a new religious order called the Congregation of Notre Dame. Marguerite served the settlers with such selflessness that she became known as the Mother of the Colony. Her feast day is January 12.

Saint Martin de Porres

St. Martin de Porres was a Dominican brother from **Peru**. He grew up poor. People were unkind to him because his parents weren't married and because he was of mixed race.

Martin spent hours praying every night and wanted to become a religious brother. Martin became a servant boy in a monastery, doing simple tasks like kitchen work, laundry, and cleaning. Even some of the brothers were mean and called him names. Martin responded with kindness and continued to pray and work hard. Eventually, Martin became a religious brother.

Martin cared for and loved people no matter what their race was, how much money they had, or whether they were sick or dirty. He founded an orphanage and was in charge of his monastery's infirmary, where sick people are treated. Martin also loved animals and could talk with them. There are stories about how he stopped two bulls from fighting and led mice out of the kitchen to the garden by promising to feed them. He loved animals so much that he didn't eat meat!

Other amazing things happened in Martin's life. When he prayed hard, sometimes he was lifted into the air. One time, there was a sickness at the monastery. The sick brothers were kept locked up so no one else would get sick. Martin was able to pass through the locked doors to care for his sick brothers. It is said he could be in two places at the same time—he was seen in other countries, but he never left Peru!

Martin was good friends with St. Rose of Lima. St. Martin de Porres died of fever on November 3, 1639, at the age of 60. We celebrate his feast day on November 3.

Saint Mary MacKillop

St. Mary MacKillop is **Australia's** first saint. She was born in 1842 in Melbourne, the eldest of eight children. She has a Scottish name because her parents had immigrated from Scotland before they met and got married.

Mary's father was a farmer, but the family suffered because there wasn't always enough money for food and clothing. Mary's education came to an end at age 16. It was necessary for her to work to help provide for the needs of her family.

For the next eight years, Mary worked at various jobs: as a store clerk, governess, schoolteacher, and then founder of a boarding school for young ladies. Through these experiences, God was preparing her for her life's work.

At age 24, Mary and two of her sisters were asked to open a Catholic school in Penola. The school building started out as a stable, but with hard work and her family's help, they made the necessary changes. Soon, they were teaching over 50 children!

It was during this time that Mary heard the call from God to dedicate her life to serving Him. She wished to do this with other women, so she founded the Sisters of St. Joseph of the

Sacred Heart. She became Mother Mary of the Cross. In just five years, 130 sisters were working with her in more than 40 schools, orphanages, and homes for the elderly, the poor, and the dying.

In 1902, Mother Mary suffered a stroke. After that, she couldn't move her right side. She died seven years later at the age of 67. Her feast day is celebrated on August 8.

Saint Monica

St. Monica was born in North **Africa** around AD 332. She and her husband, Patricius, had three children who lived past childhood: Augustine, who we now know as **St. Augustine**; Navigius; and Perpetua.

Monica was a prayerful, generous woman who gave to the poor and attended Mass. Patricius did not love God and would often get angry with Monica for her faith. He treated her very unkindly and would not allow their children to be baptized.

Patricius died when Augustine was in college. After college, Augustine refused to pray and live a Christian life. This made Monica very sad. She cried and prayed, asking God to help her son come to the Catholic Faith. For 17 years, Augustine did not go to Mass. He lived a sinful life. She always offered little

sacrifices for him and prayed often.

Finally, Augustine returned to the Faith and was baptized by St. Ambrose. Not long after, St. Monica died. Augustine went on to become a saint and one of the Doctors of the Church. In his famous book *Confessions*, St. Augustine wrote that St. Monica's many loving acts and prayers helped him return to God.

We can ask St. Monica to pray for our loved ones too, and we can ask her to help us love God more every day. Her feast day is celebrated on August 27, one day before St. Augustine's feast day.

Saint Moses the Ethiopian

St. Moses was an African born in the fourth century AD. He was from Nubia, the region between Egypt and Sudan, and he was Ethiopian by race. He lived at the same time that the Christian Faith was beginning to spread in that part of the **continent** of **Africa**. But Moses was not raised a baptized Christian.

From a young age, Moses was a slave to an important rich man in Egypt. Little by little, he began to live a very bad life. He did not have any respect for other people or their things and was caught stealing from his master.

Moses was sent away because he could no longer be trusted.

By that time, Moses was a very big, strong man, but nobody wanted to hire someone who was a thief. So he became a leader of a band of robbers near the **Nile River** in Egypt. He was a wicked man and feared by all who knew him. It is said that he even committed murder.

But one day, Moses was hiding out at a monastery in the **desert**. He saw how the monks lived their lives for God and decided that he needed to stop living a life of crime. He begged to join the brothers. He was accepted, and his new life as a monk began with baptism.

By his example, Moses converted many men from his band of thieves, some becoming monks themselves. He was put in charge of a new band, this time of brother monks. He was ordained as a priest, and not long after, he died a martyr at the hands of robbers at age 75. His feast is celebrated on August 28.

Saint Nicholas

St. Nicholas was born to wealthy Christian parents in about AD 270 in the **port** town of Patara, Turkey in **Asia**. There are not many factual records about his life, so much of what we know about him has been passed down through stories told from person to person.

Some people who study history believe that Nicholas was at the First Council of Nicaea in AD 325. They believe he was one of the bishops to sign the Nicene Creed (we still pray this on Sundays). He also preached against the belief of Arianism, which taught that Jesus was not God. As a bishop, Nicholas helped people learn about and understand the reality of the Trinity: one God in the three Persons of the Father, the Son, and the Holy Spirit.

Many stories and legends have been shared throughout the years about St. Nicholas. In one story, he calmed a storm at **sea**. In another, he saved three innocent soldiers from being killed. One of the most famous stories says that he helped a father who had lost all his money. Because he was caring and humble, the story claims that Nicholas threw a purse full of gold coins through the family's window one night. Whether this story is true or not, Nicholas' generosity and kindness to those in need were real and showed his great love for God and his neighbors.

Other stories also tell of Nicholas' secret gift-giving, including how he would put coins in the shoes that were left out for him. This practice is still celebrated by many families on December 6, his feast day.

St. Nicholas is also known as Nicholas the Wonderworker because many miracles have come about through his intercession. He is the patron of many, including sailors, archers, children, unmarried people, students, and repentant thieves.

Saint Pedro Calungsod

St. Pedro Calungsod was a teenage missionary and martyr who lived in the Philippines in **Asia** from 1654–1672. He helped start the first Catholic mission in Guam and is the second Filipino to be declared a saint.

As a young boy, Pedro lived with other boys at a school run by Spanish priests called Jesuits. He was taught many things, including the Spanish language. He learned the catechism so well that he thought one day he would become a missionary. He liked to practice doing things that would be important for missionary work, such as carpentry, acting, and artwork.

When Pedro was 14 years old, he was chosen to go to the **island** of Guam as a missionary with Fr. Diego San Vitores (who is now beatified). He knew that it would mean leaving his family and friends behind. He also knew that it would mean living a hard life—facing dangerous **typhoons**, running out of supplies, and many other hardships. He went anyway, trusting in God's care for him.

At first, the native Chamorros welcomed Pedro and Fr. San Vitores. The two missionaries baptized hundreds of people. Later, the natives' welcome turned into hate. This was because Pedro and Fr. San Vitorestold the Chamorros that if they were to live as Christians, they would have to give up doing things that the Catholic Church does not allow, like lying, cheating, and stealing. The Chamorros became very angry and didn't want to give up their old beliefs and sinful ways. So they made it very hard for the missionariesto teach and convert anyone else. This is called persecution. But Pedro and Fr. San Vitores stayed, taking many risks to continue their missionary work.

After four years on Guam, both Pedro and Fr. San Vitores were attacked and killed. St. Pedro Calungsod's feast day is April 2.

Saint Perpetua and Saint Felicity

St. Perpetua and St. Felicity were young mothers who were martyred in Carthage, now Tunisia. Tunisia is in North **Africa**. It was controlled by the **Roman Empire** at the time, so a lot of Romans lived there. They were martyred in AD 203.

Perpetua was a noblewoman with a small baby son. She and Felicity were catechumens, people preparing for the Sacrament of Baptism. Felicity was a slave who was eight months pregnant. When they refused to give up their Christian faith, they were put in prison.

Perpetua wrote a diary about her sufferings. She wrote that her pagan father would visit her and try to talk her out of being a Christian. She told him: "Do you see this pot? Can it be called by any other name than what it is? So also I cannot call myself by any other name than what I am—a Christian." She strongly believed in Christ's love for her.

While in prison, Felicity gave birth to a baby girl. Then, their babies were taken from them. Felicity and Perpetua were put to death as part of the birthday celebration for the Roman emperor. They won a glorious crown of martyrdom and went straight to Heaven!

We still have St. Perpetua's diary. Through the centuries, countless Christians who were persecuted have gained strength from its pages.

St. Perpetua and St. Felicity's names are in the first Eucharistic prayer at Mass and in the Litany of the Saints. Their feast day is celebrated on March 7.

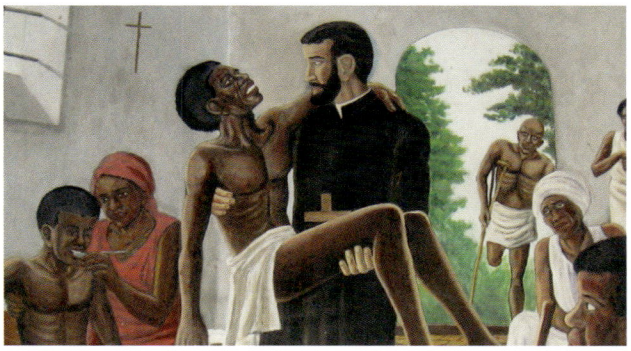

Saint Peter Claver

St. Peter Claver was a Jesuit missionary who served, baptized, and cared for slaves in **South America**. St. Peter was born in 1581 in

Catalonia, **Spain**. He decided to become a missionary after his teacher, St. Alphonsus Rodriguez, encouraged him to go to the Americas. St. Peter arrived in New Granada, which is now Colombia, in 1610. He became a priest in 1615 and spent the rest of his life caring for slaves. Because of this, he is often known as the patron saint of slaves.

When St. Peter Claver was alive, many people saw black people as less than human, just because of the color of their skin. Many Africans were forced onto ships and brought to the Americas. They were sold as slaves and made to work in fields or mines. They were treated cruelly, especially on the long journey by ship. St. Peter Claver wanted to care for them and teach them about God.

Whenever a ship arrived in **port** with more slaves, St. Peter would go on the ship with food and medicine. He took care of the sick and baptized babies and those who were dying. St. Peter also preached to the slave traders and sailors, visited hospitals, and cared for slaves working in the fields and mines.

St. Peter was greatly disliked by many people who didn't want him to help the slaves. They often made trouble for him, but St. Peter never gave up. He called himself "the slave of the blacks forever." He always defended the slaves and tried to make their lives better. He spent 44 years in Colombia and baptized more than 300,000 slaves. His feast day is September 9.

Saint Peter's Basilica

St. Peter's Basilica is the huge beautiful church in **Vatican City**, inside the country of **Italy**. It is built over the spot where St. Peter, the first pope, was buried. There was actually once a church over the same spot—the original St. Peter's Basilica—built in AD 329 by the Emperor Constantine. After more than a thousand years, it began falling down, so the Catholic Church hired artists and architects who worked together for over 150 years to build the basilica that we see today.

In front of the basilica is St. Peter's Square, a large open space surrounded by stone columns. On top of the columns are statues of different saints. In the middle of the square, there is an obelisk, which is a tall pointed monument. A cross is fixed to the top. This obelisk is thought to be the site of St. Peter's crucifixion.

St. Peter's Basilica is one of the largest churches in the world! There are many works of art inside the basilica, and the walls themselves are covered with beautiful statues, paintings, and designs. Many skilled artists and architects helped make the basilica so beautiful. For example, the painter **Michelangelo** helped design and paint parts of the basilica. The altar in the very center, where the pope often offers Mass, has a huge bronze covering called a baldacchino. This was made by the famous artist Bernini to honor St. Peter's tomb, which is directly below this altar.

Pilgrims from all over the world come to St. Peter's Basilica to admire its art, pray to St. Peter for his intercession, see the pope, and visit the tombs of the many other popes buried there.

Saint Pier Giorgio Frassati

St. Pier Giorgio Frassati is a modern saint who lived in Turin, **Italy**. He was born in 1901 and died from polio in 1925 when he was only 24 years old.

Pier Giorgio was born into a wealthy family. His father owned a newspaper and had important government jobs, and his mother was a successful painter. Even as a young child, Pier Giorgio felt compassion for people who had less than he did. One time, he gave his own shoes to a poor, shoeless child. He would even give his bus money to the poor and then run home to be on time for meals!

Pier Giorgio continued to show compassion for the poor as an adult. As a member of the Third Order of Saint Dominic, he often led charitable activities for the poor. When he was 17 years old, he joined the **St. Vincent de Paul** Society and spent much of his free time serving the sick and poor, caring for orphans, and helping soldiers who had returned from World War I. Often, he gave up family vacations, saying, "If everybody leaves Turin, who will take care of the poor?"

Pier Giorgio loved physical activities, especially **mountain climbing**. He climbed the highest peaks of the Italian **Alps**. When climbing, he was always kind and generous to his companions, often helping weaker climbers. He would keep everyone's spirits up by singing as they climbed, and he would lead prayers at night.

On a photo of himself climbing, Pier Giorgio wrote "*Verso l'alto,*" which means "toward the top." This phrase became a motto for many people after he died, encouraging them to reach for the treasures of Heaven. Pier Giorgio Frassati was canonized in 2025, and his feast day is July 4.

Saint Pio of Pietrelcina

Fondly known as Padre Pio, St. Pio of Pietrelcina is a modern saint from **Italy**. He was born as Francesco Forgione in 1887. At age five, he said he wanted to dedicate his entire life to God. At age 15, he joined the Franciscan Capuchin friars and took the name Pio.

Throughout his childhood and young adulthood, Pio faced many health challenges and was often sick. In 1918, he was marked with the *stigmata*, which are the wounds Jesus bore on the cross (bleeding from the hands and feet, a wound in the side, and pain from the crown of thorns). St. Pio was given many gifts and graces from God, including being able to heal others, the ability to be in two places at once, levitation, prophecy, the ability to read hearts, and the gift of tongues.

One story about St. Pio says that he was able to live for 20 days with only the Holy Eucharist and no other food, and that he hardly needed any sleep!

As he became well-known, many people went to him for spiritual direction. He urged everyone to try to do God's will in all things. One of St. Pio's most famous sayings is "Pray, hope, and don't worry."

St. Pio was canonized in 2002, and his feast day is September 23.

Saint Rose of Lima

St. Rose of Lima is the first person born in the

Americas to be recognized as a saint. She is called the First Flower of the New World and is the patron saint of **Peru**.

Rose was born in 1586 in Lima, the capital of Peru. Rose had many brothers and sisters. She did her best to be kind and charitable to them every day. When her parents asked her to do something, she was very obedient and did the job right away without a fuss.

Rose was beautiful from the day she was born. As she grew into a young lady, there were many young men who wanted to marry her. But she was so in love with Jesus that she made a special vow, promising Jesus that she would never get married and that He alone would be her spouse. Rose became a member of the Dominican Order just like St. Catherine of Siena, whom she greatly admired. She spent time praying and sacrificing in a tiny brick house that she and her brother built in the corner of the garden.

Rose also took care of the poor, the sick, and the hungry at her parents' home. She needed money to do this, so she made fine needlework like lace and embroidery. She sold these at the market, as well as flowers she grew in her garden. Using her talents in this way gave her much joy.

Rose died at age 31, offering all of her pain and suffering for the conversion of her country. Her feast day is on August 23.

Saint Rose-Philippine Duchesne

St. Rose-Philippine Duchesne is a saint who served the poor people in the Midwest in **North America**. She was born in 1769 and died in 1852.

Philippine was born in **France** to a rich and powerful family. She was sent to a monastery school and became interested in monastic life. Even though her family didn't want her to become a nun, she entered the Order of the Visitation of Holy Mary when she was nineteen. Then the **French Revolution** came. The monastery was shut down, and Philippine went home. She served God by helping people who were injured or suffering because of the Revolution, but she wanted to be a missionary.

After the revolution, Philippine met the founder of the Society of the Sacred Heart of Jesus, Mother Barat. Immediately, she wanted to join and asked Mother Barat to send her to America. Philippine had to wait 12 years, but eventually her dream came true!

In 1818, Philippine was sent to Missouri to found the first house of the Society of the Sacred Heart outside France. It was a log cabin! It was very cold, and there was lots of hard work to do. This cabin became the first free school west of the Mississippi. The school was for girls, who didn't always get the best education at that time. In 10 years, Philippine founded 6 more houses!

Philippine loved her work, but she wanted do more to help Native American Indians. When she was 72 years old, she got her wish. The Jesuits opened a school for the Potawatomi tribe in Kansas, and Philippine was invited along. She lived there for a year, praying for the Potawatomi, who called her Woman-Who-Prays-Always. That's a good name, isn't it?

St. Rose-Philippine was canonized in 1988. We celebrate her feast day on November 18.

Saint Teresa of Ávila

St. Teresa of Ávila was born in 1515 in **Spain**. As a young girl, Teresa loved reading about the saints, especially medieval stories of knighthood and books about gardens and flowers. After her mother's death, she grew closer to the Blessed Virgin Mary and was sent to the Augustinian nuns' school in Ávila.

After completing her education, she entered the Carmelite Convent of the Incarnation. Teresa became very sick and was in bed for almost a whole year, but she said St. Joseph miraculously made her well. After this, she began to experience spiritual ecstasies, which means she was in such a prayerful state that she became close to God in a special way. Teresa knew prayer was very important and a special way to get to know God.

Teresa and the Carmelite friar John of the Cross worked to bring important changes to the Carmelite orders for men and women, and in 1580, the two of them established the Discalced Carmelites. ("Discalced" means "shoeless.")

In 1970, St. Teresa of Ávila was the first woman to be named Doctor of the Church. She is honored as the Doctor of Prayer. Teresa wrote several books that you may want to read when you're older! She is the patroness of Spain, sick people, people in religious orders, chess, people ridiculed for their piety, and lacemakers. Her feast day is October 15.

Saint Teresa of Calcutta

St. Teresa of Calcutta (now Kolkata), lovingly remembered as Mother Teresa, had a mother's heart for the poorest of the poor. In order to care for them, she founded the Missionaries of Charity in **India**, in the **continent** of **Asia**. Mother Teresa is a modern saint who is loved all over the world by Catholics and non-Catholics alike.

Mother Teresa was named Agnes at her baptism in Albania in 1910. She was welcomed into the world by her parents, a brother, and a sister. They were a close-knit family, but before Agnes turned nine, her father suddenly died. This was a very sad time, and the family had little money to live on.

As a teenager, Agnes became more involved with her parish. She served wherever she was needed, doing "small things with great love." This prepared her for her future. When Agnes turned 18, she left her family and country to become Sr. Mary Teresa (after St. Thérèse of Lisieux, the patroness of missions). For nearly 20 years, she taught high school girls in India as a member of the Sisters of Loreto. These were happy days for her.

Then she received another call from God to leave the convent and work and live among the poor in Kolkata. So she worked in the poorest areas of the city, taught poor children, and treated the sick in their homes. It took a lot of courage and prayer because she was not welcomed by everyone.

One by one, her former students decided to join her in her work. Their group became a new religious order called the Missionaries of Charity. Mother Teresa spent her life for Jesus, seeing His face in the poor, lonely, desperate, and dying. He called her to Himself in 1997, and we celebrate her feast day on September 5.

Saint Teresa of the Andes

St. Teresa of the Andes was a young Carmelite nun of Los Andes, Chile in **South America**. She was only 19 years old when she died and went to meet Christ Jesus, her Spouse. Only one of those years was spent in the Carmelite monastery. For the other 18 years, she was known as Juanita Fernández Solar.

Juanita became a saint by treating everyone with love and kindness. She was able to do this because she made time for prayer each day. Her friendship with Jesus was deepened by her First Holy Communion.

Juanita loved the Catholic Faith so much that she wanted to share it with others. So she taught catechism lessons to the poor and those who worked for her family. She showed them how to put faith into action by caring for their needs.

Every family goes through hard times, and so did Juanita's. They lost their lands, which reduced their income, and some of her siblings lost their faith in God. But this did not stop her from being full of life and being a loving support to each member of her family.

At boarding school, Juanita missed her family very much. Instead of being sad all the time, she decided to offer this pain to Jesus and asked Him to help her to be a good student. She brought a spirit of joy and gratitude to her classmates and tried hard to set a good example.

In 1919, Juanita joined the Carmelites, and her name changed to Sister Teresa of Jesus. She kept in touch with family and friends through letters. Her words helped others to become closer friends with Christ.

Nearly a year later, Sr. Teresa became very sick and died after terrible suffering. St. Teresa of the Andes is Chile's first saint, and her feast day is celebrated on April 12.

Saint Thérèse of Lisieux

St. Thérèse of Lisieux, the Little Flower, was a Carmelite nun who lived in Lisieux, **France**. She grew up with four older sisters who also became nuns. Her mother died when Thérèse was just four years old. She missed her mother very much. About six years later, when Thérèse was ill, the Blessed Mother appeared to her, and she was cured. She joined the Carmel of Lisieux at the early age of 15. After suffering from tuberculosis, she died at age 24, in 1897.

St. Thérèse is famous all over the world. As a cloistered nun, she never left the monastery. But people in **Africa**, Ireland, **China**, Russia, and other far-away places love her because her life shows them something special: that ordinary people can become holy too.

She called her way of life the "Little Way" and wrote about it in the book about her life, *Story of a Soul*. The Little Way means doing small things with great love for God. She did not do any great deeds like those of **St. Joan of Arc**. She did small things instead. For example, she showed great kindness to a fellow nun who never showed kindness to her.

St. Thérèse lived a short life on earth, but she promised, "I will spend my Heaven doing good on earth. I will let down a shower of roses." Her feast day is on October 1. Her parents are Saints Louis and Zélie Martin.

Saint Thomas Becket

Thomas Becket was a saint born in London, England, in 1118. As a young man, he worked for the Archbishop of Canterbury, Theobald of Bec. Theobald sent Thomas on important missions to Rome and also had him study Church laws. Thomas did such a good job that he ended up working as the chancellor for King Henry

II. Thomas was in charge of the king's money and lived like royalty. Thomas and King Henry soon became good friends.

After Theobald died, King Henry wanted Thomas to become Archbishop of Canterbury, but Thomas was not a priest. Thomas also worried that being archbishop might cause trouble in his friendship with the king. Thomas knew that the king would want him to put the government first, not the Church.

Thomas did become a priest and was immediately made Archbishop of Canterbury. Right away, he began to live a simpler and more prayerful life. But King Henry wanted Thomas to help him control the Church. When Thomas refused, the king became angry. Trying to please King Henry, some of his knights captured Thomas and threatened to kill him. They tried to force Thomas to do what the king wanted, but he refused, saying, "I am no traitor, and I am ready to die." He was killed on December 29, 1170.

Just two years after his death, he was declared a saint by Pope Alexander III. Thomas' tomb has become a popular pilgrimage site. Thomas' life shows that it is more important to be faithful to God than to be pressured by friends to do the wrong thing. We celebrate St. Thomas Becket on December 29.

Saint Thomas Cathedral Basilica

St. Thomas Cathedral Basilica is a church in Chennai, **India**. It is built over the tomb of St. Thomas the Apostle. The tomb contains some relics of St. Thomas, but most of St. Thomas' remains are in Ortona, **Italy**.

Do you remember the story of St. Thomas? He wasn't with the apostles when Jesus first came to visit them after His Resurrection. Thomas didn't believe that Jesus had risen from the dead! Later, though, he saw the risen Jesus and believed. He became a great preacher of the Gospel and traveled all the way to India telling people about Jesus! Those Christians are called the **St. Thomas Christians**.

This basilica was built in 1523 by Portuguese missionaries. They traveled to Chennai to see if the story was true that St. Thomas really was buried there. The missionaries found his tomb there and decided to build a new shrine over St. Thomas' relics.

In 1545, **St. Francis Xavier** visited this church. He stayed for a year before setting out on his mission to Taiwan. The church was rebuilt by the British in 1896, so when you examine it, you may recognize the building style that was popular in England during the Victorian period. Look for the small tower in the center of the cathedral that marks the burial place of St. Thomas. Inside the basilica, also make sure to look for the spearhead that killed St. Thomas.

Saint Thomas Christians

The St. Thomas Christians are a group of people in **India** who converted to Christianity nearly 2000 years ago because of the preaching of St. Thomas the Apostle. The Saint Thomas Christians are one of the oldest branches of Christianity in the world.

Several ancient writings speak of St. Thomas' travels, missionary work, and martyrdom in India. A large cathedral, the **St. Thomas Cathedral Basilica**, now stands over his tomb in Chennai, India. Thanks to St. Thomas' sacrifice, Christianity is still practiced in India today. There are an estimated four million Saint Thomas Christians in India!

The Saint Thomas Christians are also called Syrian Christians, or the Nasrani. This is because Syriac is the language that Saint Thomas Christians use in the liturgy. *Nasrani* is a Syriac word that means "Christians." Most Saint Thomas Christians live in the Indian state of Kerala.

Nowadays, there are many different groups of Saint Thomas Christians. These groups have their own liturgies and traditions, but they all can trace their roots back to the missionary work of St. Thomas the Apostle. Some of the groups are Protestant or Orthodox, but two groups are still Catholic.

Saint Thomas More

St. Thomas More was lord chancellor to **Henry VIII**, the king of England. A chancellor is a very important servant of the king. Like **St. John Fisher**, he was martyred in 1535 for not giving in to the king's demands to disobey the pope.

Thomas' father was a lawyer who was very proud of his son. He sent Thomas to the best schools, where he studied hard. There were so many things that Thomas was interested in, like literature, philosophy, music, and languages. Later, he followed in his father's footsteps and became a lawyer himself. He turned out to be one of the most intelligent and clever people in the world! Thomas was also known for his sense of humor: he loved a good joke.

Sir Thomas was so wise that King Henry VIII made him his advisor and lord chancellor. After a while, though, he tried to force Sir Thomas to agree that he was the head of the Church in England instead of the pope in Rome.

Sir Thomas refused to agree with the king. He could not keep serving him, so he gave up being the lord chancellor. He was no longer an important man. He lost his friends. He lost his money. His family lived very poorly. Some of his own family begged him to give in to the king's wishes so he wouldn't have to die.

Because Thomas would not obey the king, he was put in prison and later beheaded. These were his last words: "I die the king's good servant, but God's first." St. Thomas More and St. John Fisher share the same feast day, June 22.

Saint Turibius of Mogrovejo

St. Turibius of Mogrovejo was born in **Spain** in 1538 and served as a missionary in **Peru** for 26 years. In Spain, he started out teaching law at a university and then became a judge in the Inquisition of Granada, a court in charge of protecting the truths of the Faith.

After being ordained as a priest and then bishop, he was ready to preach the Gospel in his new diocese. He traveled to Peru in 1581. The area he was in charge of was very large, and he usually had to travel on foot. There were many dangers for travelers in those days.

St. Turibius built many roads, hospitals, schools, churches, and convents in Peru, as well as the first seminary (a school to train priests) in the Americas. He also helped write a catechism in the native language so the people of Peru could learn the Faith. When the natives were treated badly by Spanish colonists, St. Turibius defended the natives and made sure they were treated well. Over his lifetime, he led almost half a million people to the Faith. He gave the Sacrament of Confirmation to the future **St. Rose of Lima** and probably to **St. Martin de Porres** as well. He was also good friends with another saint and missionary, **St. Francisco Solano**.

St. Turibius was given an unusual gift: God allowed him to know ahead of time the day that he would die. He died of a fever in 1606 near Lima, Peru. His feast day is March 23.

Saint Vincent de Paul

St. Vincent de Paul was a Catholic priest from **France** who lived in the seventeenth century. He was born into a poor peasant family with six children. At age 15, his father sold the family's oxen to send him to seminary. Vincent did well as a student and earned money to pay for his education by tutoring others.

Vincent was put in charge of distributing money to the poor, and later he became the pastor of a small parish. He brought food to the hungry and collected money for missionary projects. He also began many hospitals and helped slaves and people who had been hurt by wars. Eventually, he had so much work to do that he founded the Daughters of Charity to help him with his work.

Vincent also realized that priests needed help to become better leaders in the Church. Using his passion for preaching, Vincent held retreats for priests and helped train them. He also founded a group of priests known as the Vincentians. Vincentians at this time focused on missions, serving the poor, and training priests.

Vincent's dedication to serving the poor has made him the patron saint of all works of charity. Many organizations have been inspired by his example of service to others. The largest and most popular organization is the Society of St. Vincent de Paul, a French charity dedicated to serving the poor. The society works in 153 countries today. We celebrate St. Vincent de Paul on September 27.

Saint Wenceslaus

St. Wenceslaus is a saint who lived in Bohemia in the tenth century. Bohemia is part of Czechia today in Central **Europe**. Wenceslaus was the duke of Bohemia and was martyred in the year 935.

Wenceslaus was the son of Duke Wratislaw, a Christian, and Dragomir, who was a heathen. Wenceslaus' grandmother, St. Ludmilla, raised him to be a Christian. But when Wenceslaus' father died, his mother, Dragomir, began to rule Bohemia. She fought against Christianity. The people were not happy with this, and they asked young Wenceslaus to rule instead.

When Wenceslaus became a duke, he encouraged Christianity. He made peace with Germany and brought German priests to Bohemia.

Wenceslaus was a good ruler and a holy man. He stood up to neighboring dukes to protect his people and prevent bloodshed.

Dragomir was unhappy that Wenceslaus had made Bohemia Christian again. She convinced Wenceslaus' brother, Boleslaw, to kill him. Boleslaw killed and buried him. Three years later, Boleslaw repented of murdering his brother. He had Wenceslaus' body moved to holy ground in Prague. Wenceslaus' feast day is celebrated on the day of his death, September 28.

Although Wenceslaus was only a duke, Emperor Otto I gave him the title of king after he died. Wenceslaus is remembered in the hymn "*Svatý Václave*" ("Saint Wenceslaus"), which is still sung in Czechia. It was played often with the national anthem during World War II, when the Czech people were ruled by terrible enemies. In the West, we sing a similar song, the Christmas carol "Good King Wenceslas." It tells of Wenceslaus' servant following him as he walked through the snow to help the poor!

Salmon

Salmon are a type of fish that are well-known and commonly eaten throughout **North America** and parts of **Asia** and **Europe**. There are seven different species of salmon. One species lives in the Atlantic Ocean, while the other six all live in the Pacific Ocean.

Salmon can live in both fresh water and salt water. In fact, while salmon are born in freshwater streams or **rivers**, they spend most of their lives in the open **ocean**.

When adult salmon are old enough, they leave the ocean to journey back to the rivers and streams where they were first born. These journeys are part of what makes salmon so famous and so fascinating. They are able to remember where they came from, and they find these places partly by using their sense of smell. To get back to where they hatched, salmon have to swim upstream against strong river currents and even jump up waterfalls!

As salmon make the journey to their hatching grounds, their bodies change. In most kinds of salmon, males' jaws become long and hooked. In some species, their silver skin turns bright red!

After laying their eggs, some kinds, like the Atlantic salmon, can make it back to the ocean. However, most species of the Pacific salmon cannot, and they die in the rivers and streams. While this seems sad, this helps the environment, providing food and nutrients for insects, bugs, and plants, and wildlife like bears, foxes, and wolves—and for fishermen!

Samuel de Champlain

Samuel de Champlain was a Frenchman known for founding the city of **Quebec** in **Canada**. Samuel was a man of many talents. He was an explorer, a navigator, a soldier, and even a geographer who could make maps. He was born in **France** around the year 1570. In his lifetime, he sailed across the Atlantic Ocean between France and **North America** over 20 times. Samuel sailed to the land north of what would become the United States. It was here that the French had claimed some land. Today, we know this land as Canada, but back then, it was called New France.

Samuel was very good at writing down all of his findings when he explored New France. Thanks to these writings, we know about what he saw and did. One of the most important things he did was create a city from the ground up. In 1608, Champlain came to a place called the "point of Quebec." It was here that he spent time building three forts to protect the area from invaders. These buildings were the beginning of the city of Quebec. Samuel would continue to add on to the buildings of Quebec for the rest of his life. Quebec is considered one of the oldest European settlements in North America.

In his travels across New France, Samuel became partners with some of the local Native American Indians, who helped him explore the land. In this exploration, he discovered a **lake** that he named after himself. Lake Champlain is a large lake that you can visit in Canada or the United States.

Sanctuary of Las Lajas

The Sanctuary of Las Lajas is an amazing church in Colombia, **South America**. It is a shrine to Our Lady of the Rosary. It is built on the side of a beautiful **canyon**, on top of a large stone bridge that crosses the canyon. The shrine's name, Las Lajas, means "stone slabs" and comes from the flat rocks found nearby.

Almost 300 years ago, the Blessed Mother and the Child Jesus appeared to a woman named Maria and her young daughter, Rosa.

At first, only Rosa saw the Blessed Mother. She said, "Mama, the Virgin is calling me!" Maria was very surprised because Rosa had never been able to hear or speak.

Not long after, little Rosa died. Her mother brought her to the canyon and asked Mary to bring Rosa back to life. The Blessed Mother answered her prayers! When people came to see the spot where this happened, they found an image of the Blessed Mother on a flat area of the rocky canyon wall.

People immediately built a shrine around the image on the rock wall. Thousands of pilgrims come here to pray and honor the Blessed Mother. Other miracles happened here, too. Many memorial plaques (flat pieces of metal or stone with writing on them) can be seen at the shrine. These plaques thank Our Lady of Las Lajas for healing them or granting other miracles. In 1994, the shrine was made a basilica, a special honor given by the pope.

Sanctuary of Our Lady of Lourdes

The Sanctuary of Our Lady of Lourdes is one of the world's most-visited Catholic shrines. It is in the town of Lourdes in southwestern **France**. It marks the place where the Virgin

Mary appeared to 14-year-old Bernadette Soubirous in 1858. Bernadette was collecting firewood near the grotto, or **cave**, of Massabielle when Mary appeared to her. Bernadette did not know who she was and called her "lady."

Mary appeared to Bernadette 18 times. She instructed Bernadette to drink water and wash from a spring that suddenly appeared inside the grotto. Mary also told her to tell the priests to build a chapel at the grotto so people could come for processions of the Blessed Sacrament, which are still held there daily. Today, there are also three basilicas built around this site where people come to pray!

Mary's most important message to Bernadette was sharing her title of Immaculate Conception. Bernadette did not understand what this meant, but the priests did, and that is why they believed that she had seen Mary. Mary's title of Immaculate Conception refers to Mary being conceived without original sin. This meant she was completely pure and could be the Mother of Jesus.

Many people travel to the sanctuary, especially those who are sick and disabled. Lourdes water has flowed from the grotto since Mary appeared to Bernadette and is known for many miraculous healings. Visitors can even bathe in the water and collect it in bottles to bring home!

The grotto of Massabielle is the most famous site in the sanctuary. Around the world, many people have decorated small caves or created places to look like the Lourdes grotto because of their love for Mary and St. Bernadette. The feast day of Our Lady of Lourdes is February 11.

Sandboarding

Sandboarding is a lot like **skiing** and snowboarding. Instead of going down snow-covered **mountains**, a sandboarder balances on a single board like a snowboard, sliding down mountains of sand called **dunes**. This is a popular activity in the Ica Desert in **Peru**.

The dunes in the Ica Desert can reach up to 1,600 feet high. There are no ski lifts like what you might find on a snowy mountain. Instead, people get around in dune buggies. Dune buggies, locally known as *areneros*, are vehicles with special tires designed to go through the **desert** sand.

There are a few differences between snowboarding and sandboarding. One difference is it is very hot in the desert, so sandboarders must pay careful attention to the time of day they choose to be outside. Another difference is that snow is very slick, like ice, but sand is coarse and rough. This makes it more difficult to move through the sand. Before heading down each dune, a special wax must be rubbed onto the bottom of the sandboard to give speed and a smoother ride.

Huacachina is a small tourist village surrounded by dunes in the Ica Desert. Because it has a natural desert **lake**, people often refer to it as the "**oasis** of America." There are many hotels, restaurants, and opportunities to sandboard for the tens of thousands of tourists that visit each year.

Santiago de Compostela Cathedral

Santiago de Compostela Cathedral is a large church in the region of Galicia in the north of **Spain**. The cathedral is built over the relics of Saint James the Greater, one of the twelve apostles. (Santiago means "Saint James" in Spanish.) It is one of the only churches still standing that is built over an apostle's tomb! The others are **St. Peter's Basilica** in **Vatican City** and **St. Thomas Cathedral Basilica** in **India**. For hundreds of years, pilgrims on the **Camino de Santiago** pilgrimage have come to pray at the shrine of St. James.

Santiago de Compostela was built long ago, in the year 1211. It has thick stone walls and very high ceilings that are rounded at the top. When you enter the cathedral and look up, you will be amazed at the stone pillars holding up the high roof. There is a huge dome right over the altar in the center of the cathedral. Pilgrims to the Santiago Cathedral can come behind the altar to kiss a famous statue of St. James.

Santiago de Compostela has a huge censer used during special Masses. (A censer holds burning incense and is swung by a priest or server to honor holy things.) It takes eight people to swing the censer because it is over five feet high! Would you like to make a pilgrimage to Santiago de Compostela someday?

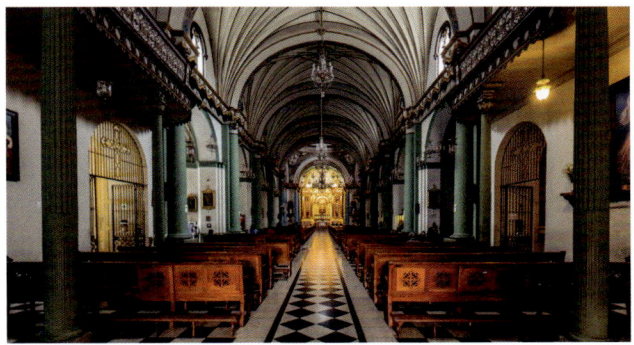

Santo Domingo

The Basilica and Convent of Santo Domingo was one of the first churches in Lima, **Peru**. The Dominicans built Santo Domingo for their missionaries in the sixteenth century. The beautiful church and convent are dedicated to Our Lady of the Rosary, but they are usually called Santo Domingo (Spanish for "Saint Dominic").

In the seventeenth century, **St. Martin de Porres** lived as a friar at the Convent of Santo Domingo. St. Martin, **St. Rose of Lima**, and St. John Macias (another Peruvian saint) are all buried at Santo Domingo! The saints' relics are displayed in a beautiful gold-covered chapel near the main altar.

Visitors to the church can pray before a statue of Our Lady of the Rosary and the Child Jesus above the main altar. St. Martin and St. Rose also loved to pray in front of this same statue! Inside the convent, there is the same wooden crucifix from the time of St. Martin.

St. Martin would sometimes pray so deeply in front of this crucifix that he would levitate (a grace given to some saints where they hover above the ground).

Santo Domingo is also known for starting the University of San Marcos, the first official university in Peru and the oldest university in the Americas. This university is now at a different location in Lima. Dominican friars still live and work at Santo Domingo today.

Saturnia Hot Springs

The Saturnia Hot Springs are one of **Italy's** natural wonders. Hot springs are springs of water that come up from deep inside the earth. The water is heated by the rock at the earth's core—or by the roots of a **volcano**. The Saturnia Hot Springs are heated by the extinct volcano Mt. Amiata in Tuscany, northern Italy. (An extinct volcano is one that will not erupt again.)

Hidden deep within the earth, these hot springs pick up natural chemicals and minerals and finally bubble up outside the village of Saturnia. For thousands of years, the hot springs have been gushing at the rate of 132 gallons of water per second. A fancy spa and golf resort has been built around the beautiful pools of water.

From the resort, the water flows into the Gorello stream for about a mile. This stream then spills out and over a cluster of natural pools and the Cascate del Mulino waterfalls. Over the centuries, the water carved these pools in the limestone rock. Far back in the Bronze Age, the Etruscans lived at these springs and enjoyed bathing in the warm pools of water. When the Romans came along, they were jealous, so they took the springs for themselves.

Today, people come from all over the world to soak in the hot springs. The water stays warm all year. Even in the winter, it is around 100°F! It does have a lot of sulfur in it, which makes it smell like spoiled eggs, but the natural beauty of the falls and the landscape make it all worth it!

Scarlet Macaw

Scarlet macaws are beautiful parrots that live in the **Amazon rainforest** and can be found in **Peru**. Their red, yellow, and blue feathers are eye-catching. They are very large birds, measuring almost three feet from beak to tail. Scarlet macaws have strong, wide wings and hollow bones that allow them to fly at a speed of 35 miles per hour.

Scarlet macaws typically live about 40–50 years in the wild, but in captivity, they can live as many as 90 years. They are rowdy birds. They make high- and low-pitched squawks and screams that can be heard from miles away.

Scarlet macaws gather in flocks at night, and in the morning, they fly great distances in small groups searching for food. They feed on fruits, nuts, seeds, flowers, nectar, insects, and larvae. Their curved beaks help them crack open nuts and shells, and their tongue can grasp what is inside. Some of the fruit they eat is poisonous to other animals. They also eat dirt and clay, and it is believed that the clay helps keep them safe from the poisonous fruit. If you ever visit a **rainforest**, look for these beautiful and noisy birds!

Scottish Bagpipes

The bagpipes are a fascinating musical instrument, also known as "the pipes." Bagpipes are really loud! You will know this if you've ever heard bagpipes played indoors. Because of how loud they are, bagpipes have been used in history to communicate over long distances. They could call men to war and intimidate enemies on the battlefield. But bagpipes can also play music that inspires people and stirs up their emotions: bagpipes are often played in Scotland at weddings, festivals, and funerals. Bagpipes can play sad melodies that make people cry, energetic marches, and joyful dance music.

Bagpipes work in an interesting way. They have a bag that holds air, and the player keeps the bag full of air by blowing into it with a tube or by using a bellows, which pumps in air. To make music, the bag is pressed, and the air comes out through a kind of flute called a chanter. The chanter plays the main melody. Since it plays the melody, the term "chanter" is derived from the Latin word *cantare*, meaning "to sing." There are usually other flute-like tubes coming from the bag that make sounds whenever the bag is squeezed. These are called drones. The drones lay against the musician's shoulder. Each drone plays a different note and harmonizes with the chanter. The bagpipe's sound is made by reeds that move quickly, making a noise, when air is blown over them.

Scotland, in the **United Kingdom**, is famous for its bagpipes, and many pipe tunes come from there. Many other places, however, have different types of bagpipes, including **Europe**, some of North **Africa**, and the Middle East. Bagpipes were probably first invented in ancient Egypt. Then, they were used in ancient Greece and Rome, and they were probably introduced to Scotland when the **Roman Empire** invaded Britain.

In the United Kingdom and its Commonwealth nations, such as **Canada**, New Zealand, and **Australia**, the Great Highland bagpipe is still frequently used during funerals and memorials, especially among fire departments or military and police forces.

Shakespeare

William Shakespeare was a great poet and playwright who lived in England. He was born in 1564 and died in 1616.

Shakespeare is probably most famous for his plays, including *Julius Caesar*, *Romeo and Juliet*, *Macbeth*, and *Hamlet*. During his life, he wrote at least 39 plays! The English loved going to see his plays, and sometimes the king or queen would invite his actors to the palace to perform their plays there. Sometimes, Shakespeare would act in his plays, too. Shakespeare told very interesting stories in his plays. Some are sad and some are funny, but they all have wisdom about life and what it means to be a human. This is what made him one of the most famous writers in history.

Shakespeare also wrote many poems called sonnets. He developed a new form of the sonnet and wrote 154 of them that we still have today. These sonnets are very thoughtful and explore topics like what it means to love someone and what kinds of things last forever.

Shakespeare's life is a bit mysterious since we don't have many historical records of him. We know he married a woman named Anne and had three children: Susanna, Hamnet, and Judith. He moved to London, wrote, and performed with a group of actors there. Oddly enough, there are seven years of his life where no one knows where he was! Some say he became a soldier, and others say that he traveled to **Italy**. We may never know more about Shakespeare's life, but we can still enjoy his amazing plays and poems.

Sheep

The sheep is a domestic animal that originally came from **Europe** and **Asia**. A domestic animal is one that has been tamed and kept by humans for many generations and no longer lives in the wild. Asia was the first place where people kept sheep, but Europe has also been raising sheep for thousands of years. Nowadays, they are kept all over the world, and there are more than one billion sheep worldwide!

There are as many as 200 different breeds, or types, of sheep. Some breeds have horns and some don't. Some are white, and some are black, brown, or spotted. Sheep live together in big flocks. A female sheep is called an ewe, and a male sheep is called a ram. A baby sheep is called a lamb. Some sheep are raised for their delicious meat or milk, while other breeds are kept for their wool, which is used to make warm clothes. Sheep farmers shave wool off the sheep when it grows long enough. The wool grows back, so one sheep can produce lots of wool in its lifetime.

Sheep are herbivores and only eat grass and other short plants. Like goats and cows, sheep have four different stomachs. A little while after swallowing their food, sheep spit up mouthfuls of grass into their mouth and chew them over again. This is called "chewing the cud." Then they swallow their food again. This method of digesting food allows sheep to get enough nutrients from the grass.

Sheshan Basilica

Sheshan Basilica is a Marian shrine in **China**. It stands on Sheshan Mountain near the busy city of Shanghai. It is very special because it was the first basilica built in eastern **Asia**.

The basilica began as a small chapel joined to a retreat house for Jesuit priests. At that time, a terrible civil war called the Taiping Rebellion was going on in southern China. The Chinese fought each other for 13 years, killing at least 20 million people. As the fighting continued, the superior of the Jesuit priests went up the **mountain** to the chapel and prayed to the Blessed Mother. He asked her to save them from the attack of the rebels. He promised that if his prayer was answered, a basilica would be built in thanksgiving for Our Lady's protection.

His prayer was answered. The fighting ended the next year. In 1873, after nine years, the

building was finished, and the bishop consecrated the new basilica. The shrine was called Our Lady Help of Christians of Sheshan. On top of the basilica stands a statue of the Blessed Mother, reminding the world that China and its people are under her protection.

Shrine of Our Lady of La Salette

The Shrine of Our Lady of La Salette marks the location where the Blessed Mother appeared to two shepherd children in **France**.

Eleven-year-old Maximin Giraud and 14-year-old Melanie Calvat saw the Blessed Virgin Mary weeping in September of 1846. They said Mary continued to cry as she told them that mankind needed to repent and that she could no longer hold back the hand of her Son from punishing sinners. She specifically mentioned the inappropriate use of Jesus' name causing much distress, and she also predicted famine.

Our Lady of La Salette is the only Marian apparition in which she was crying when she appeared.

Many modern saints were affected by the message of La Salette, including **St. John Vianney** and **St. John Bosco**. Pope **St. John Paul II** wrote, "La Salette is a message of hope, for our hope is nourished by the intercession of her who is the Mother of mankind."

Conversion of all people to Jesus is the main message of La Salette. Many shrines dedicated to the apparition and message are found outside of France, including in Portugal, Mexico, **India**, and two in the United States.

Shrine of the Canadian Martyrs

The Shrine of the Canadian Martyrs is in Ontario, **Canada**. One of six national shrines in Canada, it is a place where people go to honor a group of six priests and two ordinary people who were martyred for their faith.

In the seventeenth century, many Jesuit missionaries left **France** and went to **North America** so they could teach the Native American Indians about Jesus and the Catholic Faith. Fr. Jérôme Lalemant and Fr. Jean de Brébeuf started a missionary site where they lived and taught the Catholic Faith to the Hurons, a Native American Indian tribe.

The inside of the shrine is shaped like an overturned canoe. It was completed in 1926. Stained glass windows, Stations of the Cross, and the altar were donated by churches in Toronto, Canada and London, England. The

bones of St. Jean de Brébeuf, St. Gabriel Lalemant, and St. Charles Garnier are housed in the shrine. The shrine is closed during autumn and winter. Because it was built without insulation, it gets very cold!

Eight of these martyred missionaries are remembered at the shrine: St. René Goupil, **St. Isaac Jogues**, St. Jean de Lalande, St. Antoine Daniel, St. Jean de Brébeuf, St. Noël Chabanel, St. Charles Garnier, and St. Gabriel Lalemant. They were canonized in 1930 by Pope Pius XI. Their feast day is October 19 in the United States and September 26 in Canada.

Shrine of Saint Anne de Beaupré

The Shrine of St. Anne de Beaupré is located along the St. Lawrence River in **Quebec**, **Canada**. One of the six national shrines of Canada, it is sometimes also called the Basilica of St. Anne. The shrine was created to honor St. Anne, who is the mother of Mary. That means she is Jesus' grandmother. Think of some things you enjoy doing with your grandmother. Can you picture Jesus doing those types of things with St. Anne? How special!

Many miracles have happened to people who have visited the church. The first reported miracle happened when the shrine was being built. A man named Louis Guimond was one of the builders. He suffered from rheumatism, which makes joints such as your knees and elbows very sore. After placing only three stones for the foundation of the building, he was cured! As more people shared their miraculous stories, more people wanted to visit the shrine, so they made the building bigger. Eventually they built the basilica (a very large church), and it opened for worship in 1876. Sadly, fire destroyed the church in 1922. The basilica was rebuilt in 1926, but it took many more years before it was completed.

About half a million people visit the shrine each year. When they arrive, they can see the many canes and crutches left at the front entrance by people who say they have been miraculously cured .

One of the busiest times at the shrine is around July 26, which is the feast day of St. Anne.

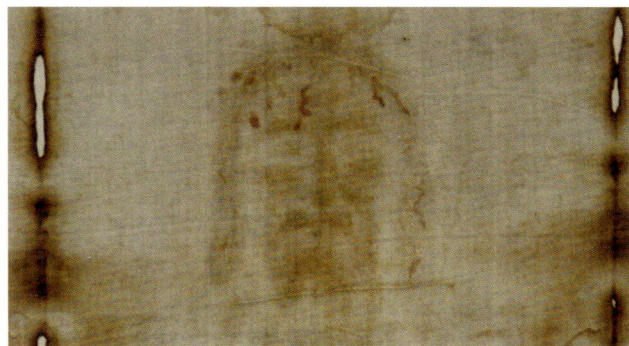

Shroud of Turin

Have you ever heard of a shroud? It is a blanket-like cloth that people used to wrap around someone after he died. The most famous shroud in the world is called the Shroud of Turin, also known as the Holy Shroud. You might wonder, why is a shroud famous? This shroud just might have the imprint of Jesus on it! This shroud is in Turin, **Italy**.

When looking at the shroud, you can see marks that look like Jesus' body as it would have been after He died. It shows a beard and long hair, His eyes are closed, and His hands are folded. There are lines that show where streaks of blood were on His face, and there are marks in the hands and feet. The image of Jesus' face on the Shroud of Turin is the basis for the devotion to the Holy Face of Jesus, and many churches have this image framed. Some people wear a medal showing this image on a necklace.

Many scientists have done studies on the shroud, learning many things about the type of cloth, the microscopic cells of plants and animals found on the cloth, and about how old the cloth might be. Some scientists think the cloth is the actual cloth that was wrapped around Jesus' body, but other scientists disagree.

The Catholic Church has never officially declared that the Shroud of Turin is or is not the real burial cloth of Jesus. What the Church does teach us is that our faith and devotion to Jesus is the most important thing.

Silk Road

The Silk Road was a series of roads connecting

China to the Middle East and Europe. In the ancient world, people traveled on these roads with things to sell and trade in other places. One country would make certain goods, such as swords, while another country would produce other things, such as silk. These countries would then make a deal to trade some of their goods. If you lived in medieval China, you could use the Silk Road to buy things that you needed and make money selling things.

China was famous for producing the finest silk. Silk is a very smooth, valuable fabric that can be made into clothing, bedding, and many beautiful things. Many other countries wanted silk, so Chinese traders traded their silk for other useful items. China traded many other important things that the Western world wanted—including tea, spices, paper, and gunpowder—and other beautiful things like jade and porcelain. The West traded things like horses, glass, and other fabrics with China.

The Silk Road wasn't just one road but many roads that stretched for more than 4,000 miles from China to Europe and even Africa. Many traders would only travel back and forth on a part of the road, taking goods to sell to another trader who would then travel farther. The Silk Road was used for trade for nearly 1,500 years. Today, you can still visit many interesting places along the Silk Road that have been preserved, including medieval cities, desert watering places, and a grove of frankincense trees!

Silkworms

Silkworms are special little creatures that come from China. They are the caterpillar form of the *Bombyx mori* moth. Silkworms eat only white mulberry leaves. They have a special ability to make a material called silk, which is thin and smooth and makes wonderful fabric.

When a silkworm is ready to turn into a moth, it will make a little house around itself out of silk, like a sleeping bag! This house is called a cocoon. It is a safe little home for the silkworm to hide in while it's changing into a moth. The whole cocoon is made from one very long, very thin piece of silk. If you were to stretch out the thread of silk, it would be anywhere between 1,000 and 3,000 feet long. That's taller than the tallest skyscrapers that have ever been built!

When the Chinese discovered that silk could be woven into fabric, they began to make things like clothing, bedsheets, and many other things out of the soft and beautiful material. China was the only place in the world where the silkworm lived, so silk could only be made in China. Because of this, China was able to trade their silk for other valuable things that other countries made. Silk is part of what made China famous throughout the world. Silkworms have been making silk in China for more than 5,000 years. These creatures now live in other places in the world, too.

Simón Bolívar

Simón Bolívar was the leader of a revolution in **South America**. He lived from 1783–1830. During his life, he led **Peru** and many other surrounding countries to freedom from the Spanish Empire.

We know him now as Simón Bolívar, but his full name was Simón José Antonio de la Santísima Trinidad Bolívar Palacios Ponte y Blanco! He was born in Venezuela to a wealthy family. Like other young men from rich families in South America, Bolívar went to school in **Spain** and lived there for a while.

While he was in Spain, Bolívar learned new, modern ideas about what makes a good life. He came to believe that people should be free and should choose the kind of government they want. So when Bolívar came back home, he decided to free South America from Spanish rule.

Bolívar began by fighting against Spain as a militia officer in the Venezuelan War of Independence. He went on to fight Spanish forces in many different battles, defeating them and freeing territories from Spain. Eventually, he united many of these territories into a new country, the Republic of Colombia. Bolívar served as the first president of Columbia, and he was also the president of Peru and Bolivia.

Today, Bolívar is remembered as an important hero of South America. The countries of Bolivia and the Bolivarian Republic of Venezuela even named themselves after him! Bolivia and Venezuela also named their currency (money) after him. Bolivia's currency is the *boliviano*, and Venezuela's currency is the *bolívar*.

Skiing

Skiing is a very popular sport in **Canada**. It is done for fun, exercise, and competition.

In order to glide across the snow, a person wears skis on his feet. Skis are made of two long, narrow boards. The skier first puts on special boots. The skis then clamp onto the boots. A pair of poles with spikes on the ends help the skier push himself forward, keep his balance, and make turns in the snow.

There are a few basic types of skiing. When a person skis down a **mountain**, it is called Alpine skiing. When a person wants to glide across flat, snowy trails, it is called cross-country skiing. Most exciting to watch is ski jumping. Ski jumpers ski down a slope and fly off a big ramp called a jump at the end, landing farther down the slope. Jumps can be as high as 300 feet!

A ski resort is a place that has a lot of mountain slopes to ski down. The resort gives the skiers different ways to get to the tops of the slopes. A popular option is cable cars or chair lifts, which carry skiers to the top in small compartments or seats that move on cables.

People like to ski in places like Canada, where the snowfall is very deep. Two of the most popular ski resorts in Canada are Banff in Alberta and Whistler in British Columbia. The ski season in Canada begins in early November and runs through late May. The Slush Cup is an exciting event that ends the season. Skiers gather together to see who can ski the farthest across a slushy, icy pool!

three colorful umbrellas, and golden lace.

Try to imagine 30 snake-shaped boats with 100 rowers in each one. The rowers paddle hard for miles, racing through the water at 90 strokes per minute. If you listen, you will hear singing and shouting. This keeps everyone paddling in fast, rhythmic motions. The singers' only job is to stand above the rowers, shouting their ancient boat songs. Everyone is in high spirits! The first to reach the end wins the prize money and is honored by all for months after.

Snake Boat Racing

Snake boat racing is a sports event that takes place in Kerala, a western state in **India**. The racing boats are made of wood in the shape of snakes and are over 100 feet long. They were first used for fighting wars in the thirteenth century.

The races are held each year during the state's harvest festival. Thousands of people come to watch the races—both locals and tourists.

Each village has a boat. The carpenter and villagers work hard to prepare their boat for the big race. They rub it down with fish oil so it will speed through the water. The people of the village are very proud of their boat. They decorate it with a flag, two or

Snake Charmer

Snake charmers are street performers who work with cobra snakes. Snake charming used to be very common in **India**. Snake charmers like to use cobras because a cobra's defensive posture makes them stand upright. The cobra also has a slow strike, which means the snake charmer can avoid getting bitten.

When performing, a snake charmer might sit cross-legged on a rug with a wicker basket in front of him. Using a flute-like instrument, the snake charmer begins to play a song. Then, a snake rises from inside the basket. To someone watching a snake charmer, it looks like the cobra is dancing as it sways back and forth to the music. But snakes are actually deaf! The snake charmer knows this, so he makes the snake "dance" through a special trick. What is actually happening is that the snake is following the instrument as it moves.

Snake charming was more common in the past. In the 1970s, it was mostly banned by the Indian government to protect cobras. However, it is still practiced in other countries.

Snow Petrel

The snow petrel is a small seabird that lives in **Antarctica** and some of the surrounding **islands**. Like other petrels, it spends most of its time flying over the open **ocean**. When it needs to rest, it sits on **icebergs** or floats on the water.

Usually, the snow petrel only goes on land to build nests and raise chicks. When on land, snow petrels form huge colonies, or groups of many birds all in one place. Snow petrel couples stay together for life and raise baby petrels together. The female snow petrel lays one egg in its nest, which is made of pebbles and usually hidden in a rocky area. After it hatches, the chick stays in the nest for about two months.

The snow petrel likes to eat fish, krill, octopuses, squids, animals like clams and snails, and dead animals like seals or whales.

Fun Facts:

- The snow petrel is tube-nosed. It has tubes (called naricorns) on top of its beak instead of nostrils.
- The snow petrel swallows a lot of ocean water, so it has a special gland for getting rid of the extra salt in its body.
- The name "petrel" might have come from the fact that these birds appear to run on the water as they take off—just like St. Peter walked on water when Jesus called to him!

Snowy Owl

The snowy owl lives in the **Arctic** in northern **Canada**, Alaska, and other cold places like Russia and Norway. They like wide, open areas, such as fields and shorelines. They are one of the largest species of owl in the world. They have soft white feathers that help them blend in with their surroundings. In winter, they look like just another patch of dirty snow! Snowy owls can make about fifteen different sounds such as chirps, clucks, squeals, grunts, and cackles. Their primary call sounds like a barking dog.

Most owls sleep during the day and are awake at night, but snowy owls are the opposite. They are active during the day and sleep at night. They spend most of their time sitting on the ground or on rocks. When they are hunting, they may perch on fence posts, telephone poles, haystacks, chimneys, and roofs so they have a good spot to look for something to eat.

One of the snowy owl's favorite things to eat is a lemming, which is a small, mouse-like rodent. They eat about three to five lemmings a day! Snowy owls have large yellow eyes that allow them to see prey from far away. Their soft feathers help them fly silently so they can sneak up on their prey. They can also use their keen sense of hearing to catch prey they cannot see.

Fun Facts:
- Snowy owls usually live about 10 years in the wild, but one lived 23 years in the wild! The oldest snowy owl taken care of by humans was 35 years old.
- The snowy owl is the official bird of **Quebec**.
- North American snowy owls like to winter in airports because they are built in flat and grassy areas. Airports are also hosts to lots of bugs the snowy owl likes to eat!

Spanish Armada

In 1588, a huge navy from **Spain** called the Spanish Armada set sail. They were on their way to England (now part of the **United Kingdom**) to defeat the English. The Spanish Armada was called the Invincible Armada because no one thought it could be beaten!

But the Spanish Armada was delayed because of weather, and the English heard they were coming. The armada arrived in the **English Channel** with 117 ships, many of which were much bigger than the English ships. The Spaniards had many more guns than the English, too. The English had more ships, but they didn't have all the supplies they needed because they weren't expecting an attack.

The navies fought for weeks in the English Channel. In battles at **sea**, you can either sink the enemy ship by hitting it with cannons or board it—go on the ship—and defeat the sailors and soldiers to win the ship. The smaller, faster English ships tried to get close enough so they could shoot the Spanish ships but not have to fight the soldiers on board. Since the Spanish ships were bigger, they had more soldiers on board and would probably win a hand-to-hand fight.

One night, when the Spanish Armada was anchored all close together, the English sent fireships. A fireship is a ship set on fire, and it can easily destroy other wooden ships nearby by setting them on fire too. The English sacrificed eight of their ships, setting them on fire with guns and supplies still on board because they didn't have time to take them out. The fireships sailed toward the armada, which scattered in terror!

After that, the English cannons sank some Spanish ships. The rest of the armada tried to get away by sailing north around the coast of Britain. Many of their ships were driven by winds and storms onto the coast of Ireland, where they were wrecked. The Invincible Armada was defeated.

Spanish Fighting Bull

The Spanish Fighting Bull is a special type of bull known for its strong muscles, bravery, and spirited nature. These bulls are raised on ranches in **Spain**, where they grow up running around in large, open fields.

Spanish Fighting Bulls have a striking appearance. They are usually black or dark brown and have powerful horns that curve upwards. These bulls can weigh up to 1,500 pounds!

These bulls are treated with great care and respect. They are given the best food and lots of space to roam. This ensures they are healthy and strong. The Spanish Fighting Bull plays an important role in Spanish culture and traditions. Some bulls are used in **bullfighting**, a very old sport in Spain. If a bull shows special bravery in a bullfight, it can be given a pardon and sent back to its ranch to live out its life with less excitement.

Fun Fact:

Spanish Fighting Bulls are often honored for their bravery. Visiting a bull ranch in Spain can be an exciting experience. You can see these majestic animals up close and learn about their importance in Spanish culture.

Spanish Conquistadors

The conquistadors were soldiers and explorers from **Spain** who lived in the fifteenth and sixteenth centuries. They traveled to **North** and **South America** and conquered many lands. This is why they are called conquistadors, which means "conquerors" in Spanish.

Conquistadors had many different reasons to travel to the Americas. Some wanted to find new ways to travel to places like **India** or **China** for trading. Others wanted power and riches. They wanted to look for silver and gold in the Americas.

When the conquistadors got to the Americas, they met many groups of people who had already been living there. In Mexico, a conquistador named Hernán Cortés led the Spanish against the Aztecs and their leader Moctezuma II (also known as Montezuma). In **Peru**, the conquistador **Francisco Pizarro** conquered the **Incas**. After the Spanish defeated the Aztecs and the Incas, they spread throughout the Americas and built many settlements.

Some of the conquistadors were very cruel to the native people they conquered. Some Spanish missionaries who came with the conquistadors defended these people and tried to make the conquistadors treat them better.

These missionaries cared for the native people and taught them about God.

Spanish Eagle

The Spanish eagle is a bird found in **Spain**. It is sometimes called the Iberian imperial eagle because it comes from the Iberian Peninsula, which is where you find Spain and Portugal. The Spanish eagle measures about two and a half feet, and its wings stretch up to seven feet wide. Adult Spanish eagles might look a bit like the golden eagle, but its feathers are a much darker brown with a bit of white along the top edges of its wings. This makes it easy to tell apart from other eagles. These white feathers on the tops of their wings are also the reason you might sometimes hear the Spanish eagle called the white-shouldered eagle.

Like other eagles, the Spanish eagle has a sharp, hooked beak and sharp talons that are perfect for helping it hunt and catch its food. The Spanish eagle shares the same favorite food as the **Iberian lynx**—the European rabbit. If there aren't enough rabbits around, the Spanish eagle has been known to eat other birds and smaller rodents. These birds like living in woodland areas. They build their nests in the trees and tend to stay as far away from people as possible so that they aren't bothered. Their nests are very large, usually over four feet across.

Spanish eagles lay two to three eggs at a time in their nests. After the baby eagles have hatched, it takes about two months for them to grow feathers and be able to fly for the first time. That's faster than a human baby learns how to walk!

Spectacled Caiman

A spectacled caiman is an animal found in **Peru** that is very similar to an alligator. There are different types of caimans that live in **South America**, but you can recognize the spectacled caiman by the ridge between its eyes. It looks like it has a pair of glasses on! All caimans are a dark color and hatch from eggs. They are carnivores, or meat-eaters, and mostly eat fish, snails, and crabs.

Spectacled caimans like to live near fresh water, including **marshes** and **rivers**. You can find them in the wetlands of southern Brazil and near the water in Peru.

There are some differences between caimans and alligators. Caimans are faster and have sharper teeth. Most caimans are smaller than most alligators, generally about half the size. Spectacled caimans communicate by making nine different calls and also by moving their tails into different positions.

Caimans have a soft side: female caimans are great mothers. A caiman mother carefully makes a nest on land, where she lays between 10–40 eggs. The shells are more like leather than the hard chicken eggs you're probably familiar with. After about six weeks, the eggs hatch. If any caiman is having trouble hatching from its egg, the mother carefully uses her sharp teeth to break open the shell. After the babies, called hatchlings, have hatched, you'll see the mother put them in her mouth—but not to eat them! Instead, she carefully carries each baby caiman, one by one, in her mouth to a shallow nursery pool where they all learn how to swim. A caiman mother stays with her babies and guards them for as long as 18 months. Caiman mothers are very protective and will fight any other predator to keep their babies safe.

Spotted Hyena

Spotted hyenas are mammals that live in **Africa** south of the **Sahara Desert**. They are found in **savannas**, grasslands, woodlands, and even **mountains**. Although they look like large dogs, they are not part of the dog family.

One of the strange sounds they make is a crazy laugh, which is why they're also called laughing hyenas. It's a high-pitched laugh or giggle that frightens people when they hear it, but hyenas usually make that sound when they're afraid.

Did you know that a group of hyenas is called a clan? Each clan has a female that's in charge. Female hyenas are larger than the males. This is very different from most mammals where the male is larger and takes charge of its group.

Hyenas are nocturnal, which means they are active at night. This is partly because it's too hot in the day to be moving around. It also makes hunting easier because they can hide from their prey better when it's dark. As you can guess, their night vision is much stronger than ours.

Spotted hyenas are carnivores. This means they eat other animals, even if they're already dead. They can eat the bones without any problem because they have powerful jaws and special stomachs to digest them. Their jaws are even stronger than a bear's!

Some people think that hyenas follow after **lions** and eat what is left over from a kill, but it works the other way around. The lions listen for hyenas' cries after killing prey and then take the food from the hyenas. Lions are hyenas' main predator, but hyenas are very smart and know how to protect themselves.

Statue of Liberty

The Statue of Liberty is a 151-foot statue of a woman that stands on Liberty Island near New York City in the United States. The statue was dedicated in 1886 to remind people of the freedoms that Americans fought for and won. It was a gift from **France** as an act of friendship between the two countries. Millions of people traveling to the United States have been welcomed by this symbol of freedom as they began their new life in America.

If you take a ferry boat across the **harbor**, you can see Lady Liberty for yourself. In one hand, she holds up a torch. It stands for progress. The tablet in her other hand stands for the law. It has the date of the Declaration of Independence written on it: July 4, 1776.

If you go to Liberty Island, you can visit the museum to learn how the statue was built. It was designed by the French sculptor Frédéric Auguste Bartholdi. The framework was made from iron, and pure copper was hammered into shape for the body of the statue. Over time, the copper color changed into the green color seen now.

Inside the statue is a spiral staircase leading to the top. Looking out from inside of the crown, you can see stunning views of the Atlantic Ocean and New York State!

Stonehenge

Stonehenge is a prehistoric monument in Wiltshire, England, part of the **United Kingdom**. ("Prehistoric" means before written history, so it's very old!) It is one of many henges found in the country. A *henge* is made of stones standing in a circular pattern, surrounded by a ridge of earth and a ditch. The largest stones at Stonehenge are around 13 feet high and 7 feet wide and weigh around 25 tons.

There is some mystery surrounding Stonehenge. No one knows who built it or why it was built in the first place. Some people think that it was used as a place to worship the sun or the moon. Others believe it was a burial site. During the summer solstice (the longest day of the year), the sunrise lines up with some of the stones. This could mean that it was a calendar used to mark the seasons of the year.

What we do know about Stonehenge is that it would have taken hundreds of people to build it. They would have been very smart and very strong. Remember, in prehistoric times, there were no roads, trucks, or trains. The wheel had not even been invented yet! The huge stones had to be moved from 20 miles away—sometimes from much farther. It is thought that the builders did this by dragging them on logs.

Stonehenge first began as a circular ditch.

Instead of digging with shovels or a backhoe, the builders used tools made from antlers. The huge stones were shaped by hand with hammerstones, a very hard rock used as a tool. Without the help of a crane, the stones had to be put in place using ropes, wooden beams, and manpower.

Today, Stonehenge is one of the most famous landmarks in the United Kingdom.

Sugarloaf Mountain

Sugarloaf Mountain is a tall hill at the mouth of Guanabara Bay in Rio de Janeiro, Brazil, in **South America**. It stands on a **peninsula** surrounded by the Atlantic Ocean.

Are you wondering why it is named Sugarloaf? Hundreds of years ago, the Portuguese called it by that name. When they first saw the hill from their ship, they thought it looked like a giant sugar loaf. At that time, sugar was sold in loaves in the shape of a rounded cone, much like the **mountain's** shape.

Sugarloaf Mountain is 1,299 feet tall at its highest point. People enjoy climbing its steep granite and quartz slopes in order to reach the top. There is also an easier way. This easier way is what made Sugarloaf famous. In 1912, a cable car was built to bring visitors to the mountain's peak. It was made of wood at first, but the one that runs now is a glass-walled car that holds about 60 people. The glass walls allow people to see some amazing views of Rio de Janeiro, the Marvelous City.

Have you learned about the **Christ the Redeemer Statue** that is only a 40-minute car ride away? If you have, then you know that Sugarloaf is not the only tall hill on the peninsula. There are several of them that make a beautiful landscape.

Surfing

Surfing is a water sport where a special board called a surfboard is used to ride a wave. Most people think of places like Hawaii when they think of surfing, but surfing is also very popular in **Peru**. The beaches in northern Peru have warm water and beautiful weather all year round because they are near the **Equator**. One beach in Peru, called Chicama, has some of the longest waves in the world. These waves are up to a mile and a half long!

A surfer first has to paddle on his surfboard out into the **ocean** to find big waves. Then he has to catch a good wave and stand up on his board. The surfer positions himself so the wave carries him along while he balances carefully. It takes a lot of practice and skill not to fall off the surfboard while riding a wave!

Modern surfing started in Hawaii, but some think that native peoples in Peru were the first to surf. Ancient Peruvians rode waves on a special kind of **reed boat** that can still be seen today. They are called *caballitos de totora*, meaning "little reed horses," because you sit on them like you would ride a horse. The native people used to ride waves on these boats while catching fish in the ocean.

Swiss Guards

Swiss Guards are soldiers who live in **Vatican City** in Rome, **Italy**. For more than 500 years, their job has been to protect the pope and keep him safe. They also guard the place where the pope lives and works, which is called the Apostolic Palace.

There are a few rules to become a member of the Swiss guard. A man must be:

- A good Catholic
- Between the ages of 19 and 30
- Healthy and in good shape
- At least 5 feet, 8.5 inches tall
- Unmarried and a native of Switzerland
- Trained in the Swiss Army

Every Swiss Guard takes an oath during a special ceremony. They swear to keep the Holy Father safe even if it means dying to protect him. Because of this promise, it's important that they keep their bodies strong. Every day, they exercise and play **football** (known in the United States as soccer).

The uniforms they wear today look like they did in the sixteenth century. On special days (for example, when they welcome the president of a country), they wear shining armor with helmets with red **ostrich** feathers. One day, you may visit the Vatican. If you need directions to a museum or a certain church, know that you can ask a Swiss Guard for help. They are easy to find in their colorful uniforms!

Sydney Opera House

The Sydney Opera House is a famous building that is built on the **harbor** in Sydney, **Australia**. In 1957, a contest was held in which people from all over the world could send in ideas about how to build the opera house. A Danish architect, Jørn Utzon, won the contest. (An architect is a person who designs buildings.) He was surprised when his design was chosen because he wasn't a famous architect!

Utzon's design for the Sydney Opera House was very unusual and difficult for the builders. The Sydney Opera House looks like big white sails or seashells. If you put all of the shells together, they would form a perfect sphere, like a giant golf ball! The building is also pretty tall. From **sea** level, the highest point of the building is about 22 stories tall.

The Sydney Opera House took much longer than expected to build because the design was so complicated. Utzon had to redo the plans for the building 12 times before it could be built without costing too much money or being too hard to build. Finally, the building was completed in 1973. It has become one of the most famous landmarks in the world. Hundreds of performances and concerts, including **operas**, are held there every year, and many tourists travel from all around the world to see this amazing building.

Taj Mahal

The Taj Mahal is a very large tomb located in **India**. It was built in the seventeenth century by King Shah Jahan in memory of his wife, Mumtaz Mahal. The Taj Mahal is one of the most famous landmarks in the world. Nearly 80 million people visit the Taj Mahal every year.

The Taj Mahal is made of white marble, a beautiful kind of rock that reflects the colors of the sunrise and sunset. The Taj Mahal's design is one of the most famous examples of the Islamic style of buildings. It has a large dome in the center, which is surrounded by four smaller domes. Four tall towers called minarets stand at each corner. At its highest point, the Taj Mahal reaches 240 feet! The Taj Mahal also has beautiful patterns all over the inside and the outside. The walls are decorated with Arabic calligraphy, which is a type of beautiful writing, and even jewels.

Inside the Taj Mahal, the tombs of King Shah and his wife, Mumtaz, are also beautifully decorated. However, these tombs do not actually house their bodies. These are more for show. The real tombs are in the lower levels of the building in a much simpler burial site.

Tarsier

A tarsier is a small monkey-like creature found in parts of Southeast **Asia**. Tarsiers are members of the primate family, which means they are similar to monkeys and lemurs. Like other primates, they spend lots of time in the trees. Tarsiers are named after the bones in their ankles, which are called tarsus bones.

Tarsiers have short, soft fur that is usually brown. They also have long, thin tails, and long fingers and toes that help them catch their prey. Tarsiers are very small, usually measuring only four to six inches long and weighing less than a pound. This means that they are so small that they could fit in your hand! Tarsiers also have very good hearing, and they can turn their heads almost all the way around the way owls can.

Tarsiers eat mostly bugs, frogs, and lizards, but sometimes they will eat small snakes and birds. Tarsiers hunt by sitting still and waiting patiently. Once their prey is close, they use their long back legs to jump from one tree to another. In this way, they can catch their prey even if it is flying.

Fun Fact:
A tarsier's eyes are bigger than its brain. These eyes are big in comparison to their small bodies, but each eye is actually smaller than a dime!

size of a small dog. It gets its name from the wild noises it makes. It lives on a large **Australian island** named Tasmania. The Tasmanian devil lives all over the island—even near the cities—but its favorite places to live are dry forests and woodlands along the coast.

The Tasmanian devil's main predator was the Tasmanian tiger until it became extinct (which means there are none living today). There are still wolves around that will sometimes prey on Tasmanian devils. Young Tasmanian devils have to watch out for eagles, owls, and wild dogs, too.

Tasmanian devils are **marsupials**, like **kangaroos**. The mothers have a small pouch where her babies stay for their first 100 days. The babies are called pups, joeys, or imps.

The Tasmanian devil usually lives by itself in a burrow, a den, or a **cave**. It is a nocturnal animal, which means it sleeps in the day and is awake at night. God gave it the ability to see in the dark. It's a carnivore, which means it eats meat. The Tasmanian devil hunts animals like small wombats, but it likes carrion most of all. Carrion is the flesh of dead animals. Because it has very strong teeth and jaws, it even eats bones!

Fun Fact:
Tasmanian devils can climb trees!

Tasmanian Devil

The Tasmanian devil is a mammal about the

Teotihuacan

Teotihuacan was an ancient city in central Mexico in **North America**. It was an important city between the first century BC and the seventh century AD. Teotihuacan was once the largest city in the Americas. Over 100,000 people lived in it! Today, you can visit its ruins just outside of Mexico City.

If you walk through Teotihuacan, you might travel down the wide street in the center of the city. This street is called the Avenue of the Dead, and there are many interesting buildings on either side of it. The most amazing buildings are three large pyramids: the Sun Pyramid, the Moon Pyramid, and the Feathered Serpent Pyramid.

The word *teotihuacan* means "birthplace of the gods." This name is actually not the original name of the city. We don't know what the people living there called it. Long after the civilization that built the city had passed away, other people who lived nearby gave it the name Teotihuacan and told many stories about the city. They thought the world had been created from the city of Teotihuacan.

Another interesting fact about Teotihuacan is that the people there lived in apartment buildings, just like many people do today! It didn't matter if you were rich or poor—everyone lived in one of these apartments. The insides of these buildings have many beautiful paintings that can still be seen today. These paintings have helped us learn about the religion and everyday lives of the people who lived there. Also, people usually lived in the same building as others who did the same kind of work. For example, if you were a builder, your neighbors would be builders, too.

Terracotta Army

The Terracotta Army is an ancient Chinese army made of clay. It was discovered underground outside the city of Xi'an, **China** in 1974 when farmers were digging for a well. Today, there are over two thousand clay soldiers uncovered for display. Experts say that there may be six thousand more still buried.

Try to imagine thousands of six-foot clay sculptures buried underground. They all stand in military order, with the commanders and common soldiers in their places. Not one soldier looks the same as another. Some carry weapons like swords or spears. Even their faces are different!

Why are they there? The terracotta soldiers were put there about two hundred years before Jesus was born, long before there were any Christians. Instead, people in China had different beliefs. They thought that after a person died, anything buried with him would go with him to another life. Around 247 BC, the first emperor of China decided that he wanted an army to protect him in the afterlife. He ordered hundreds of thousands of workers to build his underground city of soldiers.

Why are they called "terracotta"? Because the soldiers were made with terracotta. Terracotta is a clay that comes from the earth. After the body parts for the soldiers were formed, they had to be fired, or "cooked," so the soft clay would harden. In Italian, *terracotta* means "cooked earth."

Thar Desert

The Thar Desert is a huge **desert** in **India**. It is also known as the Great Indian Desert. While most of the desert is in India, part of it is also in Pakistan. Everywhere you look, the Thar is covered with sand. When the wind blows across the sand, it causes it to gather into **dunes**. These dunes are different sizes, ranging from 52 feet to nearly 500 feet tall. **Sandboarding** on the dunes is a popular sport there.

The Thar Desert's landscape is extremely dry. There is very little rain in this desert. Only one **river** flows through the desert. It is called the Luni River. During the dry season, the Luni River will completely dry up. Even though it

is so dry, the Thar Desert is the most lived-in desert in the world. The biggest city there is Jodhpur, where one and a half million people live. Some ways Jodhpur gets water are by transporting it from a nearby **lake**, using deep wells, and saving rainwater.

People come to visit from all over the world to see the Thar Desert's historic monuments and buildings. Most people in the Thar Desert live in small villages with houses made of mud and thatch roofs to keep cool. If your home was in the Thar Desert, you would probably live with your entire family, including your aunts, uncles, cousins, and grandparents. Can you imagine every day being a family reunion?

Tianchi Lake

Tianchi Lake is found on the border between North Korea and **China**. *Tianchi* means "heaven." Tianchi Lake is on top of a tall **mountain** that is called *Changbai* by Chinese people and *Paektu* by Koreans. It is a special mountain for the Korean people, and it is also very important to the Chinese and Manchu people (an Asian group in northeast China). It is very cold at the top of the mountain, so the **lake** is covered with ice a lot of the year.

Tianchi Lake is a special type of lake called a crater lake. A crater is a bowl-shaped **valley** that is often made by a meteor, a rock from outer space, hitting the ground. A crater can also be made by a **volcano**, and then it is called a caldera. Calderas are made when a volcano erupts and then the top of the volcano caves in, leaving a valley at the top of the volcano. This is how Tianchi Lake was made. Changbai Mountain is an active volcano! However, it only erupts every hundred years or so.

The giant volcanic eruption that made Tianchi Lake was over one thousand years ago. It is called the Millennium Eruption because it happened near the year 1000, the new millennium. It was one of the largest and most powerful volcanoes on earth! Huge amounts of lava flowed out of *Changbai*. When everything was over, an empty caldera was left behind where the top of the mountain used to be. When rainwater filled the caldera, this was the beginning of Tianchi Lake.

Tibetan Yak

The Tibetan yak is a long-haired, cow-like mammal that lives in and around the **Himalayas**. It is often found in Tibet and the nearby **plateaus** of **China**. Yaks like to stay together in a large group called a herd. They do this so that they can look out for each other. Their favorite food is grass, which is why you can always find yak herds in fields eating grass.

Male and female yaks stand at different heights. In the wild, male yaks are around six or seven feet tall, while female yaks are just over three feet tall. If yaks live on farms, they are usually a bit shorter, between three to six feet. All yaks have a pair of horns on their head and a thick coat of long hair all over them. Most yaks are black or brown in color, but sometimes you might see a white yak! Because they live in very cold areas with plenty of snow, yaks also have an undercoat of wool that keeps them nice and warm.

There are very few yaks living in the wild now. Most of the yaks you see today are found on farms. They are very useful creatures. Yaks are strong and can be used to carry people on their backs or pull wagons. They can also provide wool to make warm clothing, and they can even provide milk to drink, like a cow. In fact, the people of Tibet use yak milk to make butter and create a special drink called butter tea. If you lived in Tibet, you might drink up to 60 small cups of this tea every day!

Toro Muerto Petroglyphs

The Toro Muerto Petroglyphs are ancient rock

carvings found in the **desert** in Arequipa, **Peru**. Petroglyphs are rock carvings, usually made by scraping rock with something hard. At Toro Muerto, thousands of volcanic rocks have all kinds of petroglyphs carved into them. It is considered one of the largest examples of rock art in the world. No one is quite sure how old these ancient carvings are, but they are thought to be at least 1,000 years old.

If you visit these petroglyphs, you can see thousands of drawings of people and animals made using simple lines and shapes. Many of the petroglyphs seem to tell a story. The most common petroglyphs are of birds—especially **Andean condors**, snakes, **llamas**, and different kinds of cats. Another petroglyph that you can see repeated a lot is a person that researchers call "the dancer." This dancer has a zigzag for a body and wears a rectangle shape for a mask. You can try making some drawings of your own. Draw people and animals with just lines and simple shapes, and then see if your family and friends can guess what you drew!

Toucan

The common toucan is a bird that lives in **South America**. It can be found in places such as woodlands, **rainforests**, and **savannas**. If you were to go on a safari in South America, you might spot the common toucan roosting high in a tree alone or among a flock of toucans. They are very social birds!

The toucan is a popular animal at many zoos. The first thing you might notice about this beautiful bird is its large yellow-orange beak. Even though it looks heavy, it is actually light because it is mostly hollow. That is a very good thing because it can grow up to nine inches long. Its beak works to keep the bird cool: a toucan's blood flows through its beak, and this releases body heat because the blood cools down as it flows through the large, thin beak. When a toucan is too hot, its body sends more blood into its beak, and it dips its beak in water to cool down more.

Another reason God gave this huge beak to the toucan is to help it reach its food. It uses its bill to pluck tasty treats from fruit trees. It also eats insects, frogs, small lizards, and small birds and their eggs.

Fun Facts:

- Its voice sounds like a low, rough croaking that repeats every few seconds.
- It will clack its beak against other toucans' beaks to communicate with them.
- During nesting season, the parent birds carve out a hole high in a tree. The female will lay two to four eggs a year.

Tour de France

Every July in **France**, a famous bicycle race takes place called the Tour de France. It covers over 2,000 miles. This long route changes each year. It winds its way mostly through France and ends in Paris. Some parts of the route are flat, some have a lot of curves, and some have very steep **mountains**.

About 175 men join the race each year. They travel at an average speed of 25 miles per hour, which is really fast for a bicycle. The men ride hard for five to six hours a day. They keep this up for three weeks. During that time, they only get two days off to rest! The best mountain cyclist is named the King of the Mountains.

Ever since the first race in 1903, the Tour de France has been for men. But now there is also a race for women called Tour de France Femmes. In this case, the best mountain racer is called the Queen of the Mountains.

Tower of London

The Tower of London is a famous castle in London, England in the **United Kingdom**. It is located next to the Thames River. The Tower of London gets its name from the largest building in the center of the castle, the White Tower. The White Tower and the other buildings in the castle are surrounded by two rings of stone walls with many towers. A large moat surrounds the whole castle.

The White Tower is not really a tower but a keep, which is a large building at the center of a castle. A keep has four towers. The White Tower is one of the largest keeps in **Europe**. It was built near the end of the eleventh century by William the Conqueror. Over the next two hundred years, kings added more buildings and built walls and towers around them. The castle today covers almost 12 acres. That's as big as nine football fields!

The Tower of London has been used as an armory to store weapons, a treasury, and even the home of the Royal Mint, the place where English coins are made. It is also famous for being a prison for those who disobeyed the king. Saints like **St. Thomas More** and **St. John Fisher** were once kept as prisoners within its walls. It was also used as a prison during World War I and World War II.

Nowadays, the Tower of London is a popular

● ● ●

tourist attraction. Every year, millions of people visit the Tower of London. The Tower of London also displays the Crown Jewels, a collection of crowns, scepters, and gems belonging to the British royalty. There are more than 23,000 gems in the collection!

Tyburn Martyrs' Shrine

Tyburn Martyrs' Shrine is in London, England in the **United Kingdom**, and honors over 350 Catholic martyrs of the Reformation. It is named for a gallows (a place people are hanged) in London called Tyburn Tree. At Tyburn Tree, 105 Catholics were martyred for their faith.

These martyrdoms happened during the sixteenth and seventeenth centuries when it was against the law to be Catholic. Through their sacrifice, the brave Catholic martyrs turned Tyburn Tree into a symbol of hope—a Tree of Life. These martyrs include **St. Edmund Campion**, St. Oliver Plunkett, St. Margaret Ward, and many monks.

Later, people built a shrine to remember these martyrs who died at Tyburn Tree. The Shrine of the Martyrs is inside Tyburn Convent. It is very close to the original location of Tyburn

Tree, which no longer exists. At the shrine, there is a replica of Tyburn Tree and an altar called the Martyrs' Altar. The shrine also has many relics of the martyrs.

The Tyburn nuns look after the shrine. They welcome pilgrims from all over the world who want to honor and pray to these martyrs for their intercession. You can also attend Mass at the Martyrs' Altar.

Valley of the Ten Peaks and Moraine Lake

The Valley of the Ten Peaks and Moraine Lake are in Banff National Park, found in Alberta, **Canada**. The 10 **mountains** surrounding this **valley** were named by explorer Samuel Allen.

These mountains, part of the Canadian

Rockies, are jagged and covered in snow much of the year. Picture this: Lake Moraine's bright blue-green water allows for a reflection of the mountains like a mirror. There is even a **glacier**, too! It is a favorite destination for all sorts of visitors. What do you think you would like best if you visited? Maybe paddling across the **lake** in a canoe? If you like to camp and take hikes, this is a great place for it. You can even catch some fish for dinner from the lake! If you visit during winter, you can enjoy snowshoeing.

As you're out hiking, walking, canoeing, and exploring, keep a close eye out for the many different types of animals that live in the park. Stay away from the dangerous ones—wolves, **grizzly bears**, black bears, and coyotes. If you're lucky, you might catch a glimpse of river otters, elk, deer, moose, and maybe even **caribou**! Make sure to give the elk and moose some space too.

If you're really adventurous, you can climb one of the mountains around the lake. If you hike for most of the day, you can spend the night in the Neil Colgan Hut, the highest building in Canada. This hut is built on a glacier, and it has a stove and lamps so you can heat up your dinner. Brrr!

Vasco da Gama

Vasco da Gama was a European explorer who was the very first man in the Western world to reach **India** by **sea**. He was born in the 1460s in Portugal. During that time, the Portuguese were trying to figure out the best way to get to India by sea. Sailors would sail south from **Europe** and try to travel around **Africa**. No explorer made it farther than Vasco da Gama.

In 1497, da Gama set sail from Portugal with a crew of 170 men and four ships. Together with some of the best navigators (people who plan where a ship will go), da Gama sailed around the entire **continent** of Africa. After that, they used strong summer winds to get from Africa to India in only 23 days! Overall, it took da Gama almost a year to finally reach India. On the way, he and his crew discovered new waters, friendly traders, and others who were dangerous.

Da Gama's entire trip to India and back home again to Portugal was greater than the distance of the **Equator**—the longest distance anyone could possibly travel in a straight line on earth! He sailed a few more times, too. Thanks to his exploration, Portugal was able to set up important trading posts to buy and sell goods between Europe and India. He was honored with the title "Admiral of the Seas of Arabia, Persia, India, and all the Orient." There is even a crater on the moon named after Vasco da Gama!

Vatican City

Vatican City—or as it is commonly known, the Vatican—is located in Rome, **Italy**. It is the center of the Catholic Church and the home of the pope. It includes **St. Peter's Basilica**, St. Peter's Square, the Vatican Gardens, a large group of buildings called the Vatican Palace, and more.

The Vatican Palace includes the **Vatican Museums**, chapels, offices, and the papal apartments, which is where the pope lives. From one of his rooms, the pope looks out of a window at noon on Sundays to bless the crowd in St. Peter's Square below. Many other people also live and work in the Vatican, including the **Swiss Guards**.

Vatican City is actually not part of Italy. It is an independent state. In fact, Vatican City is the smallest country in the world! This means that even though it is very small—only 0.17 square miles—it has its own government, which is headed by the pope. It has its own flag, and daily newspaper, and a radio station. It even prints its own money and postage stamps!

The location of the Vatican is important because it is where St. Peter, the first pope, was martyred and buried. Vatican City is a symbol of the spiritual authority that Jesus gave to the Catholic Church. If you visit the Vatican, be sure to climb the dome of St. Peter's and enjoy the beautiful view!

Vatican Museums

The Vatican Museums are a set of buildings with a huge collection of art in **Vatican City**. There are about 70,000 works of art collected by popes over hundreds of years. The art is displayed in the beautiful rooms of the Vatican Palace. Many of these artworks have amazing histories. Some famous examples include the Sistine Chapel and the Raphael Rooms. Their walls and ceilings are covered with amazing paintings made by **Michelangelo** and Raphael, two very famous artists.

The Vatican Museums are some of the oldest and largest museums in the world. If you visit the Vatican Museums, you can see many different types of art from many different cultures and places. There are also workshops where people take care of the art that needs cleaning or repairing, but they aren't open to visitors.

The Church preserves beautiful art because it is a reflection of God's beauty. Millions of people visit the Vatican Museums every year to appreciate the beautiful art.

Venerable Matteo Ricci

Ven. Matteo Ricci was a missionary priest who was in charge of bringing the Good News to **China**. He was born in **Italy** in 1552 and grew up to become a Jesuit priest. He was very smart and learned to speak, read, and write Chinese. When he was 31 years old, he went to China as a missionary.

It was not easy to get the Chinese people to trust him and his fellow missionaries. They thought that anyone that came from outside of China was a barbarian. But they liked what Fr. Ricci brought with him. He set up a little museum of things like clocks and musical instruments. Soon, they began to ask about his picture of Mother Mary holding baby Jesus! This gave Fr. Ricci the chance to teach them about God.

Then the emperor of China heard about him. Fr. Matteo Ricci was invited to share his knowledge of math, science, and astronomy (the study of stars and planets). He was the first religious person in history to enter the emperor's palace, which was called the **Forbidden City**. When they saw his map of the world, they were shocked! Their own maps showed that China was the largest country on earth. They saw for the first time just how small it

was when compared to the rest of the world. Fr. Ricci made them new maps and labeled the **continents** and countries in Chinese.

Fr. Ricci's teaching helped the Chinese to open their minds to God. He brought many souls to believe in Him through the books he wrote in Chinese and by the way he respected their culture. After 28 years in China, Fr. Matteo Ricci died at the age of 57.

Verdon Gorge

Verdon Gorge is found in **France**. This **gorge** is over 15 miles long! The **river** that runs through Verdon Gorge has bright turquoise-green water, which inspired the gorge's name (it comes from the French word *vert*, which means "green").

Verdon Gorge is a great place to go rock climbing and hiking. In some places, the rocky walls stretch up 2,300 feet, making it the biggest gorge in **Europe**. To picture how tall that is, it would be like standing next to a building that has 212 stories! This is why Verdon Gorge is called the Grand Canyon of Europe. (The **Grand Canyon** in Arizona is almost three times as deep, but Verdon Gorge is still pretty deep!). There are lots of different paths to climb and hike.

Another fun activity to do during warm

seasons is to go kayaking in the river. After putting on your life jacket, you can take your kayak out into the green water. As you paddle, you'll probably catch sight of some fish. On the shore, you might see rare orchids or the famous 1,000-year-old juniper tree. Imagine hearing a screech echo off the rock and looking up to see eagles flying high above you. But be careful—the water current here can be strong!

be smooth, worn down by centuries of traffic. You will see ancient ruins and tombs by the side of the road, and you might have to stop to let a goat herd pass. You may get dusty and hot, but there are water fountains along the way with cool spring water. You can stop at the Catacombs of St. Sebastian, too. If you walk down the stairs into the underground rooms, you can see ancient Christian tombs and art.

Via Appia Antica

The Via Appia Antica is an ancient 360-mile-long road in **Italy**. It was called the "queen of roads." It connects Rome with Brindisi, which is a city on the eastern coast of Italy. The ancient Romans built it so that their army could travel easily through a muddy swamp filled with mosquitoes.

Via Appia Antica means the "Old Appian Way." It was named after a man named Appius who planned the road and made sure it was built. Most of the Via Appia was built in 312 BC, and it's still there! A historian once said the stones that pave the road still fit together so well that it looked like they grew together. The road is also very straight and flat, just the way Romans liked their roads.

Today, you can still walk into Rome on this ancient road. The stones under your feet will

Victoria Falls

Victoria Falls is a beautiful waterfall in **Africa** situated between Zambia and Zimbabwe. The Zambezi River flows over a huge crack in the earth, which causes Victoria Falls. In 1855, David Livingstone, a British explorer, was the first European to see the falls. He thought they were amazing and decided to name them after the British queen at the time, Queen Victoria.

Victoria Falls is known as one of the Seven Natural Wonders of the World. It is a beautiful sight, and you may even see a rainbow if you visit! Sunlight shining through the mist of the falls can make rainbows in the daytime, and when there's a full moon shining at night, you can even see a moonbow.

During the dry season, which lasts from May to October, you can walk across the top of the falls or swim in the **river** at the top. At the upper edge of the falls, a group of rocks form a natural swimming pool called Devil's Pool. November through April is the rainy season. During this time, there is lots of water and mist. It's very hard to see the falls then, but the mist can be seen 30 miles away!

Around the falls, there is a **rainforest** full of tropical plants. There, you can see elephants, **hippopotamuses**, and crocodiles. There's lots to see along the trails near Victoria Falls—just be prepared to get wet!

Fun Facts:

- In the rainy season, 300,000 gallons of water drop from the falls every second.
- Local people sometimes call the falls *Mosi-oa-Tunya*, which means "the Smoke that Thunders." This name comes from the loud sound of the water falling and the heavy mist that looks like smoke.
- One million people visit Victoria Falls each year.

the law in Vietnam to be Christian. People were made to step on a crucifix to show they weren't Christian. Anyone who refused suffered. Many Christians were forced to leave Vietnam, and at least 130,000 Christians were killed.

Some of the martyrs were Spanish or French missionaries, but most were Vietnamese. Father Andrew Dũng-Lạc, who was beheaded in 1839, is the most famous Vietnamese martyr. Another well-known martyr was a woman named Agnese Le Thi Thành, who was a mother of six children.

When Pope **St. John Paul II** canonized the Vietnamese Martyrs in 1988, thousands of Vietnamese people gathered in **Vatican City** to honor their sacrifice. The pope told them that these martyrs remind us of Christ's victory over death. The Vietnamese Martyrs are often known as Saint Andrew Dũng-Lạc and Companions. They share a feast day on November 24.

Vietnamese Martyrs

The Vietnamese Martyrs are a group of 117 bishops, priests, and ordinary people who were killed in Vietnam, **Asia** for their faith between 1745–1862. During most of the eighteenth and nineteenth centuries, it was against

Virgin Mary in the Catacombs

The Virgin Mary in the Catacombs is a fresco painting (a painting made on wet plaster on a wall) just outside the city of Rome, **Italy**. It is underground! This painting can be found in the ancient burial place called the Catacombs of Priscilla.

In ancient Rome, the **Roman Empire** didn't allow people to choose their religion. They had to follow the emperor, not Jesus. Christians had to practice their faith in secret. Many people were killed because of their belief in Christ, becoming **early Christian martyrs**. Christians built underground cemeteries called catacombs to bury their fellow Christians. They wanted special burial places so they could pray at the tombs and honor their family members who had been martyred.

The walls of these catacombs come alive with painted stories of what the early Christians believed. Their paintings encouraged Christians in their faith. The Virgin Mary in the catacombs is the oldest known painting of Mary that still exists today! Mary is pictured with a veil on her head and holding baby Jesus in her arms. Mary has a gentle look, which shows her loving ways. The baby Jesus is looking over Mary's shoulder at a man. Many people think this man could be either the prophet Isaiah or the prophet Balaam. Both men talked about the coming of Jesus in the Bible. Many people believe this painting of Mary shows the early Christians' belief in Christ as their Savior.

White Cliffs of Dover

Have you ever heard of the White Cliffs of Dover? Let's start with their location: Dover is a city in England, in the **United Kingdom**.

A cliff is a very steep wall of rock. The White Cliffs of Dover are mostly made of chalk, which is why they are bright white. They are the biggest cliffs in England. The seawater of the **English Channel** washes against the rocks there. The cliffs stretch for about 8 miles along the shore and are as tall as a 33-story building! Since they are near the narrowest part of the English Channel, they can be seen all the way in **France** on a clear day!

The White Cliffs of Dover were important during World War I and World War II. Trenches were dug across the tops of the cliffs so soldiers could hide there and see if enemy forces were approaching by **sea**. What used to be secret tunnels under the cliffs—created by prisoners during the wars with **Napoleon**—were used as a headquarters by Winston Churchill during World War II.

More than three million people visit the White Cliffs of Dover each year to learn about their history and beauty.

White Stork

The white stork is a large bird that lives in **Europe**. What makes it stand out from many other birds is its long, thin legs and extra-long, pointy beak. These help the white stork walk in the shallow water in a **lake** or a pond and catch its favorite foods—fish, insects, frogs, and other reptiles.

The white stork's wings stretch five to seven feet wide. That means many storks' wingspans are probably wider than your dad is tall! White storks don't make the usual squawking sounds you might expect to hear from a bird. Instead, they make snapping sounds with their beaks to talk with other storks.

White storks are known for traveling very long distances during certain times of year. In the warmer months, white storks live in Europe. There, they spend their time in grassy meadows and wetlands with shallow water. As it gets colder, white storks will fly to **Africa**.

This way, the white stork can enjoy warm and sunny weather all year long.

Fun Fact:
Storks appear in European folktales, carrying babies to parents who want children. This is why you might see illustrations of a stork carrying a basket or bundle in its beak!

Wild Boar

A wild boar is a type of pig that lives in many parts of the world, including **Africa**, **Asia**, and **North** and **South America**.

They have large heads and rough, spiky hair called bristles. Male boars have tusks, which are very long teeth that look like horns. They use their tusks to fight off other animals. Wild boars eat mostly plants, but sometimes they eat a small amount of animal meat. They like to live in wooded areas with a water source nearby.

In most of the world, human beings are the main predator of wild boars. Humans often hunt them for meat or to help keep their numbers down. If there are too many boars, there aren't enough plants for them to eat.

Before guns were invented, wild boars were very hard to kill. Group boar hunts in **France** and other European countries were big and serious events. Even today, wild boars can be hard to hunt because they are good at hearing people coming and may attack to protect themselves.

Fun Facts:
- Over a hundred years ago, people used boar bristles to make toothbrushes!
- Today, you can use hairbrushes and paintbrushes made with boar bristles.

Windsor Castle

Windsor Castle is a castle in Berkshire, England in the **United Kingdom**. It is the largest and oldest castle in the world that is still used as a family residence. The British royal family owns this magnificent castle and still uses it as its home, although the family sometimes stays in other places. Visitors have been welcomed for hundreds of years to tour the castle and see great art from the Royal Collection.

In 1066, William the Conqueror wanted to be king of England. He and his army marched from **France** into England, fighting many battles. He was crowned king on Christmas Day that year. To hold power over the country, William had many castles built all over the land. One of those was Windsor Castle, near the Thames River.

At first, Windsor Castle was made of wood.

Do you think wood is a good material to use for a castle? Over time, the wood either rotted or burned in a fire. Eventually, the wood had to be replaced with stone.

The castle eventually became very strong, and soon, more buildings were added to the castle. In the thirteenth century, King Henry II built a very expensive palace inside the castle walls. Three kings later, the palace was rebuilt again. It was made even more grand! Ever since St. George's Chapel was added in the fifteenth century, there have been many royal weddings and burials held there.

Wombat

A wombat is a **marsupial** found in **Australia**. A wombat's joey (baby) stays in its mother's pouch for eight to nine months while it finishes growing.

Other marsupials, such as **kangaroos**, have pouches that open toward the front, but wombats have pouches that open toward their back legs. This is because wombats walk on all fours and use their strong claws to dig burrows. If the wombat's pouch opened toward the front, it would get filled with dirt!

Wombats can live in many different kinds of places, such as forests, grasslands, and **mountains**. They eat grass and other plants, and they can even chew tough stems, bark, and roots. Wombats defend themselves from predators like **dingoes** or **Tasmanian devils** by kicking and biting. They can also quickly run into their burrows. If the predator tries to follow the wombat into its burrow, the wombat uses its rear end as a shield. The wombat has very tough skin on its rear, which protects it from being bitten by predators from behind!

Fun Facts:

- The wombat's closest relative is the **koala**.
- "Wombat" comes from the name that was used by the native Darug people of Australia.
- Wombats have short, stubby tails.

Zebra

A zebra is an African horse from south of the **Sahara Desert** in **Africa**. As an herbivore, it grazes on grass but will also eat fruits, leaves, and vegetables. It is a very social animal, so it lives with other zebras in herds. **Lions**, **spotted hyenas**, and crocodiles find that a zebra makes a delicious meal. But they have to work for it! The zebra will run away the moment it thinks it's being hunted. If it can't get away, it tries to fight off predators with deadly kicks.

There are three main species: the plains zebra, the mountain zebra, and the Grevy's zebra. Here are some easy ways to tell them apart. The plains zebra, the most common, is the only one with stripes on its belly—the others have white bellies. The mountain zebra is the only one that has a flap of skin, or dewlap, on its throat. The Grevy's zebra is the only one that does not have stripes on its tail.

Scientists are still doing research to find out why God gave zebras stripes. They have come up with a lot of ideas. Three of them are more likely to be true than the others. The first one is that the zebra's stripes act as camouflage (something that helps it blend into its surroundings and be harder to see). The second one is that they keep deadly disease-carrying African flies away. This is because the strips confuse the flies' eyes, and they have a hard time seeing where exactly the zebra is—so they often fly past or bump into the zebra instead of landing on it. The third idea of why God gave zebras stripes is that they might keep zebras cooler in hot climates. Maybe God gave them stripes for all those reasons!

Fun Facts:

- A herd of zebras is called a zeal or a dazzle.
- Each and every zebra is born with its own unique pattern of stripes, just as you have your very own set of fingerprints!

Zebu

A zebu is a type of cow from **India** and parts of Southeast **Asia** that is known for having a hump on its back close to its neck. They are often called humped cattle.

Zebu are very good at surviving in high heat since their native areas are very hot. Zebu release a lot of heat from their bodies through their loose skin folds. Because of their short hair, it is harder for them to get used to colder temperatures. They can eat many kinds of grasses, including grass difficult for most cows to digest. Zebu are known for being very healthy, and they do not get diseases easily. They even keep bugs away with their thick skin.

In Hinduism (a religion common in India), zebu are considered to be very special. In fact, it is against the law to kill cows in much of the country. Hindus do not eat beef. Zebu are very useful for pulling wagons or carts and for riding.

Fun Facts:
* In Madagascar, an **island** off the coast of **Africa**, there are more zebu than people!
* Miniature zebu are sometimes kept as pets.

Zhangye National Geopark

Zhangye National Geopark is in the **province** of Gansu in **China**. *Geo* means "earth," so a geopark is a park for dirt or rocks. A whole park for dirt and rocks? Yes! Zhangye National Geopark has special rock formations that are important for science.

The geopark is visited by many tourists who want to see its colorful striped rocks, called *danxia* landforms. (*Danxia* means "red sky glow" in Chinese.) The reddish striped cliffs of the **Grand Canyon** in the US look similar. However, the Zhangye National Geopark is much more colorful. The rocky hills look as if a giant came and painted stripes on them with a big brush!

Actually, the stripes are made when underground layers of red sandstone and other rock are pushed to the surface. Over time, rain, wind, and floods wash away parts of the land. Left behind are amazing cliffs, pillars, towers, and **valleys**, all with colorful stripes. Geologists (scientists who study rocks) say the *danxia* landforms at Zhangye National Geopark were formed over millions of years!

You probably noticed from the image that the stripes, or layers of rock, are diagonal (tilted) rather than flat. This is because the layers

● ● ●

of rock were pushed up at an angle. Imagine a seven-layer caramel cake made with raspberry filling. If you put a slice of cake on your plate, you can see the golden and red layers stacked on top of each other. If you lift up one side of the cake plate, the cake layers will be tilted. This is just like the *danxia* landforms at Zhangye National Geopark (but much more delicious!).

Glossary

Aqueduct

An aqueduct is a man-made trough, or **canal**, that carries water from one place to another.

Canal

A canal is a man-made waterway.

Archaeology

Archaeology is the practice of studying the past by digging up old things that are underground, like bones, pots, and structures.

Canyon

A canyon is a deep ravine, or crack, in the land.

Arctic

The Arctic is an area around the North Pole that is mostly covered with ice.

Cape

A cape is a large, narrow piece of land that sticks out into a body of water.

Cave

A cave is a natural underground space large enough to crawl into.

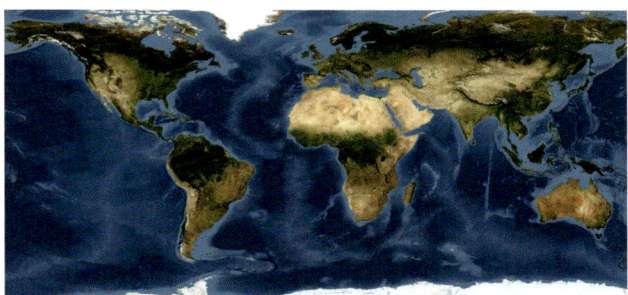

Continent

A continent is one of the seven main areas of land on earth. Any land too small to be considered a continent is an **island**.

Coastal Plain

A coastal plain is a flat area of fields and wetlands along a seashore.

Desert

A desert is a very dry area of land that gets little to no rain.

Communist State

A kind of government in which all the power belongs to a small group of people called Communists. Communists believe that rich people are always bad. Communists don't believe in God, and they don't think human beings have souls. Often, people who live in a Communist state don't have a lot of freedom and aren't allowed to practice their religion as they choose.

Dictatorship

A kind of government in which the people don't have a say in how their country is run. In a dictatorship, one person rules (the dictator), usually because he has enough power to make everyone else obey him. People who live in a dictatorship aren't always allowed to live, work, or worship as they choose.

Dike

A dike is a barrier, or wall, to hold back water.

Elevation

Elevation is how high above **sea** level (the level of the **ocean**) something is. **Mt. Everest's** elevation is 29,032 feet.

Dune

A dune is a large hill of sand that changes shape with the wind.

English Channel

The English Channel is a narrow strip of the Atlantic Ocean that separates England from **France**.

Earthquake

An earthquake is a sudden and often dangerous shaking of the ground.

Equator

The Equator is an imaginary circle that divides the northern and southern parts of the earth equally.

Fjord

A fjord is a long, narrow body of **ocean** water that reaches far into the land and is bordered by tall banks or cliffs.

Gorge

A gorge is a narrow **valley** between high cliffs. A gorge is the same as a **canyon**, but it is usually narrower and less deep.

Glacier

Glaciers are huge, thick layers of ice that have formed from snow that doesn't melt all the way in the summer. Glaciers are **rivers** of ice: they move downhill very slowly as the ice partly melts and freezes again.

Gulf

A gulf is a large part of the **ocean** that comes into the land, surrounded by land on three sides.

Glen

A glen is a narrow **valley**.

Habitat

A habitat is a natural home, or environment, where an animal or plant lives.

Harbor

A harbor is a safe place to keep a boat, usually protected from wind.

Ice Sheet

An ice sheet is a permanent layer of ice that covers a large area of land, especially near the North or **South Pole**.

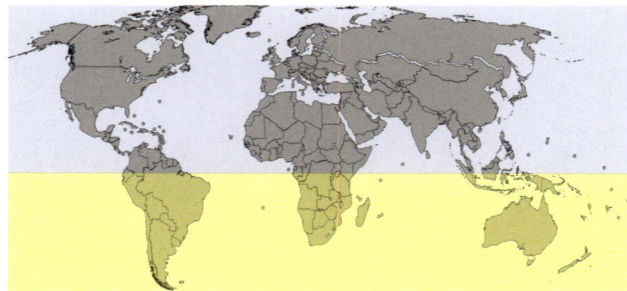

Hemisphere

A hemisphere is a half of the earth; for instance, the Northern Hemisphere is the half of the earth that is north of the **Equator**. The earth can also be divided into the Eastern and Western Hemisphere.

Inuit (Eskimo)

Inuit is the name of the native people living in the **Arctic**.

Iceberg

An iceberg is a huge section of ice broken from a **glacier** and floating in the **ocean**.

Irrigation

Irrigation is a man-made system of watering plants when there isn't enough rain.

Island

An island is an area of land that is smaller than a **continent** and entirely surrounded by water.

Loch

Loch is a Scottish and Irish word for a body of water mostly or completely surrounded by land.

Jungle

A jungle is a hot and humid area of land that is thickly covered with trees and other plants.

Lowlands

Lowlands are mostly flat lands near the level of the **ocean**.

Lake

A lake is a body of water surrounded by land.

Marsh

A marsh is a wetland, often at the edge of **lakes** and **rivers**, where grass, reeds, and plants grow.

Marsupial

A marsupial is a mammal that is carried in its mother's pouch because it is not finished growing when it is born.

Monsoon

A monsoon is a seasonal change in the wind. In tropical places, it brings heavy rain.

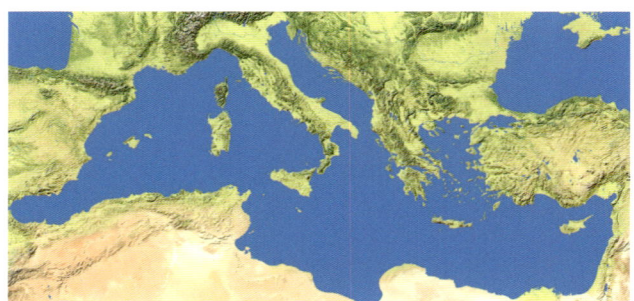

Mediterranean Sea

The Mediterranean Sea is a large **sea** mostly surrounded by land that separates **Europe** and **Africa**.

Mountain

A mountain is an area of land that rises far above the land around it.

Monarchy

A monarchy is a kind of government that has a monarch, which is a special word for king or queen.

In an absolute monarchy, the king or queen has a lot of power and is in charge of the country.

In a constitutional monarchy, the king or queen doesn't have much power. Instead, the country is run by leaders who are elected by the people. The people vote for who they want to run the country.

Mountain Range

A mountain range is a group of **mountains** connected in a line.

Oasis

An oasis is a place in the **desert** with water and plants.

Outback

The Outback is a large area of **plains** and **desert** in **Australia** where not many people live.

Ocean

The ocean is a large body of saltwater that covers the earth between the **continents**. We call the five main parts of the ocean by different names: the Arctic Ocean, the Atlantic Ocean, the Indian Ocean, the Pacific Ocean, and the Southern Ocean (sometimes called the Antarctic Ocean). Sometimes, the ocean is called "the **sea**."

Pagoda

A pagoda is a tall building, or tower, often used for religious worship in **Asia**. Each floor has a roof that curves upward at the edges.

Parliamentary Democracy

A parliamentary democracy is like a **republic**, but it can be combined with a constitutional **monarchy**. For example, **Canada** is ruled by leaders who are elected, but Canada also has a monarch. Whoever is king or queen of the United Kingdom is also the king or queen of Canada. The king or queen of Canada doesn't have much power, though.

Parliament, a group made up of elected members, has the most power in the government. They make laws and decide what the government can spend money on. The parliament is run by a prime minister.

Peninsula

A peninsula is an area of land that is surrounded on three sides with water.

Plain

A plain is a flat area of land with few trees.

Peat Bog

A peat bog is a wetland with spongy ground made up of very old plant matter called peat.

Plateau

A plateau is a flat area of land that rises sharply above the land around it.

Port

A port is a place along the water where ships can dock and unload their cargo.

Raja

A king or prince is called "raja" in **India**.

Province

A province is a large division of a country, like a state in the United States. Provinces usually have their own local governments, like states do.

Reef

A reef is a raised area of rock or coral just beneath the surface of the **ocean**.

Rainforest

A rainforest is a forest that gets very heavy rainfall.

Republic

A republic is a kind of government in which the people elect, or vote for, their leaders. They have a say in how their country is run.

Rice Paddy

A rice paddy is a flooded field used to grow rice.

Sari

A sari is the traditional dress worn by women in **India**.

River

A river is a large stream of fresh water that flows from higher ground to lower ground.

Savanna

A savanna is a grassy **plain** with a scattering of trees and shrubs.

Rupee

The rupee is the main form of money used in **India**.

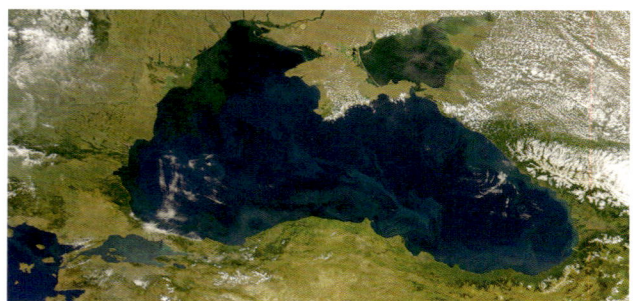

Sea

A sea is a smaller part of the **ocean** that is completely or mostly surrounded by land. Sometimes, the ocean is called "the sea."

South Pole

The South Pole is the southern-most point on earth.

Summit

A summit is the highest point of a hill or **mountain**.

Steppe

A steppe is a dry, grassy **plain** in **Europe** or Siberia, an area of Russia.

Territory

1. An area of land governed by a country. **Canada** has both **provinces** and territories. The ten provinces are divided across the lower two thirds of Canada, while the three territories make up the northern third of Canada. The provinces have their own governments, like the states in the United States, but the territories are just governed by Canada's national government.

2. Land that is owned by a country but is outside that country's borders

3. The area that an animal treats as its home. Sometimes it will warn or fight other animals that enter its territory.

Strait

A strait is a narrow body of water that connects two larger bodies of water.

Typhoon

A typhoon is a huge storm that brings high winds and flooding.

Vineyard

A vineyard is a garden of grapevines.

Valley

A valley is a low area of land that rests between hills or **mountains**.

Volcano

A volcano is a **mountain** or hill with an opening at the top where ash and hot, fiery lava sometimes pour out.

Index

Animals

Culture and Activities

Historical People and Events

Mary and Saints

Places and Landmarks

Image Credits

Images not listed below are in the public domain.

Key to Abbreviations: t. = Top, b. = Bottom, l. = Left, r. = Right, m. = Middle, CHC = Catholic Heritage Curricula

Special thanks to:

François-Marie Héraud at the Sanctuaire de Sainte-Anne-de-Beaupré for the photo of Sainte-Anne-de-Beaupré, pg. 260.

The Canossian Daughters of Charity for the photo of St. Josephine Bakhita, pg. 229.

Maps on pages 9, 12, 15, 18, 21, 24, 27, 32, 36, 39, 44, 46, 50, 52, 56: © CHC

Topographic background to alphabet letters throughout: © themefire/Envato Elements

Front cover and title page: Background © Dima Zel/ Shutterstock; t.l. © Nadezda Zavitaeva/ Shutterstock; t.m. © neelsky/ Shutterstock; t.r. © Mark Schwettmann/ Shutterstock; b.l. © Pete Niesen/ Shutterstock; b.r. © buteo/ Shutterstock

Back cover: Yevgeny Pashnin, CC BY-SA 3.0, https://commons.wikimedia.org/w/index.php?curid=2088600

Interior: 3: © Paul Banton/Shutterstock; **6-7:** t.l. © FamVeld/ Shutterstock; t.m. © SALMONNEGRO-STOCK/Shutterstock; t.r. © Leon Rafael/Shutterstock; m. © juan68/Shutterstock; b.l. © ChameleonsEye/Shutterstock; b.m. © Jon Chica/Shutterstock; b.r. © Oni Abimbola/Shutterstock; **8:** t. © James Karuga/ Shutterstock; b.l. © Oni Abimbola/Shutterstock; b.r. © Media Lens King/Shutterstock; **10:** t.l. © Elen Marlen/Shutterstock; t.r. © Vanessa Champion/Shutterstock; m.r. © Oscar Espinosa/ Shutterstock; b. © AlexAnton/Shutterstock; **11:** t. © slowmotiongli/Shutterstock; b.l. © Alexey Suloev/Shutterstock; b.r. © juan68/Shutterstock; **13:** t. © sljones/Shutterstock; m.l. © Gonzalo Solari Cooke/Shutterstock; m.r. © Thomas J Mitchell/ Shutterstock; b. © juan68/Shutterstock; **14:** t. © The Green foto/ Shutterstock; m. © xamnesiacx84/Shutterstock; b.l. © Supermop/Shutterstock; b.r. © Asifgraphy/Shutterstock; **16:** t. © xamnesiacx84/Shutterstock; m. © Narantungalag Dashtseren/ Shutterstock; b. © Jon Chica/Shutterstock; **17:** t. © John Crux/ Shutterstock; b.l. © ChameleonsEye/Shutterstock; b.r. © Jackson Stock Photography/Shutterstock; **19:** t. © Mino Surkala/ Shutterstock; m. © Nicole Patience/Shutterstock; b.l. © B Lamb/ Shutterstock; b.r. Andrew Mercer (www.baldwhiteguy.co.nz), CC BY-SA 3.0, https://commons.wikimedia.org/w/index.php?curid=31037276; **20:** t. © muratart/Shutterstock; m. © FooTToo/Shutterstock; b.l. © FamVeld/Shutterstock; b.r. © domhnall dods/Shutterstock; **22:** t. Giles Laurent, CC BY-SA 4.0, https://commons.wikimedia.org/w/index.php?curid=143032186; m.l. © laraslk/Shutterstock; m.r. © Joao Paulo V Tinoco/ Shutterstock; b.l. © Boris Stroujko/Shutterstock; b.r. © THONGCHAI.S/Shutterstock; **23:** t. © Chris LaBasco/Shutterstock; m. © Leon Rafael/Shutterstock; b. © Susanne Pommer/ Shutterstock; **25:** t. © Caleb Jones Photo/Shutterstock; m. © Benoit Daoust/Shutterstock; b.l. © tayfos/Shutterstock; b.r. © IrinaK/Shutterstock; **26:** t. © SALMONNEGRO-STOCK/ Shutterstock; m. © Mario Chipev/Shutterstock; b.l. © Cacio Murilo/Shutterstock; b.r. © Ale Curtinhas/Shutterstock;**28:** t. © BTK/stock.adobe.com; b. © MarinaTP/Shutterstock; **29:** © BETO SANTILLAN/Shutterstock; **30-31:** t.l. © Maria Wold/Shutterstock; t.m. © Rudra Narayan Mitra/Shutterstock; t.r. © SuxxesPhoto/ Shutterstock; m.m. © PitukTV/Shutterstock; m.r. © Mazur Travel/ Shutterstock; b.l. © Yudina_Elena/Shutterstock; b.m. © Nadezda Murmakova/Shutterstock; b.r. © Zhukova Valentyna/ Shutterstock; **33:** l.© Wandering views/Shutterstock; r. © Kim D. Lyman/Shutterstock; **34:** t. © Kate Scott/Shutterstock; b. © Nadezda Murmakova/Shutterstock; **35:** t. David Stanley from Nanaimo, Canada, CC BY 2.0, https://commons.wikimedia.org/w/index.php?curid=71501372; b. © Rick Wang/Shutterstock; **36:** b. © QinJin/Shutterstock; **37:** t. © Nickolai Repnitskii/ Shutterstock; b. © Robert Way/Shutterstock; **38:** © PitukTV/ Shutterstock; **40:** t.l. © FreeProd33/Shutterstock; t.r. © Rasto SK/ Shutterstock; b. © oksana.perkins/Shutterstock; **41:** t. © EQRoy/ Shutterstock; b. © Ralu Spatareanu/Shutterstock; **42:** t. © Zhukova Valentyna/Shutterstock; b. © Pierre Laborde/ Shutterstock; **43:** t. © Zvonimir Atletic/Shutterstock; b. © ABHISHEK BASAK 90/Shutterstock; **44:** b. © Zvonimir Atletic/ Shutterstock; **45:** t. © Mohammad Shahnawaz/Shutterstock; b. © Rudra Narayan Mitra/Shutterstock; **47:** t.l. © maziarz/ Shutterstock; t.r. © illpaxphotomatic/Shutterstock; b. © Dudaeva/Shutterstock; **48:** t. © Christopher Moswitzer/ Shutterstock; b. © Maria Wold/Shutterstock; **49:** t. © Neale Cousland/Shutterstock; b. © SCStock/Shutterstock; **50:** b. © Yudina_Elena/Shutterstock; **51:** t. © Diana Guevara/ Shutterstock; b. © Viktorus/Shutterstock; **52:** b. © Gena Melendrez/Shutterstock; **53:** t. © Juanmi80/Shutterstock; b. © Mazur Travel/Shutterstock; **54:** t. © Juan Enrique del Barrio/ Shutterstock; b. © BearFotos/Shutterstock; **55:** t. © Antonia Gros/Shutterstock; b. © SuxxesPhoto/Shutterstock; **56:** b. © Pete Hancock/Shutterstock; **57:** t. © jimmonkphotography/ Shutterstock; b. © Sampajano_Anizza/Shutterstock; **58-59:** t.l. © Peter Zaharov/Shutterstock; t.m. © Mari Jensen/ Shutterstock; t.r. © Jarno Gonzalez Zarraonandia/Shutterstock; m.l. © Sportsphotographer.eu/Shutterstock; m.m. Thorvaldsson, CC BY 3.0, https://commons.wikimedia.org/w/index.php?curid=6367812; b.l. © Patrick Wang/Shutterstock; b.m. © Benson HE/Shutterstock; b.r. © PHOTOCREO Michal Bednarek/ Shutterstock; **60:** b.l. Winky from Oxford, UK, CC BY 2.0, https://commons.wikimedia.org/w/index.php?curid=990298; r. © Vadim Petrakov/Shutterstock; **61:** © Villiers Steyn/Shutterstock; **62:** l. Antony McCallum: Who is the uploader, photographer, full copyright owner and proprietor of WyrdLight.com, CC BY-SA 4.0, https://commons.wikimedia.org/w/index.php?curid=65009148; r. Holger Uwe Schmitt, CC BY-SA 4.0, https://commons.wikimedia.org/w/index.php?curid=156888873; **63:** l. © Ervin Monn/Shutterstock; r. Gilloteaux, CC BY-SA 3.0, https://commons.wikimedia.org/w/index.php?curid=40494712; **64:** l. © enricodevita/Shutterstock; r. Neil Palmer/CIAT, CC BY-SA 2.0, https://commons.wikimedia.org/w/index.php?curid=28393993; **65:** l. © Mike Treglia/Shutterstock; r. © Jeffrey B. Banke/ Shutterstock; **66:** © Jupiterimages/Thinkstock; **67:** l. Hugo Pedel, CC BY-SA 3.0, https://commons.wikimedia.org/w/index.php?curid=10810107; r. Rod Waddington from Kergunyah, Australia, CC BY-SA 2.0, https://commons.wikimedia.org/w/index.php?curid=29767401; **68:** l. Yosemite, CC BY-SA 3.0, https://commons.wikimedia.org/w/index.php?curid=65920; **69:** © Olga_i/Shutterstock; **70:** l. © cynoclub/Shutterstock; r. User:Jean-Pol GRANDMONT (Collection personnelle/Private collection), CC BY 2.0, https://commons.wikimedia.org/w/index.php?curid=114166; **71:** l. © Mogens Trolle/Shutterstock; **72:**

Sputnikcccp, CC BY-SA 3.0, https://commons.wikimedia.org/w/index.php?curid=433265; **73:** l. © Tadeusz Ibrom/Shutterstock; b.r. kallerna, CC BY-SA 3.0, https://commons.wikimedia.org/w/index.php?curid=20438652; **74:** l. © FloridaStock/Shutterstock; r. Nima Sareh from Bangalore, India, CC BY 2.0, https://commons.wikimedia.org/w/index.php?curid=2805313; **75:** Rosario Fernandes, CC BY-SA 4.0, https://commons.wikimedia.org/w/index.php?curid=35072830; **76:** l. © Vadim Petrakov/Shutterstock; r. ಕಾ‌ಕ‌ ಕೆ, CC BY-SA 4.0, https://commons.wikimedia.org/w/index.php?curid=36801626; **77:** l. Jiuguang Wang, CC BY-SA 3.0 es, https://commons.wikimedia.org/w/index.php?curid=21690293; r. Didier Descouens, CC BY-SA 4.0, https://commons.wikimedia.org/w/index.php?curid=58176551; **79:** l. © Patrick Wang/Shutterstock; r. © Aleksandar Todorovic/Shutterstock; **80:** l. Massimo Roselli, CC BY-SA 3.0, https://commons.wikimedia.org/w/index.php?curid=47400830; r. © Steve Heap/Shutterstock; **81:** l. © Daniel Rose/Shutterstock; r. © F. JIMENEZ MECA/Shutterstock; **82:** l. © Allison Herreid/Shutterstock; r. © emin kuliyev/Shutterstock; **84:** r. © lunamarina/Shutterstock; **85:** l. Gregory "Slobirdr" Smith, CC BY-SA 2.0, https://commons.wikimedia.org/w/index.php?curid=40573659; r. "Stalactite formations at Borra Caves" by Rajib Ghosh [CC-BY-2.0], https://flic.kr/p/e3rMQw; **86:** l. © Gary Unwin/Shutterstock; r. dbking, CC BY 2.0, https://commons.wikimedia.org/w/index.php?curid=151847140; **87:** © Natursports/Shutterstock; **88:** b.l. © Fernando Cortes/Shutterstock; r. "Camargue" by Josef Grunig [CC-BY-2.0], https://flic.kr/p/p33ps1; **89:** © Dmitry Pichugin/Shutterstock; **90:** losmininos- Flickr [CC-BY-2.0], via Wikimedia Commons; **91:** l. Chuck Szmurlo, CC BY 2.5, https://commons.wikimedia.org/w/index.php?curid=1815133; r. © istvanffy/Shutterstock.com; **92:** l. Egg, CC BY-SA 2.5, https://commons.wikimedia.org/w/index.php?curid=1223612; r. © Stu Porter/Shutterstock; **94:** l. "2046-Praia das Catedrais en Ribadeo (Lugo)" by Jose Luis Cernadas Iglesias [CC-BY-2.0], https://flic.kr/p/9LJMa6; **95:** Maxima20, CC BY-SA 3.0, https://commons.wikimedia.org/w/index.php?curid=19624782; **96:** r. © Captain Mario Küntzler Chief of Belgrano II Base 2013 Staff; **98:** © silky/Shutterstock; **99:** l. © Stu Porter/Shutterstock; r. Pavel from Sydney, AU, CC BY 2.0, https://commons.wikimedia.org/w/index.php?curid=24659766; **100:** l. © choikh/Shutterstock; r. Bairuilong, CC BY-SA 4.0, https://commons.wikimedia.org/w/index.php?curid=48923904; **101:** l. Moastoode, CC BY-SA 3.0, https://commons.wikimedia.org/w/index.php?curid=18674526; **102:** l. Robert444444 aka Philip K (Flickr), CC BY-SA 4.0, https://commons.wikimedia.org/w/index.php?curid=138663337, r. © Sergei Bachlakov/Shutterstock; **103:** © Mark Schwettmann/Shutterstock; **104:** r. © meunierd/Shutterstock; **105:** © Framalicious/Shutterstock; **106:** l. Neil Ward, CC BY 2.0, https://commons.wikimedia.org/w/index.php?curid=36174483; r. © Hans Jeitner/Shutterstock; **107:** © FCG/Shutterstock; **108:** l. Jerzystrzelecki, CC BY 3.0, https://commons.wikimedia.org/w/index.php?curid=3022227; r. © Rahul Sapra/Shutterstock; **109:** l.b. © Benson HE/Shutterstock; r. © Mhai Little Arts/Shutterstock; **110:** l. © muroPhotographer/Shutterstock; r. © worldswildlifewonders/Shutterstock; **111:** © ian woolcock/Shutterstock; **112:** r. Aaron "tango" Tang from cambridge, ma, usa, CC BY 2.0, https://commons.wikimedia.org/w/index.php?curid=38450049; **113:** © pisaphotography/Shutterstock; **114:** l. Draceane, CC BY-SA 4.0, https://commons.wikimedia.org/w/index.php?curid=152961452; r. Ввласенко, CC BY-SA 4.0, https://commons.wikimedia.org/w/index.php?curid=85083756; **115:** r. Ingo Mehling, CC BY-SA 4.0, https://commons.wikimedia.org/w/index.php?curid=37509203; **116:** l. © Jeremy Richards/Shutterstock; r. © TravelMediaProductions/Shutterstock; **117:** © Mari Jensen/Shutterstock; **118:** l. © mauribo/iStockphoto; r. © aabeele/Shutterstock; **119:** b. Johann-Nikolaus Andreae, CC BY-SA 2.0, https://commons.wikimedia.org/w/index.php?curid=6355623; **120:** l. © De Visu/Shutterstock; **121:** © Johnny Lye/Shutterstock; **122:** l. © Jack.Q/Shutterstock; r. © Pagina/Shutterstock; **123:** l. © muzsy/Shutterstock; r. © 06photo/Shutterstock; **126:** b.r. Miguel303xm~commonswiki, CC BY-SA 2.5, https://commons.wikimedia.org/w/index.php?curid=943206; **127:** l. © Danita Delimont/Shutterstock; r. © FCG/Shutterstock; **128:** © Hung Chung Chih/Shutterstock; **129:** l. © Paul Banton/Shutterstock; r. © Nickolay Stanev/Shutterstock; **130:** l. © Luciano Mortula- LGM/Shutterstock; r. EditQ, CC BY-SA 4.0, https://commons.wikimedia.org/w/index.php?curid=136061119; **131:** © Josemaria Toscano/Shutterstock; **132:** l. © melissaf84/Shutterstock; **133:** l. © WitR/Shutterstock; r. © Daily Travel Photos/Shutterstock; **134:** © Hung Chung Chih/Shutterstock; **135:** l. © Richard Seeley/Shutterstock; **136:** © Jule_Berlin/Shutterstock; **137:** l. Flominator, CC BY-SA 3.0, https://commons.wikimedia.org/w/index.php?curid=1006375; **139:** l. © Sam DCruz/Shutterstock; r. © Martin Mette/Shutterstock; **140:** l. © robbosphotos/Shutterstock; r. © Anton_Ivanov/Shutterstock; **141:** l. © MKworldphoto/Shutterstock; r. © Axel Meineke/Shutterstock; **143:** b.l. http://www.lynxexsitu.es, CC BY 3.0 es, https://commons.wikimedia.org/w/index.php?curid=27380411; r. © Kletr/Shutterstock; **144:** l. © Scott Prokop/Shutterstock; r. © gary718/Shutterstock; **145:** Charles J. Sharp, CC BY-SA 3.0, https://commons.wikimedia.org/w/index.php?curid=19058335; **146:** r. © Jack.Q/Shutterstock; **147:** © percom/Shutterstock; **148:** l. Valdiney Pimenta from Campinas, CC BY 2.0, https://commons.wikimedia.org/w/index.php?curid=15661626; r. © sergioboccardo/Shutterstock; **150:** r. © KreativKolors/Shutterstock; **152:** b.l. © Volodymyr Burdiak/Shutterstock; **153:** © Skynavin/Shutterstock; **154:** r. © Liv Falvey/Shutterstock; **155:** l. © Daily Travel Photos/Shutterstock; r. aussiegall from sydney, Australia, CC BY 2.0, https://commons.wikimedia.org/w/index.php?curid=24660875; **156:** l. Vatican, http://www.vatican.va/news_services/liturgy/saints/ns_lit_doc_19840506_103_martiri_coreani_photo.html, GFDL, https://commons.wikimedia.org/w/index.php?curid=5192176; **157:** b. © jordache/Shutterstock; **158:** l. © Rafal Cichawa/Shutterstock; **159:** © alech/Shutterstock; **160:** r. © Keith Levit/Shutterstock; **161:** l. © andreanord/Shutterstock; r. Sam Fentress, CC BY-SA 2.0, https://commons.wikimedia.org/w/index.php?curid=210104; **162:** Aditya Laghate, CC BY-SA 3.0, https://commons.wikimedia.org/w/index.php?curid=33915818; **163:** l. © Sampajano_Anizza/Shutterstock; **164:** © Tupungato/Shutterstock; **165:** b.l. Jerzy Strzelecki, CC BY 3.0, https://commons.wikimedia.org/w/index.php?curid=3023384; r. Colegota, CC BY-SA 2.5 es, https://commons.wikimedia.org/w/index.php?curid=805781; **167:** r. Dan Lundberg, CC BY-SA 2.0, https://commons.wikimedia.org/w/index.php?curid=25314699; **168:** r. © testing/Shutterstock; **170:** © José Luiz Bernardes Ribeiro, CC BY-SA 3.0, https://commons.wikimedia.org/w/index.php?curid=31509660; **171:** l. KarlMoor, CC BY-SA 2.0, https://commons.wikimedia.org/w/index.php?curid=2008463; r. Radomił, CC BY-SA 3.0, https://commons.wikimedia.org/w/index.php?curid=29347; **172:** l. © Galyna Andrushko/Shutterstock; r. © S.R. Maglione/Shutterstock; **173:** l. El fosilmaníaco, CC BY-SA 3.0, https://commons.wikimedia.org/w/index.php?curid=5518195; r. © Chubykin Arkady/Shutterstock; **174:** © Peter Zaharov/Shutterstock; **175:** l. Paul